NEW from Idea Group Publishing

Excellent additions to your library!

Distance Learning Technologies: Issues, Trends and Opportunities

Senior Editor: Mehdi Khosrowpour
Managing Editor: Jan Travers
Copy Editor: Brenda Zboray Klinger
Typesetter: Tamara Gillis
Cover Design: Connie Peltz
Printed at: BookCrafters

Published in the United States of America by
        Idea Group Publishing
        1331 E. Chocolate Avenue
        Hershey PA 17033-1117
        Tel: 717-533-8845
        Fax: 717-533-8661
        E-mail: jtravers@idea-group.com
        Website: http://www.idea-group.com

and in the United Kingdom by
        Idea Group Publishing
        3 Henrietta Street
        Covent Garden
        London WC2E 8LU
        Tel: 171-240 0856
        Fax: 171-379 0609
        http://www.eurospan.co.uk

Library of Congress Cataloging-in-Publication Data

Distance learning technologies : issues, trends, and opportunities / [edited by] Linda Lau.
        p. cm.
    Includes bibliographical references and index.
    ISBN 1-878289-80-2
    1. Distance education--Computer-assisted instruction. 2. Educational technology. 3.
World Wide Web. I. Lau, Linda, 1958-

LC5803.C65 D57 2000
371.3'5--dc21   99-048171

British Cataloguing in Publication Data
A Cataloguing in Publication record for this book is available from the British Library.

Distance Learning Technologies: Issues, Trends and Opportunities

Table of Contents

Preface

In 1991, the World Wide Web (WWW) was conceptualized at the European Particle Physics Laboratory (CERN) in Geneva, Switzerland, with the sole purpose of making research findings and scientific materials available to the academic and scientific community on a global network. Since then, the Internet has become an important communications medium for both giant corporations as well as individuals, and lately, as an innovative instructional and distance learning tool for academic institutions. Actually, distance learning was pioneered at Stanford University more than 30 years ago to meet the increasing demand for high-tech engineers and computer scientists at Silicon Valley. Today, nontraditional bachelor and master's distance learning programs are offered by more than 150 accredited academic institutions in this country. According to the United States Distance Learning Association (USDLA), an organization committed to promoting and developing distance learning, there were no significant differences in effectiveness between distance learning and the traditional learning techniques. Hence, this book was written to provide both academicians and practitioners with a body of knowledge and understanding regarding the distance learning technologies.

This book is divided into three sections. The first four chapters provide the theoretical foundation of distance learning, commencing with Valerie Morphew's proposed constructivist approach to Web-based learning and instruction, followed by Rita Purcell-Robertson and Daniel Purcell's descriptive analysis of interactive distance learning. While Dat-Dao Nguyen and Dennis Kira summarize and evaluate the effectiveness of Internet-based teaching, Zane Berge and Donna Smith focus on implementing corporate distance training using change management, strategic planning, and project management.

The second section describes the conceptual aspect of distance learning in seven chapters. William Rayburn and Arkalgud Ramaprasad introduce three strategies for using distance learning technology in higher education, and also describe the alliances of distance learning in higher education. While Lore Peyton introduces eight elements that will contribute to the success of a distributed/distance learning program, Lynne Schrum describes several issues that will contribute to the design of successful on-line instruction. Mitchell Adrian, on the other hand, develops a learning environment that is capable of applying technology and TQM to Distance Learning. Digital video is often utilized as an important tool in the education system; hence, Major Todd Smith and Captain Scot Ransbottom discuss the use of digital video in the modern classroom, with a focus of learning. Finally, Caroline Howard and Richard Discenza conclude this section with an empirical study of a group decision support system typology.

The final section of the book provides five cases of practical implementation of distance learning. Eric Adams and Christopher Freeman describes the commuting of distance learning at Pepperdine University, while Sherif Kamel illustrates a successful Internet endeavor in Egypt. Jens Liegle and Peter Meso attempt to examine the Web-Based Instruction Systems (WBIS) from the systems' perspective, describing its components and interfacing technologies, critical problems, issues, and a taxonomy for classifying the various types of WBIS. Ira Yermish, on the other hand, describes a case study via video-conferencing at St. Joseph's University. Finally, Janet Hugli and David Wright evaluate the training requirements of the network marketing industry, based upon the industry needs and availability of training resources.

I would like to extend my greatest thanks and appreciation to all the contributing authors and the editors at Idea Group Publishing, without whom, the writing of this book would not have been possible.

Linda K. Lau

Chapter I

Web-Based Learning and Instruction: A Constructivist Approach

Valerie N. Morphew
West Virginia Wesleyan College

INTRODUCTION

The precipitous rise in Web-based education and employee training speaks volumes of technology's far-reaching potential. While most agree that Web-based instruction can be cost-effective and convenient, few academicians and practitioners have examined the efficacy of Web-based learning in terms of constructivism, the most widely accepted model of learning in education today.

The constructivist approach to learning acknowledges that both teacher and student bring prior knowledge to the learning experience. Over time and through interaction with others in the learning environment, the student co-constructs new meaning as a knowledge-building process—piece by piece, new knowledge is built onto former knowledge. This differs from the former notion of learning that considered children as empty vessels waiting to be filled (*tabula rasa*). While constructivism is widely accepted by educators in theory, it is not always evident in teaching practices, including Web-based instruction.

To help academicians and practitioners provide effective constructivist learning experiences for students and employees, the following issues will be addressed:

CONTEMPORARY CONSTRUCTIVIST THOUGHT

The constructivist perspective dominates learning theory today. Constructivists view knowledge as something that a learner actively constructs in his/her environment. Through meaningful learning experiences, a learner co-constructs new knowledge in tandem with those who share his/her learning environment. Knowledge is built piece by piece, and connections arise to join related pieces. In this view, knowledge is subjective—a learner's cumulative construction is uniquely erected.

Constructivism has its roots in various disciplines such as education, psychology, philosophy and the history of science. John Dewey, Jean Piaget, Edmund Husser and Thomas Kuhn are only a handful of theorists whose work impacts constructivist thought.

Dewey's emphasis on the role of experience in learning is significant to the constructivist perspective:

> When we experience something we act upon it, we do something with it; then we suffer or undergo the consequences. We do something to the thing and then it does something to us in return: such is the peculiar combination. The connection of these two phases of experience measures the fruitfulness or value of the experience. . . . Experience as trying involves change, but change is meaningless transition unless it is consciously connected with the return wave of consequences which flow from it. When an activity is continued *into* the undergoing of consequences, when the change made by action is reflected back into a change made in us, the mere flux is loaded with significance. We learn something (Dewey, 1944, p. 139).

Similarly, the mechanisms of knowledge development suggested by Piaget are significant to constructivist understanding. Piaget believed that thought developed by growing from one state of equilibrium to another. He believed that when a thinker encounters an experience consistent with prior beliefs, he simply needs to add it to his store of information. If an inconsistency arises, however, the thinker either ignores the new experience, modifies the experience in his mind to fit, or modifies his thinking to fit the experience. Progress in conceptual thinking occurs when the latter process is engaged (Baker & Piburn, 1997).

In the philosophical realm, Husserl's phenomenology similarly relates the construction of knowledge. In phenomenology, the subject's perceptions involve the transaction between the subject and the subject's field where things outside the subject are transformed into meaningful entities (in Morphew, 1994, from Tiryakian, 1973). When a subject experiences phenomena and perceives, meaning is possible (Morphew, 1994).

Husserl distinguished between types of meaning: meaning-intention and meaning-fulfillment. Meaning-intention corresponds to the ability of an expression to be meaningful and meaning-fulfillment to the possibility or impossibility of that meaning being carried to fulfillment (Husserl, 1970a, 1970b). Mohanty (1969) provides examples that illustrate meaning-intention and meaning-fulfillment: "Abcaderaf," "The present King of France," and "This white wall before me." "Abcaderaf" is meaningless and is not animated by meaning-intention. "The present King of France" is animated with meaning-intention as is "This white wall before me." They differ, however, in the possibility and nature of meaning-fulfillment since France no longer has a monarchy (p. 36, and Morphew, 1994).

According to Mohanty (1969), "Husserl would say that whereas thinking consists in the meaning-intending act, knowing consists in the appropriate fulfillment of the meaning-intention. So long as the meaning-intention is not fulfilled, we do not have knowledge" (p. 37). This exchange between the subject and the subject's field makes possible the learning experience.

In a collective process of learning, Kuhn (1962) described the process of acquiring new scientific understanding through his discussion of paradigm shifts. Kuhn uses "paradigm" to mean a world view involving models of explanations and models for the behavior of scientists. Most of the science done on a routine basis is normal science, a type of scientific puzzle solving. Normal science is carried out by scientists who perceive the world to operate in a particular fashion. If anomalies ("persistent failure of the puzzles of normal science") or counter-instances (new observations) arise and persist, the prevailing paradigm may be called into question and reexamined. Paradigm breakdown and blurred rules may open the door for the emergence of an alternate paradigm and for extraordinary research. As a result, a scientific revolution may emerge. This collective process of maintaining and modifying scientific thought is analogous to constructivist learning for individuals.

For the sake of this chapter, constructivism will follow the thinking of Husserl's phenomenology where meaning is defined as the co-created sense one makes of phenomena through the interaction of the subject and the subject's field (Morphew, 1994). In other words, constructivism is defined as the co-construction of meaning in the learning environment.

CONSTRUCTIVIST LEARNING AND INSTRUCTION IN THE TRADITIONAL CLASSROOM

Instruction includes planning, implementing, and evaluating the curriculum or the material covered in scope and sequence. The scope of the curriculum includes the breadth and depth of what is taught, and the sequence is the order in which it will be taught. Together the scope and sequence of the curriculum steer the act of instruction, though practically speaking, curriculum and instruction are inseparable (see Figure 1).

Theoretically, the curriculum that is taught should equal the curriculum learned (Passe, 1999). Unfortunately, in reality this seldom occurs. Instead, the difference in what is taught and learned shows itself in poor test scores and gross misconceptions. To bring the taught and learned curriculum closer together, the experiences made avail-

Figure 1: Scope and Sequence Steering the Act of Instruction

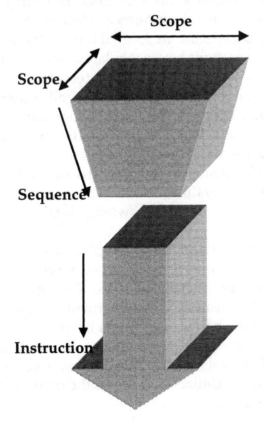

able to the learner must be amenable to what Dewey called "the flux" in learning. This attention to the experiences offered to learners helps ensure the act of co-construction of meaning.

In order for the learner to co-construct meaning, he/she must be open to the process of co-creation. To some degree instructors may influence the willingness of learners to learn, though much of this is intrinsically motivated. To a greater extent, instructors may impact the learning experience. Thus, the question arises, "What experiences should an instructor provide to help facilitate the act of co-construction?"

In traditional classrooms, instructors have adopted various teaching practices that maximize the potential for this flow by creating dynamic learning experiences. A number of experiences will be described that have proven effective.

Concept Maps and Semantic Webs

Concept maps are a visual representation diagramming concepts and relationships among concepts. Concepts are arranged hierarchically so that the most general concepts are located at the top of the diagram, and the most specific are located toward the bottom (Baker & Piburn, 1997). Connections between related concepts are shown in Figure 2. Semantic webs are also visual representations of concepts, yet they are not hierarchical in nature. Rather all concepts emanate from one overriding concept, showing relationships between the subordinate concepts and the main concept (Baker & Piburn, 1997). Figure 3 illustrates a semantic web for the skull. Concept maps and semantic Webs may be created by either the instructor, learner or both and may be introduced any time relationships among existing knowledge are made, or whenever new knowledge is constructed.

Venn Diagrams and Other Graphic Organizers

Venn diagrams, like concept maps and semantic webs, help show the connection between related concepts. They can be simple or complex and may be created by the instructor, learner, or both to accentuate connections between concepts or attributes of concepts (see Figure 4). Venn diagrams are a type of graphic organizer: any visual representation used to help make the abstract concrete. Figure 5 illustrates a graphic organizer that shows the patterns of inductive and deductive reasoning.

Figure 2: Concept Map of Dogs

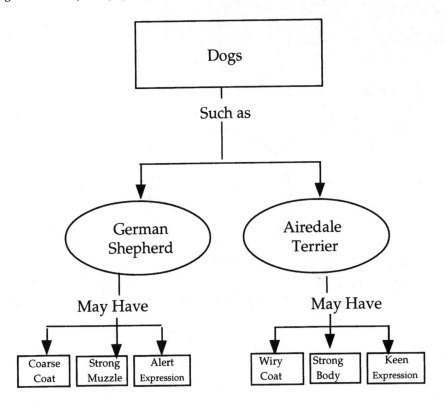

Models

Creation and utilization of models is another experience that provides learners with concrete examples of connections and relationships. For instance, relief maps help learners understand connections between flat topographic maps and changes in land elevation. A model of the solar system showing relative location and distance of the planets to the sun may be used to make the abstract concrete.

Analogies and Metaphors

Analogies and metaphors are helpful in making connections between prior knowledge and new knowledge. For example, a learner may benefit from understanding that the transmission of messages in a computer system is like the transmission of nerve impulses in the

Figure 3: Semantic Web of the Skull

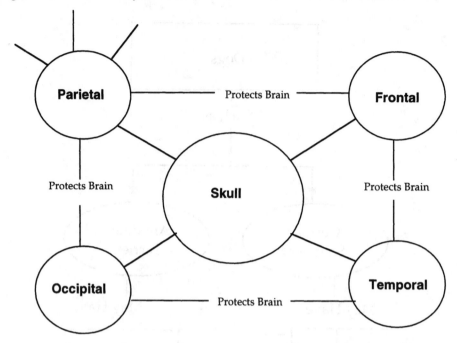

Figure 4: Venn Diagram Showing That All Dogs Grow Hair

Figure 5: Graphic Organizer Showing Inductive and Deductive Reasoning Patterns

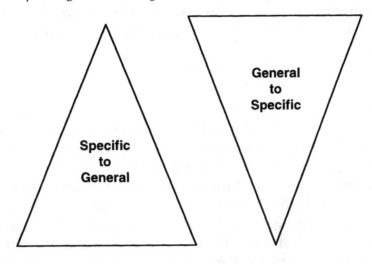

human body. Similarly, conceiving the human life span as a journey may help a learner more easily grasp the meaning of this experience.

Hypothesis Making and Testing

Hypothesis making and testing are experiences that help facilitate co-construction of meaning by requiring the learner to draw from a vast store of previously learned concepts to make inferences about new ones. Hypotheses are statements that show a cause and effect relationship between two or more factors. They are often written in the if-then format. "If temperature is increased, then pressure will increase." "If blue is added to red, then purple will result." These statements are meaning-building in their creation but also in their testing. In testing hypotheses, the learner must experiment to co-create new concept formation. This new knowledge will later be a part of future hypotheses making.

Integrated Themes

The relevancy of connections becomes apparent to learners when themes and concepts are integrated holistically. For example, the learner who constructs meaning about the life style of colonists during the American Revolution at the same time she learns about the science of that time and place has a better chance of building connections than if she were taught these concepts in isolation. Elementary instructors more often teach integrated thematic units than secondary instructors. Unfortunately, the traditional isolation of secondary teaching faculty doesn't allow for integrated planning and thus, presentation to learners.

Journaling

Journaling is the process of reflecting on a given statement or question to make sense of it in terms of the learner's past and current experiences. For example, learners may begin a journal at the beginning of a unit on space travel. Early in the journal learners may be asked to reflect and write on what it would be like to leave their familiar planet to journey for a new life wrought with uncertainties. As the learners progress through the unit, preferably thematically, they are asked to reflect on their travels as they journey farther and farther away from planet Earth. How are their survival needs being met? What kinds of hardships are they encountering? What improvements to their quality of life are they discovering? Like hypothesis testing, analogies, and metaphors, this type of experience forces the learner to reach back into her prior learning to co-construct meaning of the new.

Portfolios

Portfolios are a system of organizing various documents so that connections among the documents and their conceptual meaning may be made. Portfolios may contain paradigm statements or declarations of what students understand about a concept at that place and time in their life. For example, beginning teachers are often asked to document their educational philosophy early on in their careers and to revisit those statements as they grow up in the profession. By reflecting on where they have been, where they are, and where they might be going, connections can be made between prior, present, and future knowledge and experiences.

Another example may be at the beginning of a unit on particle physics; learners might be asked to explain their current understanding of the atom. As new concepts are introduced in their learning experience, the students would record how these concepts measure up to new ones in the process of co-construction of meaning.

Other instruments may be used to analyze current conceptions. Questionnaires, surveys and checklists may be periodically completed and updated as students move through the study of a concept. These documents may be added to the portfolio to help the learner understand how he/she constructs knowledge most fully. This act of self-observation and interpretation is called metacognition and is consistent with constructivist thought.

Dialogue and Cooperative Learning

Dialogue with others and cooperative learning provide students with experiences where the act of co-creation of meaning can occur simultaneously with other learners. When learners are asked to engage in dialogue, their prior knowledge is called up and constantly challenged as new concepts are introduced. In the cooperative learning experience, where groups of learners work together to construct meaning toward the solution of a given problem, similar connections are made.

For example, a cooperative group of learners, given the task of building a better mousetrap, will exchange prior knowledge about the construction of typical mousetraps. Different learners will likely be familiar with different types of traps. Together, the exchange of dialogue helps learners share and build new meaning. Cooperatively, the learners will test possible prototypes of new mousetraps and modify their existing understanding of what a mousetrap means.

Learning Cycle Lesson

The learning cycle lesson is a process of presenting material so that the learner capitalizes on the constructive nature of learning. The learning cycle lesson has several phases to its delivery. The first phase is the exploration phase, where students are given an opportunity to explore components of the curriculum. In a science lesson, students may be given different shells to observe. The students will be asked to record their observations and begin to make inferences about their observations.

The next phase is the explanation phase, where the instructor helps the student co-construct meaning of the observations and inferences. This phase, also known as the Term Invention phase, is where sense is made of the phenomenon. Here terminology, explanation and connections will make up the learning experience. In our example, perhaps the shells might be described in terms of their biological attributes. Connections to remains of other sea life would likely be addressed to connect former knowledge with new knowledge, and to help students discard any preconceived ideas that they now realize are incorrect.

The expansion phase, also known as the Concept Application phase, is where students are given an opportunity to apply what they just learned. Here students might develop a family tree of the shells and compare to the actual taxonomic relationship delineated by scientists. Learners would then have the opportunity to compare previous understanding with new and see how they measure up to one another.

In some versions of the learning cycle, an additional phase is listed. This phase, the evaluation phase, is actually an ongoing act of assessing for the co-construction of meaning. Student responses, questions, records and actions are all considered when assessing learning.

RECOMMENDATIONS FOR WEB-BASED CONSTRUCTIVIST LEARNING AND INSTRUCTION

The foregoing discussion on experiences used by constructivist instructors in the traditional classroom has numerous implications for distance learning education. With some creativity, much of the same experiences that stimulate thinking and facilitate the co-construction of meaning in traditional settings can be made available to the distance learner.

For example, as a distance learning educator plans for instruction, he/she must keep in mind that the experience is paramount in the constructivist learning process. But before the experiences can be selected, the scope and sequence of the curriculum must be decided. Questions such as, "What knowledge of this topic is worth knowing and significant to understanding other concepts?" and "What depth of understanding is essential for learners to make important connections?" will be helpful in narrowing down the plethora of material on a given topic.

Next, the distance learning educator must decide what planning will be necessary to deliver the curriculum. Choices must be made regarding related Web sites, CD-ROMs and other technology that will be used to help make the curriculum deliverable.

Once the technology is selected, careful attention must be paid to the experiences that will be provided to learners to make meaning possible. The appropriateness of every experience described previously should be evaluated to determine the degree to which it would bring the taught curriculum closer to the learned curriculum.

Following this planning, the distance learning educator must orchestrate all the technologies and experiences for the implementation phase of instruction. During this phase, educators should closely monitor the growth in the learners and efficacy of the program by keeping abreast of journal responses, paradigm statements, or whatever other experiences are being used as part of the distance learning education program. Instructional plans should be modified based on this feedback to most fully ensure co-construction of meaning by the learners. This process of monitoring and modifying should be ongoing throughout the distance learning education program.

During the evaluation phase of instruction, the distance learning educator should review growth of the learners in terms of meaning construction and should assess how closely the curriculum taught and the curriculum learned match. In this way, evaluation of the learner and program can be accomplished simultaneously. Figure 6 illustrates a conceptual model of constructivist learning and instruction via Web-based instruction.

FUTURE RESEARCH OPPORTUNITIES

Jonassen, Peck, and Wilson (1999) propose a conceptual model of learning environments for technology. According to their model, Constructivist Learning Environments (CLEs) should engage students in investigation of the problem, critique of related cases, review of information resources, development of necessary skills, collaboration with others and use of social support in implementation of the learning experience. Perhaps merging of the conceptual model of constructivist distance learning education described in this chapter and that presented by Jonassen, et al. will better serve distance learning educators and learners alike. Learner and program evaluation will testify to the efficacy of Web-based constructivist learning and instruction.

The degree to which this process will bring about the desired learning is a question for future study. Most Web-based instruction today is based on behaviorism, viewing the learner as an empty vessel waiting to be filled. Distance learning educators should acknowledge constructivism as the new paradigm for learning and must also be

Figure 6

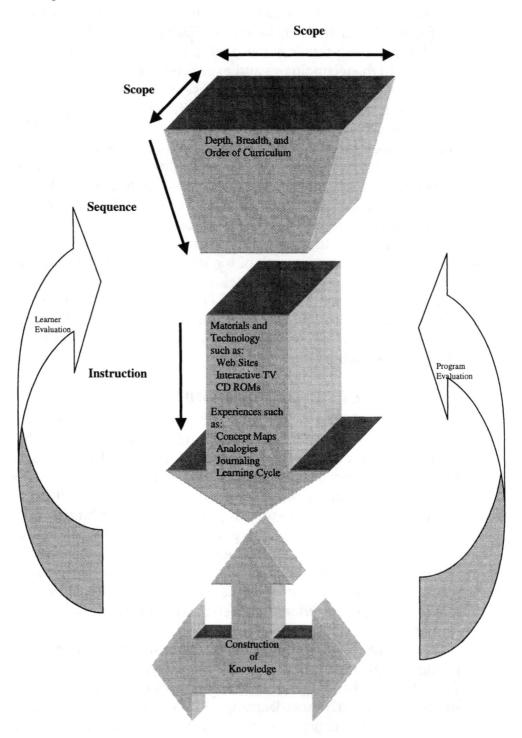

willing to shift their teaching practices for consistency and constructivist learning.

REFERENCES

Baker, D. R., & Piburn, M. D. (1997). *Constructing science in middle and secondary school classrooms*. Boston: Allyn and Bacon.

Dewey, J. (1944). *Democracy and education*. New York: The Free Press.

Husserl, E. (1970a). *Logical investigations, Volume I* (J. N. Findlay, Trans.). New York: Humanities Press. (Original work published 1921-22).

Husserl E. (1970b). *Logical investigations, Volume II* (J. N. Findlay, Trans.). New York: Humanities Press. (Original work published 1921-22).

Jonassen, D. H., Peck, K. L., Wilson, B. G. (1999). *Learning with technology: A constructivist perspective*. Upper Saddle River, NJ: Prentice Hall, Inc.

Kuhn, T. S. (1962). *The structure of scientific revolutions*. Chicago: The University of Chicago Press.

Mohanty, J. N. (1969). *Edmund Husserl's theory of meaning*. (2nd ed.). The Hague: Martinus Nijhoff.

Morphew, V. N. (1994). *Change in meaning, change in action: A phenomenological study*. Unpublished doctoral dissertation. West Virginia University, Morgantown.

Passe, J. (1999). *Elementary school curriculum* (2nd ed.). Boston: McGraw.

Tiryakian, E. A. (1973). Sociology and existential phenomenology. In M. Natanson (Ed.), *Phenomenology and the Social Sciences, Volume I* Evanston: Northwestern University Press, 187-222 .

Chapter II

Interactive Distance Learning

Rita M. Purcell-Robertson
Arcadia Group Worldwide, Inc.

Daniel F. Purcell, Sr.
University of Phoenix Online

INTRODUCTION

One of the major criticisms of distance education is the perception of inferior interaction between professor and students. Although the question of sufficient interaction is just as valid in a traditional classroom setting, the very nature of distance education serves to exacerbate the problem. This doesn't have to be the case. There are strategies an instructor can employ to ensure the interaction is maintained at a high level. In fact there is a type of distance learning structure where interaction is even higher than in a traditional classroom. This chapter will facilitate faculty in enriching the quality of the communication exchange by assisting professors in enhancing the "high touch" aspects of pedagogy when using "high tech" media.

BACKGROUND

A very dramatic statement about the state of interaction in a traditional classroom can be seen in the film *Back to School*. The series of scenes start by showing a lecture hall full of students and a professor lecturing at the board. In the next scene, some of the students have been replaced by tape recorders. As the scenes progress, more and more students are replaced until the professor is lecturing to a room full of tape recorders. In the final scene, the professor is gone and there is a tape recorder lecturing to tape recorders. Clearly an exaggeration, this does, nevertheless, identify a possible problem in interaction. If such is the case in a traditional classroom, there is an even greater potential for problems in distance education where the student is already physically removed from the instructor.

Repman and Logan (1996) said "interactions lie at the heart of any learning situation and remain critical to active learning" (p. 35). Wolcott (1996) said "it is time we shift our attention from how to work around the distance in its physical sense, to how to keep from further distancing learners in a psychological and social sense" (p. 23). There are strategies that can be employed to ensure that interaction is maintained and learning is achieved. The University of Phoenix has instituted policies and training to assist the instructor in achieving a highly interactive environment.

FACULTY TO STUDENT INTERACTION

As in the example from the film a student can feel disconnected even in a traditional classroom environment. Wolcott (1996) pointed out that "combining both physical and psychological distance makes for a potentially troublesome mix" (p. 23). The instructor in the film adopted a "sage on the stage" methodology for transmitting information. Combining this with a medium in which a student may be sitting all alone in front of a computer in their home invites feelings of being disconnected from the learning. At least in a traditional classroom the student can feel a sense of community with the others in the room.

Many believe (Repman and Logan, 1996; Wolcott, 1996; Gibson and Herrera, 1999) that the way to combat this feeling of being disconnected is to establish a learner-centered environment. How does one move from the teacher-centered environment to the learner-centered environment? The role of the instructor becomes quite different.

In a learner-centered environment, the instructor is not the "star" or the "sage on the stage." In the learner-centered environment the instructor becomes the "guide on the side," with sometimes unexpected opportunities to reflect on his or her instructional style and philosophy (Repman and Logan, 1996, 36).

The learner-centered teacher encourages students' personal growth and emphasizes facilitation of learning over transmission of information (Wolcott, 1996, 25).

When discussing the program at the University of Phoenix, Lewis and Hedegaard said, "instructors are viewed by students more as peers and facilitators than as 'professors'" (1993, p.69). Gibson and Herrera were glad that they scheduled 18 months to take a traditional class on line in part because the change in mindset was such a big step for traditional faculty (1999, p. 59). To put it simply, the instructor must "check their ego at the door." The role of facilitator vice professor sometimes requires you to hold off on answering a question in favor of guiding the class to the discovery of the answer. It means the use of leading questions and comments to draw out comments from the members of the class. It may also mean sitting back and letting the class thrash things about until they have reasoned it out. Without the traditional time restrictions of a set amount of time for the class, the instructor is normally free to take more time in a distance education environment. You are a guide or a partner in the learning instead of an imparter of wisdom.

How can you achieve this peer-like association with the students? Wolcott (1996) emphasizes building rapport, "rapport, both teacher-to-student rapport and student-to-student rapport, is crucial in creating a sense of community among learners" (p. 26). Repman and Logan (1996) tell students about themselves and give students opportunities to share information about themselves. This is the same approach used by the University of Phoenix Online. At the beginning of each session, the instructor and the students, post a biography for everyone to read, allowing them all to feel connected. To carry this one step further, the instructor can highlight information from a biography, welcome the student to the class and comment on the information. Much more than could be done in a traditional classroom.

FEEDBACK

The lack of immediate feedback is another way that learners can feel disconnected. Lewis and Hedegaard (1993) noted that University of Phoenix Online students in end-of-course surveys frequently mentioned faculty feedback as a concern. The student who doesn't receive a timely response to their comments may feel as though they are crying out in a wasteland and no one cares.

Wolcott (1996) suggests that to enhance interaction to "provide timely feedback; respond to questions and 'turn-around' assignments promptly" (p. 27). Repman and Logan (1996) go further to specify "feedback should be prompt, focused, and constructive" (p. 37). The University of Phoenix took the comments of their students to heart because their contract for faculty reads that, among other things,

The Instructor Will:

- Respond to students' questions within 24 hours from the time received.
- Return all student assignments bearing a grade and comments within one week from the date the assignments are received. If, due to extenuating circumstances, these conditions cannot be met, the faculty member will establish an alternative which will be clearly communicated to the students.

Feedback is a two-way street. Just as a student needs feedback from the instructor, the instructor needs feedback from the student. The instructor needs to know if the student comprehends the information. Students in a traditional classroom offer many nonverbal feedback cues. These cues may not be available in a distance education environment, especially a text-based one. That means that another mechanism for student feedback must be devised. One such mechanism is a weekly summary submitted by the student. The summary identifies what the student learned during the previous week and also discusses any aspects of the delivery that worked or didn't work. A key to the success of these summaries is for the instructor to read them and try to incorporate appropriate changes. Although a weekly summary works in the case of the University of Phoenix, it doesn't mean it will work in all cases. The instructor must find a mechanism and timeframe that fits their own particular style and the medium being used.

An end-of-course survey is a valuable feedback device no matter what instructional format is used. These surveys can often provide good information as they did in the case of University of Phoenix and instructor feedback. Another example is taken from a visual-based distance education format. The instructor had a local class and included other students in distant locations via a video hookup. During one particular lecture the instructor held a paper from which she was lecturing and the camera was focused such that the paper was the only thing on the screen at the distant site. Feedback from the students revealed that the instructor was inadvertently moving the paper. Since the paper filled the screen, the motion had the effect of making some of the off-campus students seasick. The instructor hadn't even realized she was moving the paper.

STUDENT TO STUDENT INTERACTION

Interaction among the students is also important to a meaningful learning experience. Repman and Logan (1996) point out that "students interacting with other students increase their participation and enhance their motivation and learning" (p. 37). Wolcott (1996) emphasizes that "the lack of rapport among participants can have a reciprocal effect on classroom interaction" (p. 24). Wolcott (1996) goes on to say "student's reticence threatens spontaneity and lessens the amount and frequency of interaction: in turn, the lack of interaction can retard the development of rapport" (p. 24). Just as important as fostering good interaction between students and faculty is fostering good interaction between students and students. The instructor and students must work together to build this community. (Repman and Logan, 1996, p. 37)

An asynchronous, text-based distance learning environment lends itself to more interactions than a voice environment such as a traditional classroom. In a voice environment, a strong speaker can monopolize the discussion and shyer people can just sit and observe without participating. The asynchronous, text-based environment not only allows interaction but also requires it. Lewis and Hedegaard (1993) point out that "social loafing becomes much more conspicuous because an uninvolved group member literally disappears" (p.69). This aspect of online education makes it preferable to a traditional environment. Kiesler identified that "interaction in online groups tend to be more evenly distributed relative to face-to-face groups" (Lewis and Hedegaard, 1993, p. 69).

Fostering this interaction means that you must recognize that the students need to socialize. In a distance environment this means that the way of socializing should be made available. In a text-based environment this could take the form of a special chat room for this specific purpose. In a visual/verbal environment it could take the form of having the equipment available for a specified period before and after the actual meeting time of the class. These mechanisms are analogous to the hallway or break room in the traditional environment.

CONCLUSION

In a distance learning environment, maintaining interaction is difficult but not impossible. We must recognize the importance of this interaction and employ techniques to encourage it to happen.

Some techniques are:

- Establish a learner-centered environment.
- Be a "guide by the side" not a "sage on the stage."
- Provide regular, meaningful feedback.
- Ask for and heed student feedback.
- Make provisions for student-to-student interaction.

REFERENCES

Gibson, J.W. & Herrera, J.M. (1999), How to Go From Classroom Based to Online Delivery in Eighteen Months or Less: A Case Study in Online Program Development. *T.H.E. Journal*, 26(6), 57-60.

Lewis, C.T. & Hedegaard, T. (1993), Online Education: Issues and Some Answers. *T.H.E. Journal*, 68-71.

Repman, J. & Logan, S. (1996), Interactions at a Distance: Possible Barriers and Collaborative Solutions. *TECHTRENDS*, 35-38.

Wolcott, L.L. (1996), Distant, But Not Distanced: A Learner-Centered Approach to Distance Education. *TECHTRENDS*, Vol(issue), 23-27.

Chapter III

Summative and Formative Evaluations of Internet-Based Teaching

Dat-Dao Nguyen
California State University, Northridge

Dennis S. Kira
Concordia University, Montreal

INTRODUCTION

Teaching is a communication process in which a body of knowledge is delivered from an instructor to students (Gagne, 1985). This communication traditionally takes place in a classroom. With the proliferation of computer software and hardware at low costs and the ease of access to the World Wide Web, one should expect that the use of Internet and related information technologies will foster an alternative teaching environment. Previous works have reported on various Internet-based teaching aids such as using e-mail, posting information on a Web page and using the Internet to search for additional class materials. Integrating these teaching media in a larger framework of Distance Learning and Virtual Class (Hiltz, 1994), they would provide a synergistic effect in helping students acquire the desired body of knowledge efficiently. From this perspective, we discuss a framework for summative and formative evaluations of Internet-based teaching in higher education. The timely evaluation is necessary for the development and implementation of a new teaching/learning environment. It will assure that the technology meets the intended pedagogic goal of teaching by taking into account feedback from student-users.

INTERNET-BASED TEACHING MEDIA

In general, one may classify Internet-based instructional technologies in the following three types: electronic communication, electronic posting and course Web site. The classification represents an evolution of the use of these technologies. However, these types are not mutually exclusive since one can always aggregate them in a larger framework of Distance Learning and Virtual Class.

Electronic Communication

Some computer networks have the facility of allowing their users to communicate online between two parties or among a group. This feature is convenient when a group of students cannot meet at a same location but could be online at the same time to exchange information. A group member will access his/her network account and then "talk" to other party via teletyping.

E-mail is another electronic communication which has been widely used by instructors and students outside the classroom. The communication varies from a one-to-one message to one-to-many messages sent to a distribution list. The advantage of using e-mail is that both parties can send and answer messages at their convenience without physically disturbing the other party as in telephone calls. Electronic files can be attached to an e-mail message. A message can be edited and then forwarded to another party. However, the response to an e-mail may not provide necessary timely feedback if one party delays his/her response. In the current state-of-the-art of telecommunication technology, e-mail should be considered as another messaging medium like an answering machine. Nevertheless, e-mail can be incorporated effectively in a larger framework of Internet-based teaching.

Electronic Posting

An instructor may make the course material available in the storage of his/her own account or a group account on a computer network. Computer software is usually used for the management of message transactions within a group account. Certain files of an individual account can be made available for public accessing. With authorization, students can extract material from the instructor's account. Or students can have personalized identifications to access the group account where class material is stored.

An interested instructor may also create a Web page to post his/her course syllabus, class announcements, lecture slides, assignments, help information, solutions and templates. This delivery mode is passive since it is a replacement of printed class handouts. The instructor simply converts the course material into an HTML or a portable file (PDF) format and then posts it on his/her Web page. The information can be viewed with an Internet browser or a reader, downloaded, and printed by students. The communication may be conducted via a link to the instructor's e-mail address. However, there are no online discussions and no pointers to other available instructional resources on the Internet.

Course Web site

In this type, students are offered a structured Web site featuring instructional materials, links to other related Internet resources, online tutorial (with or without audio-video enhancement), online tests, and online discussions. Communication within the class could be in passive and/or active modes.

In a *passive* communication mode, published material in the course Web site provides additional information in formats other than an HTML (or PDF) version of a class handout. Students may access the course Web site for posted information, review/practice the course material with interactive tutorials and tests. They can follow suggested links to other related instructional resources on the Internet.

In an *active* communication mode, online discussion is facilitated with instructor's virtual office hours and virtual group meetings. In the first case, the instructor is online at a specific time schedule to answer immediately students' e-mail. In the second case, the whole class is online and discussion takes place via a chat-box. This instructional environment emphasizes on an active role of Internet-based teaching and an active participation of students in the knowledge acquisition process.

SUMMATIVE EVALUATION

The aim of this evaluation is to justify the implementation of an instructional technology (Hiltz, 1994). Summative evaluation seeks to answer the following questions: (1) What are the most effective Internet-based teaching and learning processes and how differences in these processes relate to comparative outcomes between new and traditional environments. (2) What are the advantages and disadvantages of this delivery mode in attaining specific educational goals as compared to other traditional means. (3) How the merits vary with the characteristics of students, subject matter, teaching methods and teaching equipment.

Effective Learning-Teaching and Related Media

Some researchers view the instructional technology primarily as made up of technical knowledge to operate the medium in terms of hardware and software. Others concentrate on the accessibility of devices and material to users. Still others focus on the questions of what good does a particular instructional technology provide for education and what characteristics make it of particular values for the promotion of learning. Gagne (1987) believed that the view of this third group would foresee the promise of instructional technology. The conditions for effective learning include not only capabilities and qualities of an individual learner, but also other important issues related to the media used in teaching and learning (Gagne, 1987). However, the focus of designing and implementing an instructional technology is not just on technology *per se* but should be on how to improve performance resulting from learning. From this perspective, the choice of an effective teaching method or an instructional technology is subject to the course content, the needs of the instructor as well as those of students (Flagg, 1990; Leidner and Jarvenpaa, 1995).

Gagne (1987) noted that in studying instructional technology one should aim at revealing (i) the ways in which existing media can be most effectively employed in promoting effective learning; (ii) the conditions of optimal learning, including the properties and characteristics of media that can be used to establish such conditions; and (iii) novel techniques of designing and delivering instruction that can be shown to improve its effectiveness.

Since the purpose of instruction is to foster effective learning, the central focus for rational derivation of instructional techniques should be on the learner. Development of rationally sound instructional procedures must take into account the learner's characteristics as parameters of the design of any particular program of instruction (Gagne, 1987).

Effective learning is not simply about the efficient transfer of a

Figure 1: Learning Environment and Media

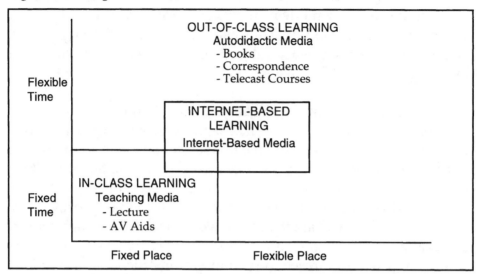

body of knowledge from an instructor to his/her students. Bloom (1956) proposed that, in an effective learning process, a learner should at first acquire facts and information and be able to recall them. Then the learner understands the basic use of acquired knowledge and can use abstractions to apply knowledge in other situations. In a higher stage, the learner is able to decompose his/her knowledge into hierarchical and related constituent elements (analysis) and can put together facts and information into a new structure of knowledge (synthesis). In the final stage, the learner can provide quantitative and/or qualitative judgements about the appropriateness of material and methods for a given purpose. From this taxonomy, effective teaching should be learner-oriented, active and in context to assist the intellectual development of learner.

Learning can happen in an in-class and/or out-of-class environment. The boundary of learning environment is defined in terms of time and place. In-class environment is constrained with fixed time and fixed place. The characteristic of this environment is the physical presence of an instructor and learners. The most common in-class teaching medium is face-to-face lecture, with or without audiovisual aids. In an out-of-class environment, one can learn at flexible time schedule and place. In this environment, a learner acquires knowledge with autodidactic media, such as books, correspondence and telecast educational programs, with or without help from an instructor. Help and feedback from instructor in out-of-class environment is asynchronous since one does not have an instant answer for a spontaneous question. With the proliferation of information technology, one can define an alternative learning environment, which is overlapping of the two traditional ones (Figure 1). Through the use of information technology, in particular the Internet-based one, a learner can acquire knowledge either inside or outside the classroom environment.

The impacts of information technology on learning can be captured in process and outcome dimensions of a taxonomy proposed by Leidner and Jarvenpaa (1995). Process dimensions relate to the control of pace and content of learning (instructor vs. student) and the purpose of instruction (knowledge dissemination vs. knowledge creation). Outcome dimensions cover impacts on motivation and self-efficacy (ephemeral vs. long term), levels of learning (factual/procedural vs. conceptual), levels of cognition (lower vs. higher-order thinking), participation, attention (high vs. low) and performance (improvements on factual/procedural tests vs. improvements on conceptual assessments). Consequently, depending on a pedagogic goal, one can implement appropriate instructional media.

In instructional technology literature, there is a debate on the performance evaluation of instructional media (Vargo, 1997). The *media efficiency* view holds that the media used to deliver an educational program can only affect the efficiency of the delivery, not the effectiveness of the outcomes (Clarke, 1994). In contrast, the *media effectiveness* view maintains that the effectiveness of media should reflect both the capabilities of media and the complexities of social situations within which they are used (Kozma, 1994). In fact, one should evaluate the performance of instructional technology from a system perspective. In a learning system, as a complex social setting, a learner will use various learning methods and media. As such, all of components of instructional technology should provide a synergistic effect on the learning outcomes (Jonessen et al., 1994).

Therefore, the task of an interested and innovative educator is to build an effective Internet-based teaching environment based on knowledge of learning and available features of the World Wide Web. This environment will promote a deep approach to learning so that what students learn are the deep understanding of subject content, the ability to analyze and synthesize facts and information, and the development of creative thinking and good communication skill

(Alexander, 1995). This learning experience should improve not only personal skills and abilities but should also prepare the learners to engage in a collaborative work of real life. In addition, it should develop learners into independent and competent persons in a life-long learning process.

Classroom Teaching

The main advantage of this type of teaching is in the *immediate control* on the learning process of students by the instructor. In classroom teaching, the boundary of relevant knowledge is defined, the learning process is scheduled from lecture to lecture, and the criteria for performance evaluation are preestablished. With guidance and evaluation, an instructor can provide students with instant feedback to assure a correct acquisition of the desired knowledge. One expects that once students complete the class, they will acquire the intended volume of knowledge.

For an instructor, there is no other preparation beyond the assemblage of related material to be lectured in class. Audiovisual aids may be used to enhance the communication in the delivery process. In any case, the delivery of course material could be controlled immediately in order to adapt to a specific audience and/or situation in the classroom environment.

Immediate interaction with teacher and peers in a classroom motivates the interest in learning and reinforces the knowledge acquisition process. Learning in class is characterized by the physical proximity, which may create a sense of belonging and exchange of emotional support (Hiltz and Wellman, 1997). However, the social atmosphere of a classroom may nurture a tendency of group conformity to the opinion expressed by the instructor and peers. In addition, a student with initiative may have to moderate his/her progress to the pace of the class. Consequently, individual creativity may not be supported or encouraged.

The major disadvantage of this teaching environment is in its *limited access* of time and place. A class lecture can only be available for a group of students at a scheduled time in a specific classroom. As one wishes to enlarge the classroom to accommodate more students efficiently, one may encounter a trade-off between quality and quantity of teaching outcome. From a student's perspective, attending a class can be very time consuming as one has to either wait or move among classrooms. Sometimes, commuting takes more time than the time actually spent in a class lecture.

Autodidactic Media

If for some personal constraints, a learner could not attend a traditional class, he/she can learn with other media such as reading books, enrolling in a correspondence or telecast course.

Learning from Books

Learning from books, and other printed media, is a popular traditional autodidactic method. The learning process is flexible since one can have access to the instructional material, in this case the book, anytime and anywhere. Books on related topics provide students with unlimited boundary knowledge. This learning environment promotes individual creativity since students use their own judgment to process information. This active selection of relevant information will reinforce the acquired knowledge.

This learning process does not emphasize on the interaction with instructor and peers, if any. There is no or only minimal feedback during the learning process. The learning environment requires a self-motivation from students. For a student with initiative, it can promote fast progress since the student can make up his/her own learning schedule and proceed accordingly. But for others, without the guidance of an instructor or a self-defined study plan, it may take longer time to locate and acquire relevant information. In addition, without self-discipline, these students may not be able to keep up with the progress of a normal class schedule.

The evaluation of student performance is usually in the form of an examination at the end of learning period. Depending on learning behavior and personal effort, the level of knowledge of students after training may not be the same even they have taken a common final examination.

Learning by Correspondence

This type of learning is similar to learning from books. A student enrolls in a correspondence course and receives instructional direction and material by mail. Learning activities could be scheduled in order to define certain milestones of achievement in the learning process. The reinforcement of learning could be enhanced by having regular feedback from an instructor in the form of correction on assignments and/or question-answer correspondence. One may have performance evaluations during the course or at the end of the learning period.

Learning with Telecast Course

The telecast course could be conducted with radio or television. The use of this medium is limited by a fixed schedule. Teaching with television is in fact a replication of in-class teaching. The advantage is one can use audio-video aids intensively to enhance the lecture. However, teaching style of a lecturer is very important in the delivery of course content. Students may not have a choice to study with a particular instructor as in a traditional school setting. The telecasting could be boring if it is simply a recording of an in-class lecture. In addition, the course is a one-way communication between lecturer and his/her audience. Since the lecture is prerecorded, an instructor cannot moderate the delivery of course content corresponding to the instant response of students.

Overall, the merit of out-of-class learning and autodidactic media is in the provision of a *flexible environment* in which a learner can progress at his/her own pace. However, these environments and media lack frequent helpful interaction with instructor and peers. Then the feedback from instructor may not be timely to provide the necessary guidance. At last, the student needs some degree of self-motivation in order to progress successfully through the learning process.

Internet-based Teaching

The prominent advantage of this learning environment is in the *unlimited access* to the class contents. In fact, students can access the "class" anytime from anywhere. This learning environment is *flexible* since students do not have to commute a long way to attend the class at a specific time. The environment provides a permanent access to the course material as the information is always online as long as one can access the Internet. There is no fixed schedule on the delivery of course content. As such, a student can progress at his/her own pace. This learning is *creative* since students participate actively in selecting relevant information and developing knowledge from their own perspective. This teaching also offers *unlimited boundary* of relevant knowledge. Unlike accessing printed media, the use of Internet may take shorter time to get relevant and up-to-date information. At last, the learning process could be *enjoyable* with the interactive audio-video enhancement of the course Web site. Consequently, Internet-based instructional technology may serve as a major teaching aid in a classroom or become the main medium for learning in an out-of-class environment.

However, the learning process in this environment is *unstructured*. Without a self-motivation and a clear study plan, a student may get discouraged due to information overload. Similarly, without self-discipline, the student may get distracted when navigating through various sources of information. In addition, the feedback may be delayed as one does not have immediate interaction with instructor and peers. This may increase the perception on the lack of physical proximity and the impersonal nature of the method.

The most commonly cited drawback of Distance Learning is the *asynchronous communication* with instructor and peers. Students may not get instant answers to their questions on a certain topic of the material and they do not have real-time feedback on their response in order to reinforce the learning. However, a counter-argument is that instant feedback may not be helpful to the learning even in a face-to-face meeting. This counter-argument is based on the fact that interaction in class is dominated by a small group of students and it could be disruptive. Then a spontaneous question may not reinforce learning as well as if the question is asked after some effort is made by students to clarify the subject matter by themselves (Collis, 1996). In fact, with the development of Internet-based communication technology, one can have online and real-time feedback with instructor and peers.

From the above summative assessments, Internet-based teaching has both merits of traditional in-class learning and autodidactic environments. In addition, students may benefit from the flexible schedule and unbounded instructional resources in order to progress at their own pace. In an Internet-based learning environment, students could have similar feedback and interaction with instructor and peers as in a classroom to reinforce their learning.

FORMATIVE EVALUATION

Formative evaluation investigates the feedback on any factors that affect teaching and learning processes, and then designing and implementing the instructional technology appropriately. The development of Internet-based teaching could be considered from a systems design and analysis perspective. As such, formative evaluation should be conducted at every stage of a systems development life cycle to improve the functionality and ease of use of the final design. These evaluations should be conducted on a regular basis at pre-course, in-course and post-course stages. As indicated in Figure 2, the efficiency of a teaching/learning system, measured by Learning Outcome, is affected by Content, Audience and Design issues.

Content Issues

In considering content issues, one should address questions such as what is the need for a greater understanding of subject matter, the content to be communicated, and the justification in choosing this content for the new technology given limited resources (Flagg, 1990). With a specific pedagogic goal, such as intellectual development or skill training, one defines an appropriate curriculum on which subjects are to be taught. Then one develops the syllabus on which topics are to be covered and in what sequence.

To deliver the instructional material, Internet-based media can be a teaching aid to make classroom meetings more efficient. It can also become an alternative instructional medium, besides other autodidactic media, to deliver effectively the course content to learners in an out-of-class environment. The implementation of Internet-based teaching requires an evaluation on content issues, which should be investi-

Figure 2 : Formative Evaluation of Teaching/Learning System

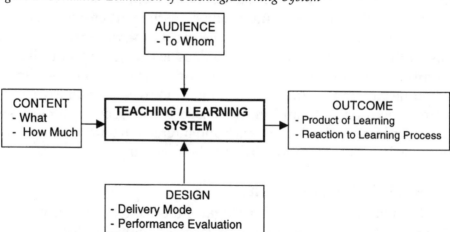

gated in a specific instructional context considering the needs and capabilities to meet these needs from the instructor's as well as students' perspective. Consequently, one has to decide on what subject matter and how much should be delivered via Internet-based communication technologies to the intended audience. Teaching with the Internet may create an unnecessary extra burden for instructors and students if the content can be delivered effectively and efficiently with other traditional instructional means.

Audience Issues

These issues address questions such as who needs the content, what are the characteristics of intended audience with respect to the course content and the size of target group to justify the effort (Flagg, 1990). Literature in educational psychology is useful to investigate the learning focus and motivation of the intended audience. Some students take courses to meet the requirements of a degree for their professional advancement. They might just study enough to pass the course. Others enjoy the subject matter and seek it for an intellectual development. There are also differences in learning style and learning attitude. Some students are confident, independent and responsible in their study. They can be selective in acquiring and exploring the topics of interest. Other students may take *in verbatim* whatever is being delivered in the course and need close supervision and guidance to proceed through the course.

In an Internet-based learning environment, students who have either a disability or family and job constraints cannot attend and spend time in a traditional class. The aptitude of these students in learning may be affected by their characteristics such as gender, age, and occupation. Some demographic groups may be more enthusiastic with the use of a computer in general and with Internet access in particular. Consequently, teaching with the Internet tends to be more favorably accepted by a specific audience. The attitude on willingness to learn independently, self-regulation versus hands-on and close supervision may be different across demographic groups. In learning with the Internet, students are responsible for the completion of course work without close supervision from the instructor. As such, learning in this environment requires a certain level of self-motivation and self-organization from students (Leidner and Jarvenpaa, 1995; Hiltz and Wellman, 1997).

Also, one should consider the students' computer competency and accessibility to the Internet outside the classroom. The difficulty in using a computer may cause a negative perception on the comprehensiveness of content. It has been shown that lack of skill in searching relevant information may develop a feeling of information overload (Hiltz and Wellman, 1997).

Design Issues

The design issues address questions such as which content needs can be best met with the technology, and what format can be best applied to communicate the content efficiently. These issues relate to the appropriateness of delivery and performance evaluation modes.

Delivery Related Design Issues

We observe the following typical design issues in developing the interface of a course Web site.

- How to organize the instructional material in terms of content, pages, frames and links. Whether the text should be represented linearly or with the use of hyperlinks.
- Which other information on the Internet is relevant to students so that one can provide them with sufficient pointers to related resources.
- How to organize group activities and facilitate group works with the choice of communication media such as e-mail distribution list, electronic bulletin board, and online discussion.
- How the design of a Web page such as background color, headings, font size and type will enhance the learning. Whether animated graphics and "bells and whistles" are useful or will distract students from learning.
- Ease of navigating through the course Web page with logical presentation of material, well-organized linked pages, enhanced graphics and related links.

Performance Evaluation Related Design Issues

Once the general learning goal for the whole course and the specific learning objectives for each segment of the course are defined, performance standards for completing the course should be implemented appropriately. In particular, specific performance standards have to be specified such as deadlines for every activity of the course work and evaluation scheme for assignments. The acquisition of course content could be evaluated with assignments of different types, ranges, and numbers. Particularly, one should ask questions on how much homework should be assigned, what types of assignments are appropriate, what level of difficulty and mastering of content one could expect from students, and how to design an online assignment and evaluation. One also has to provide appropriate measures to assure the integrity of the students' class work such as whether the final evaluation should be conducted with traditional means.

Outcome Issues

These issues relate to the measurement of student performance in order to assess the efficiency of an instructional technology. One can evaluate the efficacy of learning environment and media in terms of product of learning and reaction to the learning process. Thus, one should measure how much students have learned from the course and how well students feel about the acquired knowledge and the learning process. These quantitative and qualitative measurements of learning outcome should be compared across various teaching environments and media to assess the effectiveness of the implemented medium.

Product of Learning

Once proceeding through the course, a learner is expected to acquire improvements in personal beliefs, actions, skills, and abilities. One could measure the mastering of intended content by the degree of completion of the course requirements. Since the criteria for performance evaluation have been defined, one should be able to assess how much students have learned from the course through their assignments and examinations.

Reaction to Learning Process

Reaction to the learning process can be assessed by the course evaluation of students on their progress before and after taking the course. The evaluation intends to measure the satisfaction of students on the acquisition of course content and the delivery of this content.

- *Satisfaction with the results of learning*: Learners perceive that the outcome of learning should correspond to their effort in time, work and other opportunity costs in order to take the course. The outcome should be useful for learners in their personal develop-

ment in terms of intellectual and/or socioeconomic advancement. Ideally, as the results of learning, students should not only
learn new ideas and skill but also be able to change their behavior
and the behavior of others. In this evaluation, students should be
able to provide a qualitative assessment on the usefulness of
content and make comparisons across other learning experiences taken inside as well as outside the classroom environment.

- *Satisfaction with the delivery process*: One should consider the
perceived easiness and/or difficulties in using the learning medium in order to evaluate the acceptance of technology. From a
student's perspective, ease of learning includes the comprehensiveness of course content, the feedback from the instructor and
the communication with peers. The course content should be
appropriate for an average participant of the target audience.
Timely feedback from the instructor should be available to refine
the knowledge acquisition process by focusing on relevant information. Frequent interaction with instructor and peers is necessary to reinforce the acquired knowledge, enhance the learning
interest and broaden the students' view on subject matter.

CONCLUSION

Internet-based teaching is an information system in which end
users are students. Therefore, one should complete the process of
systems development in the design and implementation of this teaching medium. In a summative evaluation, one should justify the
effective use of teaching method. In a formative evaluation, one
should analyze the needs of student-users and then design an appropriate system to satisfy their needs efficiently. A poorly designed and
implemented Internet-based course will do more harm than good as
it may satisfy the needs of an instructor for being online and up-to-
date with the technology but it does not help his/her students in
learning.

Teaching with the Internet should not be the individual incentive
of an interested instructor. The institution should assist the effort with
appropriate infrastructure to provide easy access from within and
outside to its communication networks. To be more effective, the
method should be integrated into a framework of Distance Learning
and Virtual Class to foster a favorable learning environment. The
design and implementation of Internet-based teaching should meet a

well-defined pedagogic goal supported by the institution. It should offer a specifically designed course to students who have personal constraints such that they cannot come to a traditional classroom on a fixed schedule. The method is intended for a larger audience than the one of traditional in-class teaching.

In any case, Internet-based teaching is an efficient means to introduce the intended audience to unlimited information resources available on the World Wide Web. In the short term, besides delivering the course content, it prepares students to the future business practice of electronic commerce. In the long term, it develops them into independent learners in a lifelong learning process.

REFERENCES

Alexander, S. (1995). Teaching and Learning on the World Wide Web. *Proceedings of the First Australian World Wide Web Conference*, Southern Cross University, Lismore, NSW, Australia.

Bloom, B.S. (Ed.)(1956). *Taxonomy of Educational Objectives*. New York: Longmans, Green and Co.

Clarke, R.E. (1994). Media Will Never Influence Learning. *Educational Technology, Research and Development*, 42(2), 21-29.

Collis, B. (1996). *Tele-Learning in A Digital World : The Future of Distance Learning*. London: International Thomson Computer Press.

Flagg, B.N. (1990). *Formative Evaluation for Educational Technologies*. Hillsdale, N.J: Lawrence Erlbaum.

Gagne, R.M. (Ed.) (1987). *Instructional Technology: Foundations*. Hillsdale, N.J. : Lawrence Erlbaum.

Gagne, R.M. (1985). *The Conditions of Learning and Theory of Instruction (4th Ed.)*. New York: Holt, Rinehart and Winston.

Hiltz, S.R. (1994). *The Virtual Classroom: Learning without Limits via Computer Networks*. Norwood, N.J. : Ablex Pub. Corp.

Hiltz, S. and Wellman B. (1997). Asynchronous Learning Networks as A Virtual Classroom. *Communication of the ACM*, 40(9), 44-49.

Jonassen, D.H., Campbell J.O. , and Davidson M.E. (1994). Learning with Media: Restructuring the Debate. *Educational Technology, Research and Development*, 42(2), 31-39.

Kozma, R.B. (1994). Will Media Influence Learning? Reframing the Debate. *Educational Technology, Research and Development*, 42(1), 7-19.

Leidner, D. and Jarvenpaa, S. (1995). The Use of Information Technology to Enhance Management School Education: A Theoretical View. *MIS Quarterly*, 19(3), 65-291.

Vargo, J. (1997). Evaluating the Effectiveness of Internet Delivered Coursework. *Proceedings of the Third Australian World Wide Web Conference*, Southern Cross University, Lismore, NSW, Australia.

Chapter IV

Implementing Corporate Distance Training Using Change Management, StrategicPlanning and Project Management

Zane L. Berge
University of Maryland, Baltimore County

Donna L. Smith
T. Rowe Price Associates, Inc.

As businesses expand to become more globally competitive, their needs grow to train geographically dispersed employees in a cost-effective manner. What must businesses do to implement distance education? An important role of the training and performance specialists in business is to help management solve complex problems within an organization. Still, distance education is usually not accomplished by a single group within an organization, nor through a single process. To change the way training is done, performance managers must use what is known about change management, strategic planning and project management in order to successfully implement technology-enhanced learning globally. One of the methods being used increasingly in the workplace is distance training.

Early in the company's implementation of distance training, it is useful to think about two approaches: a change approach and a project approach. As the level of the organization's maturity with distance training grows, (i.e., as distance training becomes institutionalized), the amount of change by definition decreases, and reliance shifts from change management to strategic planning. Similarly, as distance training permeates the organization, the shift is away from "individual events" and toward distance training as simply "how the organization does business."

Offered here is a perspective for implementing distance education which integrates strategic planning, change management and project management as critical to successful overall implementation. Rather than prescribe specific models, this approach identifies the essence of what each discipline contributes to the process of implementing distance education.

WHAT IS CORPORATE DISTANCE TRAINING

Distance training and distance education are used synonymously throughout this article unless otherwise noted. Essentially, we mean that the training or teaching function is implemented remotely using some type of technology and two-way communication system. This is especially in contrast to in-person training. Our focus is on how to introduce and sustain technologically-mediated learning in the workplace. Included are applications such as internet/intranet, computer-mediated communication, video-conference, satellite broadcast, audiographics and e-mail. Corporate distance training is defined differently by different authors, but here it means bringing together resources and learners to address the business problems in which training is at least part of the solution. This needs to be done in a cost-effective, timely manner. An emphasis is on the business challenge of training geographically disperse employees and managing resource and productivity across the system.

In addition, we view corporate distance training as an "innovation" (Schreiber and Berge, 1998). We propose an approach where training at a distance represents a significant departure from how the business currently conducts training activities—a change which will meet some level of resistance. This results not only in applying new technology but also "creating a different kind of structure for learning and teaching" (Kearsley, 1998, p.49). The decision to implement distance education must be made during strategic planning, where it is determined whether distance education programs fit into the mission of the institution and how best to integrate it into the mainstream (Berge and Schrum, 1998).

THE NATURE OF DISTANCE EDUCATION IMPLEMENTATION

What does distance education "implementation" mean? Fowler and Levine (1993) define implementation as the process of putting an innovation or technology into use in an organization's or individual's work environment. Schreiber (1998) distinguishes between a technologically mature company's making distance education part of the *profile of the organization* compared with a less technologically mature organizations implementation of distance learning *events*. Many change models see implementation as synonymous with "adoption" (DLRN Technology Resources Guide, Chapter 8). Early technologically based models show implementation as the last (or nearly last) step in a linear process—framing it as a discrete step or event. Dormant (1992) notes that "the problem with the implementation-comes-last approach is that. . . it separates those involved in implementation from those making decisions about development" (p. 168). Implementation is closely tied to adoption by end users. It is gradual, sporadic, and accomplished over time. Projects are one major means of accomplishing implementation, although the complexity of distance education's impact on an organization requires careful attention to how implementation is carried out.

LESSONS LEARNED

Much of the research for implementing distance education is being conducted by higher education institutions. In borrowing what is learned from higher education for application in business, care must be taken to respect the similarities and differences of each environment, so that the integrity of the generalizations is maintained. As a preface to "mixing" experience from education and business, the fundamental missions of the two should be considered (Chute, Thompson, and Hancock, 1999). Traditional education is focused on individuals, with a secondary mission to achieve productive results. Business is focused on productivity, with a secondary mission of educating individuals, as a means to the corporate end of profitability. However, in both cases, leaders concern themselves with creating an atmosphere, relationships and processes that will achieve the organization's goal—whether it is learning as a direct or indirect goal.

Business and higher education can each pull from principles of strategy, change management and project planning to implement distance education.

CRITICAL COMPONENTS OF IMPLEMENTING DISTANCE EDUCATION

The framework here (see Figure 1), recognizes the unique contributions of the three disciplines of change management, strategic planning and project management.

Context: Change management provides the *context* for making strategic decisions and setting up projects. By context, we mean the necessary circumstances and linkages to theory which predict patterns of behavior. One significant theory underlying change management models is "diffusion of innovation." By this is meant the process by which an innovation is communicated through certain channels over time among the members of a social system (Rogers, 1995). The process used to communicate innovation provides the backdrop for making decisions about time lines, resources and human factors. Managing change can thereby guide strategy decisions, thus connecting strategic planning to the end users implementing distance training projects. Change management and diffusion theory are critical models that place in context that which strategy makers interested in sustaining changes in the organization must work.

Conditions: Strategic planning provides conditions under which

Figure 1. Critical Components of Implementing Distance Training

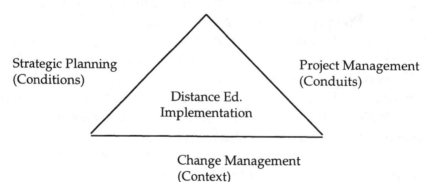

Strategic Planning
(Conditions)

Project Management
(Conduits)

Distance Ed.
Implementation

Change Management
(Context)

distance education is implemented. Conditions are any constraints or limitations imposed upon the organization because of their mission, goals, values, priorities, etc., including time, budget, and culture. Strategic plans give rise to funding allocations, assignment of resources and the elevation of distance education by the company's leaders to a critical goal. It also facilitates the identification of issues and constraints around funding, resources, infrastructure and organizational readiness. Many strategic planning models also have processes for connecting users and implementers to the plans early in the development process. Involving the implementers, as change theory tells us, will facilitate adoption. This linkage of strategy makers and users provides a reality check for distance education implementation.

Conduits: Early in an organization's use of distance training, projects function as conduits for implementation. Projects function as vehicles for realizing tangible results and measurement which are needed for justification and reinforcement in the context of corporate culture. For any large scale innovation, such as distance education, projects are also critical because of the cross-functional nature of project management. Project participants develop learning that serves as feedback for strategic planing. Change models and strategic plan models both incorporate projects as a way to implement change. Projects that run concurrent to strategic planning provide methods to track status, monitor progress, manage resources of time, money, people, and measure results. Thus, the success of distance education depends on project implementation.

CHANGE MANAGEMENT AS CONTEXT FOR DISTANCE EDUCATION IMPLEMENTATION

Change management provides a context in which to implement distance education activities. Rogers' (1995) work provided a foundation for diffusion of innovation theory, which underlies the discipline of change management. His work provides guiding principles for types and rates of adoption of an innovation (early adopter/innovators, middle adopters/opinion leaders, late adopters/laggards). The work also provides predictable patterns of adoption (s-curve) with implications for time lines, resources and other logistical considerations. These can help managers avoid "rash" actions and decisions in the name of getting results quickly. Change management for distance education capitalizes on involving early adopters in strategic projects such as first attempts and pilots of new technology. It also includes consideration of adoption rates in planning for large capital expenditures or resources and planning for sequence and locations of early projects, as well as planning for overcoming barriers in throughout.

Change management helps in focusing on human nature as a business consideration and also provides guidelines for managing the human side of implementing distance education. Surry (1997) cites problems with diffusion of instructional technologies due to ignoring the many factors that influence adoption of innovations. In distance training, these factors include lack of comfort with the nature of teaching and learning in distance environments; lack of trust among different functions with different expertise; lack of skill with technologies; lack of resources; or poor learning design. These and other factors which influence adoption must be identified and included in planning so persons charged with implementation can explain, predict and account for those issues that facilitate or impede an organization's acceptance of the innovation.

Related to this impact on people and why this affects long term acceptance is the notion of cultural change. Implementing distance training and new technologies is often considered a "cultural change" or organization development (OD) initiative. For example, Finney (1997) notes that the intranet's many-to-many communication model forces companies out of a hierarchical structure and towards individual empowerment. Strangelove (1994) addresses this cultural impact by stating that any new form of communication creates a new cultural paradigm, such as the internet's creation of "mass participation in bidirectional, uncensored mass communication" where "audience and content provider act as one" (p.7). There are many other examples, but the view of distance education implementation as requiring change management is implied in Wagner's (1992) listing of technological integration and organizational readiness as areas which influence successful diffusion of distance education technologies. He cautions that organizations not ready to show how these solutions improve the current state will find "diffusion of the innovation slow and disruptive" (p. 521). Competency in change management and understanding of diffusion theory improves the context in which distance education can be implemented, providing guidelines, predictive patterns of behavior and focus on human issues. It creates the context for implementing distance education.

STRATEGIC PLANNING FOR DISTANCE TRAINING

With regard to implementing distance training, strategic planning provides the conditions, or constraints, of the organization as they are derived from the mission, goals, values, priorities, etc. Powers (1992) defines strategic alignment as the "systematic arrangement of crucial business systems behind a common purpose" and lists the following strategic alignment model components: mission, values, aims and goals, objectives, job roles, selection, expectations, tools, training, feedback, rewards, financial and other management systems, for quality performance (p.258). Organizations must take time to establish a "big picture" on how implementing distance education will change the organization, and also how it will fit the organization, asking many questions up front to address issues like need, cost savings, audiences, technical requirements, infrastructure, resources, communication, incentives, support, etc. (Wagner, 1992).

Pearson (as cited in DLRN Chapter 7) identified 20 critical factors for implementing distance training. In rank order, the top ten were based on human and fiscal resources such as time, people, and funding. But the top critical factor for implementing distance education is to identify the need for it. Assuming that exploration of distance education is triggered by an implied or expressed need for distance education, managers should plan for and commit resources; contract with executive "sponsors;" and investigate any existing internal drives to apply distance education technology in a similar fashion to other business functions of the company (e.g. intranet, internet, e-mail communication, etc.). While some exploration and demonstration of concept is needed, it may be dangerous in the long run to view distance education technologies as a quick fix solution until the impact upon the organization is considered using the strategic planning process. Otherwise, among other things, organizations risk unnecessary resistance to the changes implied by the adoption of distance education.

The strategic planning team must assess organizational readiness by looking at factors such as numbers and locations of potential users; projected demand for distance education delivery; and technology's perceived value to the organization, to managers and to trainers themselves (Wagner,1992). Other factors to consider might be prerequisite skill sets of learners and trainers; barriers relating to accessibility of distance education; whether other major changes are distracting employees and resources; etc. Wagner cautions that it is "not sufficient to provide people with solutions without also showing them how these solutions can be applied to improve on the ways in which things have always been done" (p. 521). Jellison (1998) goes even further advocating "progressive transformation," a way to break down emotional barriers by changing people's actions in small ways instead of trying to make them believe they should change all at once. An example here may be using technology in meaningful ways in conjunction with in-person training as a stepping stone for training at a distance.

Once it is determined that the organization has a true need for distance education as a business solution, the strategic planning process must connect to the end users and/or implementers (Berge and Schrum, 1998). We characterize implementation as something that is local, must be accomplished by end users usually using a gradual, iterative process rather than a discrete event in a linear chain. If distance education is directly connected to the mission and goals of the organization, then implementers can make strong argument for management support, and users will support it to the extent they support strategic plan (Dormant, p. 174).

Noblitt (1997) notes that "top-down folks" are charged with administrative or institutional duties concerned with infrastructure while "bottom-up people" are charged with instructional or research duties and demands for time and resources to get their projects done. Their deep mutual dependency carves out different roles for each. The top-down program advocate relies on success stories to justify large investments in technology and the bottom-up project advocate needs a well-conceived and reliable working environment for successful implementation for innovative concepts (pp. 38-39). Noblitt also calls for a context-sensitive implementation plan, and this means that top-down and bottom-up people must work together on setting priorities (p. 43). For distance education, this applies as end users (trainers and learners) and strategic planners (executive management) working together with sensitivity to how changes caused by distance education can be smoothly integrated with involvement of all stakeholders (Pollack and Masters, 1997; Vazquez and Abad, 1992).

PROJECTS AS CONDUITS FOR DISTANCE EDUCATION

Change management and strategic planning both value projects as a way to manage change. Projects connect adopters, users, or implementers to the distance education initiative. In this way, projects function as the conduits for implementing distance education. Early in an organization's attempts to implement distance education, project management tools and techniques help structure distance training (Formby and Ostrander, 1997) within good business practice focusing on schedule, cost and scope issues.

The Project Management Institute (Duncan, 1996) defines a project as a "temporary endeavor undertaken to create a unique product or service" (p. 4). A project has a beginning and end; is performed by people; constrained by limited resources; and planned, executed, and controlled. Wideman's (1991) typical project life cycle includes the four stages of Concept, Development, Implementation and Termination. Within each phase are activities, methods, tools and formats reflecting classical project management techniques. Examples include feasibility study, risk analysis, scope, work breakdown structure, resource allocation, schedule, etc. Since implementation of learning technologies results in a business product with cost, schedule and scope elements to be managed and economics as an influence on successful diffusion (Wagner, 1992), it can benefit in many ways from having individuals who are competent in project management. Projects function as the conduit not only for tactical implementation of strategy but also for the change management process. Jackson and Addison (1992) note that:

> any project activity will represent some degree of change for virtually everyone affected... A critical responsibility of the project manager is to help ensure that the changes introduced by project activities are as easy and rewarding as it is feasible to make them. More than one technologically sound project has been seriously damaged simply because people in the organization saw the process as unnecessarily difficult, unpleasant, or time-consuming" (p. 71).

Projects also function as the conduits for the organizational learning that informs strategy. Nadler (1994) contends that structure leads to strategy which emerges over time from a pattern of decisions. In the process, project groups help develop new relationships and new learning within the organization (Systemic Reform, 1994, p. 3). So projects carry learning between the "top" and the "bottom" of the organization. When informed by skills in change management, project managers play a key role in successful distance education implementation. Additionally, projects are good for distance education because of their interdisciplinary nature. Schreiber and Berge (1998) cite overcoming barriers to interdisciplinary efforts as critical to successful implementation and institutionalization of distance education since it requires managers, educators, and technologists to evolve the organization into a sophisticated user of technology.

Project management as a practice provides a rigorous discipline for getting results. Schaffer and Thomson (1992) distinguish between activity-centered and results-centered programs and recommend introducing innovations in increments to support specific performance goals. With tangible results, managers and employees can enjoy success and build confidence and skill for continued improvements. They recommend using each project to test new ways of managing, measuring, and organizing for results. Marrying long-term goals with short-term projects helps turn strategy into reality. Eventually, implementation and integration of distance education into the business and training culture will result to the extent distance training aligns with strategic planning in the organization. Each design project has its own project manager, project schedule, scope, budget and objectives which "dovetail" with the concepts laid out in strategic planning. Targeted distance education projects aligned with business strategies, learner needs, and corporate objectives will move the organization toward acceptance.

CONCLUSIONS

Our approach views the implementation of distance education as a long term strategic change in the organization. Especially at the beginning stages, projects provide a structured way to synthesize what is learned and connect users to persons charged with strategic planning. Practice of the three disciplines is simultaneous and nonlinear, with overlapping aspects. Diffusion of innovation and change theory provide a background (context) for making strategic and tactical decisions, increasing likelihood of positive results. The strategic planning results (conditions/constraints) are continuously informed by what is being "learned" and evaluated in the projects (conduits).

In short, distance education must not be explored or conceived as a solution waiting for a problem. Consideration of conditions and constraints of the organization, as raised by the strategic planning process, are critical to successful implementation. The primary consideration is that distance education arises out of true need. Once this is established, the planning process is informed by connection to users. To implement distance education requires overcoming barriers and dealing with complex issues. Training and performance stakeholders can benefit from leveraging existing skills of project management, change management, and strategic planning and applying these disciplines to distance training.

REFERENCES

Berge, Z.L. & Schrum, L. (1998). Strategic planning linked with program implementation for distance education. *CAUSE/EFFECT*. 21(3), 31-38. [Online.] http://www.educause.edu/ir/library/html/cem9836.html.

Chute, A.G., Thompson, M.M., and Hancock, B.W. (Eds.) (1999). *The McGraw-Hill Handbook of Distance Learning*. New York: McGraw-Hill.

DLRN Technology Resource Guide. Steps of change: basics of innovation diffusion. Chapters 7 & 8. [Online.] http://www.wested.org/tre/dlrn/plan.html.

Dormant, D. (1992). Implementing human performance technology in organizations. In H. Stolovitch and E. Keeps (Eds.) *Handbook of Human Performance Technology*. San Francisco: Jossey-Bass, 167-187.

Duncan, W.R. (1996). *Guide to the project management body of knowledge*. Project Management Institute Standards Committee, 130 South State Road, Upper Darby PA19082 USA.

Finney, M. (1997, February). Harness the power within. *HR Magazine.*, 66-74.

Formby, S. and Ostrander, G. (August, 1997). Managing change the project management way. *PM Network.*

Fowler, P. and Levine, L. (December, 1993). *A conceptual framework for software technology transition*. Carnegie-Melon University. Software Engineering Institute.

Jackson, S. and Addison, R. (1992). Planning and managing projects. In H. Stolovitch and E. Keeps (Eds.) *Handbook of Human Performance Technology*. San Francisco: Jossey-Bass, 66-76.

Jellison, J. (1998). PIA human relations conference preview: Change is emotional. [Online.] http://www.printing.org/prhrpre.htm.

Kearsley, G. (1998, April) Educational technology: A critique. *Educational Technology*, 47-51.

Nadler, D. (1994, Set.-Oct.) Collaborative strategic thinking. *Planning Review*. p.31

Noblitt, J. (May-June 1997.) Top-down meets bottom-up." *Education Review*. 32(3), 38-43.

Pollock, C., and Masters, R. (1997). Using internet technologies to enhance training. *Performance Improvement*. 36(2), 28-31.

Powers, B. (1992). Strategic alignment. . In H. Stolovitch and E. Keeps (Eds.) *Handbook of Human Performance Technology*. San Francisco: Jossey-Bass, 247-258.

Rogers, R. (1995). *Diffusion of innovations*. (4th. ed.). New York, N.Y.: Macmillan.

Schaffer, R. and Thomson, H. (January-February 1992). Successful change programs begin with results. *Harvard Business Review*.

Systemic Reform: (1994, September). Perspectives on Personalizing Education http//www.ed.gov/pubs/EdReformStudies/SysReforms/stiegel7.html

Schreiber, D.A. & Berge, Z.L. (Eds.) (1998). *Distance Training: How Innovative Organizations are Using Technology to Maximize Learning and Meet Business Objectives*. San Francisco, CA: Jossey-Bass Inc., Publishers.

Schreiber, D. (1998) Best practices of distance training. In D. Schreiber and Z. Berge (Eds.) *Distance Training: How Innovative Organizations are Using Technology to Maximize Learning and Meet Business Objectives*. San Francisco, CA: Jossey-Bass Inc., Publisher. pp. 393-409.

Strangelove, M. (1994, December) The internet as a catalyst for a paradigm shift. *Distance Education Magazine*, 8, 7.

Surry, D.W. (1997, February 20,). Diffusion theory and instructional technology. [Online.] http://intro.base.org/docs/diffusion/, 1-11.

Vazquez-Abad, J., and Winer, L. (1992) Emerging trends in human performance interventions In H. Stolovitch and E. Keeps (Eds.) *Handbook of Human Performance Technology*. San Francisco: Jossey-Bass, 672-687.

Wagner, E. (1992). Distance education systems. In H. Stolovitch and E. Keeps (Eds.) *Handbook of Human Performance Technology*. San Francisco: Jossey-Bass, 513-525.

Wideman, R. (1991). A framework for project and program management integration, preliminary edition. The *PMBOK Handbook Series. 1.*

Chapter V

Three Strategies for the Use of Distance Learning Technology in Higher Education

William E. Rayburn
Austin Peay State University

Arkalgud Ramaprasad
Southern Illinois University

INTRODUCTION

"University A" is a small, private liberal arts school with a religious affiliation. Located in a large city, it draws locally and from its particular religious group. With an enrollment under 3,000, it carries a Carnegie Classification of Baccalaureate II and has its own board of trustees. The school has pushed the use of new technology in instruction. For instance, it was one of the first schools in its area to install a fiber optic network across campus. Programs such as business feature the active use of technology to enhance learning. For example, in an international business course, students develop links with fellow students in other countries. However, University A differs from other schools that have embraced new information and communication technology; it has rejected some uses as not appropriate to the mission of the school. For instance, University A will not use videoconferencing to send instruction to remote sites. Why? School leaders feel that a significant part of a student's experience at University A comes from faculty providing role models, and that role modeling cannot be done through a television monitor.

"University B" is a regional public university located in a small town in a heavily rural portion of its state. The nearest small city is an hour's drive away, and it draws students regionally, mostly from nearby counties. With an enrollment under 10,000, the school carries a Carnegie Classification of Master's I. For years, University B has used its Continuing Education program in aggressively serving the region, beginning with such means as "circuit rider" faculty who traveled to remote sites to teach classes and broadcast television instruction through local public television. The school has continued its aggressive outreach with new technology. In the 1990s, University B quickly moved into videoconferencing (compressed video) to phase out at least some of the circuit rider faculty. At the same time, the school has expanded the off-campus sites to which it sends instruction. Lastly, University B has augmented its MBA program by bringing in a health care administration concentration from another university via videoconferencing, and it has been considering the future servicing of majors in declining programs such as geography by outsourcing instruction.

Officers at the two universities described above were among those at several schools who participated in a series of case studies (Rayburn, 1997). The two schools use distance learning technology (DLT) in very different ways, but they do share at least one common trait: they have clear pictures of how to use available technology. Put another way, they have identifiable strategies for using technology that conform to the missions of the schools.

The point of this chapter is to identify and describe strategies for using distance learning technology (DLT) at higher education institutions. Research suggests three major strategies, the "Guest Lecturer" strategy, the "Automated Correspondence Course" strategy, and the "Large Lecture Hall" strategy. All three strategies have antecedents in the recent history of higher education, and each has its own implications for the future. The next section looks at literature and field research on the strategic use of DLT.

BACKGROUND

The literature provides many examples of how institutions have used distance learning technology (DLT). The case study research that included University A and University B, while adding to the body of knowledge on distance learning from an *organizational* perspective, also suggested a useful working taxonomy of DLT strategies. Both history and current literature support this taxonomy.

Schools employ DLT to achieve different goals. Those goals also have antecedents elsewhere in academe. Broadly speaking, the goals fall into three major categories: making instruction more effective, reaching new students and making programs more efficient. These goals translate into the three strategies mentioned in the introduction. An historic antecedent lends its name to each strategy.

Guest Lecturer Strategy

Institutions with the first goal, making instruction more effective, pursue the Guest Lecturer strategy. Just as with business, schools seek to improve the quality of their product (Baldwin, 1991), although some see DLT as a threat to a quality product (Jacobson, 1994b). The choice of the Guest Lecturer title does not suggest that its exclusive use is only to bring in a guest who could not otherwise attend class; rather, it is just an archetype. Examples of the Guest Lecturer strategy include digital libraries and archives (Basinger, 1999; Blumenstyk, 1998b; Guernsey, 1998), virtual communities (Glassman, 1997), on-line conferences for students and faculty (Kiernan, 1998; Morrison, 1997), Web-based simulations (Robbin, 1996), electronic field trips (Carey, 1991; Hawkins, 1991), the telecommuting of personnel (Berge, Collins, and Day, 1995), "cultural context" in language instruction (Lambert, 1991) and of course guest lecturers and outside experts (Carey, 1991; Berge and Collins, 1995). The case study research added the viewing of satellite programs to the list as well. DLT used this way serves as a catalyst to improve the learning experience itself. Here the antecedent is the guest lecturer whose input enhances the value of the class to the student. In its most extreme use, DLT can transform the process (how the instruction takes place) (Dede, 1991). In this regard, the potential impact of DLT on instruction conforms to the concepts of Zuboff and Scott Morton. Zuboff stated that information technology impacts beyond mere automation; she proposed that the technology had the power to *informate* processes (Zuboff, 1988). Scott Morton took Zuboff's idea further, saying that information technology has the power to *transform* process and organization entirely (Scott Morton, 1991).

Automated Correspondence Course Strategy

The second goal, reaching new students, manifests itself in business terms as seeking new markets (newly available student groups) and/or gaining existing market share (students who would otherwise attend another school) (Albrecht and Bardsley, 1994). Schools that pursue this goal use the Automated Correspondence Course strategy. With this strategy, institutions seek to expand availability and provide flexibility to previously unserved or under-served groups (Johnstone and Jones, 1997; Keller, 1997; Vines, Thorpe, and Threlkeld, 1997). Examples of the Automated Correspondence Course strategy include reaching students physically remote from on-campus programs (Schmidt, 1999), serving students constrained not only by place but also by time (Blumenstyk, 1998a) and providing students with greater choice in programs, perhaps appealing to them with niche programs (Lively and Blumenstyk, 1999; Mangan, 1999). The case study research confirmed efforts at outreach. An antecedent for this goal is the traditional correspondence course offered to students who could not come to a central campus. DLT provides the opportunity for schools to deliver classes to remote sites and at different times from the campus schedule (Godbey, 1993).

Large Lecture Hall Strategy

The third goal, making programs more efficient, mirrors productivity concerns in business. Schools seek to reduce costs or increase revenues—they act to leverage instructional resources. With this goal, institutions follow the Large Lecture Hall strategy. The Large Lecture Hall strategy reveals itself in concerns to deliver instruction more productively *at less cost* (Gubernick and Ebeling, 1997; Schmidt, 1999) or to more students for greater revenue (Biemiller and Young, 1997; Green, 1997). An antecedent for this goal is the movement to house lower-level or survey classes in large lecture halls so fewer instructors can teach more students. DLT provides schools with the means to leverage instruction—increasing the number of students who take any one instructor's class (Ohler, 1991). However, DLT also incurs its own unique costs such as equipment and new staffing which a school must consider when using DLT (Threlkeld and Brzoska, 1994).

Links to Porter's Strategies

Evidence from the case study research also links the three strategies for using DLT to Michael Porter's three competitive strategies - the introduction of new products and services, the enhancement of existing products and services, and the altering of industry structure (Porter, 1980; Stair and Reynolds, 1998). First, the Automated Correspondence Course strategy resembles Porter's new products and services strategy. Here the strategy affects the scope of instruction: the breadth of what the school offers students. When DLT provides the means for one school's MBA program to import a Health Care Concentration from a second school, that illustrates Porter's new products and services strategy. In fact, schools using this strategy can be both providers as well as receivers. For instance, the same institution that imports a special MBA concentration can in turn provide special instruction to area high schools via DLT. Finally, schools can both send and receive instruction in the same program, whether it is just a simple exchange of two accounting courses one semester or a collaboration of two schools' unique strengths to plan a joint graduate nursing program.

Second, the Guest Lecturer strategy mirrors Porter's strategy of improving existing products. When schools use DLT to change the process of instruction or how they go about the actual instruction, they are enhancing an existing product or service. Moving from traditional lecture to automation to transformation under the Zuboff and Scott Morton framework illustrates the enhancement of the product. When a school uses DLT to link its students to resources outside the boundary of the classroom, or when it uses DLT to connect students and instructors in content-rich exchanges outside the classroom setting, it follows the Porter strategy of improving an existing product. Some schools eschew all other applications of DLT and consciously focus only on using technology to improve the product they now have.

Third, the Large Lecture Hall strategy corresponds to Porter's strategy of altering industry structure. When schools use DLT to change scale (how many students receive instruction), they often follow the Porter strategy of altering industry structure. When schools seek to leverage on-campus instruction by sending it to one or more remote sites, they follow this strategy. Using remote sites to gain a cost advantage conforms to altering the industry structure. The case study research found multiple instances where a school takes existing classes and sends them to other classrooms. For example, one school uses compressed video to send its instruction not just to other area schools but also to businesses, and extensive networks promote this change in where learning takes place. Even more dramatic are Internet-based courses to provide instruction anytime, anywhere. With these methods, the boundaries of space and time and the constraints of the old classroom disappear.

The three option framework provides a means for exploring the strategic use of DLT and its implications for higher education. It is supported by the literature and confirmed by case study. The next section considers strategic issues in detail.

MAIN THRUST OF THE CHAPTER

Technological innovation of any sort affects its environment. Distance learning technology (DLT) does not differ in its potential to affect higher education. This section looks at issues surrounding the use of distance learning technology. Some of these issues are general and some pertain to only one or two of the three defined strategies. Broadly, these issues fall into the categories of personnel, funding, markets, competition, fraud and alliances. An overarching concern is the relationship between the school's mission and available technology. Each issue is examined in turn, beginning with personnel.

Personnel

The personnel category breaks down into four issues: faculty skills required, new personnel needed, "faculty recompense," and resistance to technology. First, using DLT in any strategy requires certain training for effective use. When considering teaching skills in both the routine and the creative use of technology, schools must address two challenges: they must adequately train current faculty to use DLT effectively and they must weigh what technology-based skills they look for in future faculty. The Guest Lecturer strategy stresses the creative use of DLT to enhance the student's experience, such as with the current spotlight on multimedia. On the other hand, both the Automated Correspondence Course and the Large Lecture Hall strategies demand skill in translating "old-style" teaching into a wider, perhaps non-interactive realm. Examples of this need found in the case study research include learning to instruct through compressed video. The need exists for Web-based courses as well. Schools must commit funding to train, support, and perhaps recruit faculty to use DLT in a manner compatible with their goals.

Second, higher education institutions must adapt personnel beyond just the faculty. These include support personnel: technicians to maintain equipment (Parisot and Waring, 1994), proctors to manage remote sites and classes (Moses, Edgerton, Shaw, and Grubb, 1991; Jordahl, 1995; Parisot and Waring, 1994) and staff to train faculty and prepare materials (Rayburn, 1997). Interview comments during the case study research suggested that new personnel may also include a management team to establish and promote DLT use. Again, schools must commit funding for staff. Technology, be it mainframe computers in the 1970s, microcomputer labs in the 1980s, or DLT in the 1990s, requires enough trained personnel to make the investment worthwhile. As one school officer in the case study research pointed out, institutions have often embraced innovation and bought into technology yet failed to support equipment with needed staff. Concerns about support personnel focus on the Automated Correspondence Course strategy because of its reliance on DLT such as compressed video. However, staff support also impacts the Large Lecture Hall strategy and to a lesser extent the Guest Lecturer strategy.

A great unresolved issue about personnel called "faculty recompense" begins with the question, "What does an instructor get in return for teaching in a DLT environment?". This issue transcends just monetary compensation; it includes a variety of concerns such as tenure, release time and course load. Together, these concerns come under the umbrella term "faculty recompense." First of course comes money: schools vary in how much if any premium instructors get paid for teaching via DLT. Some would hold that teaching with DLT is but one of many forms of teaching and nothing to merit higher pay, while others advocate extra compensation due either to the larger volume of students or to special teaching demands beyond that of the traditional classroom. Inconsistency about release time and course load mirror that of money. They all vary from one school to another, and the philosophy behind school policy varies as well. For instance, one view holds that teaching twenty students on campus and another twenty off campus at a remote site via compressed video equates to two courses not one. As such, that course with DLT counts as two in figuring course loads. As for release time, some schools acknowledge the need to adapt instruction to the DLT classroom and set aside schedule time at least for those new to teaching via DLT. Finally, some raise the idea of separate tenure tracks from the traditional one. There might be a special tenure track for teaching in a technology-rich environment, focusing efforts on the development of new tools and techniques. While an important issue in using any of the three DLT strategies, faculty recompense applies especially to the Automated Correspondence Course strategy when an instructor may be teaching in a mixture of the traditional classroom and the DLT realm. DLT instruction calls into question old views of course load, pay scales and job expectations.

Finally, higher education in the late 1990s has seen an increase in faculty resistance to technology. Any prior technology mixed into instruction has caused resistance, and DLT is no different. The rise of microcomputing in the 1980s saw resistance as well. Opposition to using DLT in the late 1990s has three levels. First, some faculty express discomfort with using DLT itself (Young, 1997). The history of DLT such as compressed video, with frequent downtime and faulty equipment, has bolstered such resistance. This type of resistance is possible with any of the three DLT strategies used. Second, some contend that a vital part of the educational experience is lost or distorted using DLT (Biemiller, 1998; Blumenstyk, 1998a; Neal, 1998). They worry that the interaction between instructor and student, which they consider part of the learning experience, diminishes or vanishes. This type of concern would occur when a school uses the Automated Correspondence Course strategy or the Large Lecture Hall strategy. With the Automated Correspondence Course, some would worry about the sacrifice made in instruction to reach new markets. Third, and even more profound, some see DLT instruction as a threat to them specifically and also to their accustomed way of academic life (Monaghan, 1998; Selingo, 1999; Young, 1998). An increasing use of the Large Lecture Hall strategy, minimizing costs and maximizing revenues, provokes these fears. While institutions and governing boards do not directly speak of such, some faculty have perceived that technology could and perhaps would indeed threaten not just individual faculty but also institutions themselves (Ives and Jarvenpaa, 1996). In a nutshell, they fear replacement by software.

Current policies regarding personnel, especially faculty recompense, appear ad-hoc at best. Schools must clearly assess the demands of teaching through DLT compared to traditional teaching and resolve questions on pay, tenure and course load. If schools enter into DLT-enabled courses and programs full-scale, they must reconcile these new labor concerns. Also, schools must recognize, define, and adequately staff new personnel categories such as remote-site facilitators, technicians and producers and course development specialists. Merely acquiring DLT without matching it with labor resources creates new problems. A final challenge is to integrate new or modified personnel types into the overall organization.

Funding

Funding concerns the commitment and allocation of financial resources. As with other information and communication technology, DLT is not cheap. Further, as with computers, the equipment becomes dated quickly. Success in using DLT comes with commitment. One academic officer interviewed in the case study research described a philosophical change of view: more and more, schools should view information technology as an *operating expense*, not a capital expense. Apart from specific accounting rules, this idea points schools toward an ongoing duty to maintain and replace hardware as needed. Threlkeld and Brzoska (1994) support the idea that DLT has higher fixed costs versus lower variable costs in comparison to traditional instruction.

Markets

Market issues involve changes in the quantity, location and nature of students. In particular, the Automated Correspondence Course strategy affects enrollments. DLT usage to reach new students means that those students will be greater in number, remote from campus (Schmidt, 1999), nontraditional (Green, 1997) or some blend of those traits. To reach those students, schools have to adapt not just to DLT but to student schedules, locations, and finances. Market issues have a less direct link to the Guest Lecturer and the Large Lecture Hall strategies; rather, competition is more important with them.

Competition

Technology changes competition: it resets boundaries, strengthens or weaknesses current rivals and opens the door to new parties. All three DLT strategies affect competition. The Guest Lecturer strategy impacts competition based on quality. As one officer at a large private school in the case study research pointed out, students who choose among that school and similar rivals look at how those schools use DLT to enhance the basic instruction. Those students regard creative or cutting-edge use of DLT as a plus when they compare schools. With the Automated Correspondence Course strategy, schools are trying to reach those students they could not before. Those new students could be either ones no school could reach before due to constraints such as time or distance, or ones who would have taken courses from some other school. In either case, the school would be building market share in business terms. Using the Large Lecture Hall strategy, a school or other entity alters the long-standing structure on which competition is based.

Institutions face varying degrees of competition, and DLT affects that degree of competition. Schools compete for the same students based on certain criteria such as intellect, geography, career interests and finances. Even if unacknowledged, each institution has an understood set of competitors. However, DLT has the potential to alter "groupings" of competition. The removal of geography as a competitive criteria is the most obvious example.

Literature frequently cites how DLT can change competition. New levels of competition may come from three sources. First, the competition with existing competitors may intensify (Dede, 1991). DLT can make one institution's programs more attractive due to factors such as program enhancement, time flexibility or location expansion. Second, other established institutions may enter markets previously unavailable to them (Albrecht and Bardsley, 1994; Godbey, 1993). The MBA degree market is a leading example, with "brand-name" schools offering courses and programs on-line (Mangan, 1999). Schools can now enter attractive new markets that they could not reach before (Jacobson, 1994a; Deloughry, 1996). State public schools may fight over and redefine "territories" within their states based on using DLT. Across state borders, the competition is less regulated and more intense. For example, in part using DLT, one school can locate a satellite program just across the state line from another school and tap into an attractive market (Gold, 1998). Third, new entrants such as for-profit programs can come into the market. One leading example as of this writing is the University of Phoenix (Fischetti, Anderson, Watrous, Tanz, and Gynne, 1998).

Fraud

Related to the changing competitive environment is academic fraud. Fraud relates in particular to the Automated Correspondence Course strategy, and it of course is not new. Getting a degree through the mail a generation ago would raise suspicion, getting it on-line from certain sources does the same today. DLT can facilitate a scam degree operation and also obscure it (Guernsey, 1997; Lord, 1998). With a rush into on-line programs by established institutions, the large volume of choices can mask a bogus operation in the eyes of the public (Lord, 1998).

Alliances

Finally, DLT promotes alliances. These alliances take many forms, the most transforming of which is the virtual university (Johnstone and Jones 1997). An option when schools pursue the Large Lecture Hall strategy is to enter an alliance with other schools. Alliances provide the means to bring courses and programs to students without having to add teaching resources. For example, two schools can enter an alliance using DLT that draws on both their resources to jointly offer a program, as were the plans of one school in the case study to join with a second school in starting a graduate nursing degree. Otherwise, the schools in the alliance would duplicate instructional resources.

FUTURE TRENDS

Two trends that apply to all three strategies are (1) distance learning technology (DLT) will continue to both evolve and then standardize and (2) DLT will continue to require a learning curve. Technology of all sorts goes through periods of growth and a certain degree of chaos, but over time certain standards form. Both personal computers, moving from over thirty different systems to now only two (IBM-compatible and Apple Macintosh) and VCRs, moving to the VHS format and away from the Beta format, provide recent examples. DLT will likely follow the same path, perhaps later rather than sooner. Regardless of what DLT equipment wins out, schools and staff will continue to endure a learning curve in using DLT.

Changes in tenure may occur, prompted by the DLT teaching environment. Though some have championed change over the years, tenure has remained mostly unaltered. However, technology serves as a catalyst of change and one might be in tenure. Diverse tenure tracks could address special situations such as teaching (and developing curriculum) in a DLT environment. Certainly if a school moves to the Automated Correspondence Course or Large Lecture Hall strategy, the school might use a special tenure track to push (rapid) development of "marketable products."

The market will continue to change. In particular with the Automated Correspondence Course strategy, schools will be looking to increase enrollment. The enlarged needs of the marketplace, for example, may come from geographically remote students (Gransden, 1994; Watkins, 1994) or from new demand for higher degree programs (Baldwin, 1991). It is interesting but perhaps logical that greater availability of courses and programs might itself stimulate bigger market for higher degrees.

The most radical change in the higher education landscape may come from use of the Large Lecture Hall strategy. One outgrowth of trying to reduce instruction cost or to spread that cost over more students might be outsourcing. Colleges and universities, while lagging behind industries such as manufacturing, have increasingly used outsourcing to hand over operations such as food services (King, 1997a; King 1997b), information systems and services (Wallace, 1997), bookstores (Freeman, 1997) security, and custodial services (Nicklin, 1997). A typical reason given is that cost pressures force administrators to look elsewhere, and that outsourcing allows the institution to focus on its core function: instruction. What if, as part of a Large Lecture Hall strategy, a school defined its core function more precisely? For instance, a state engineering school might define its mission strictly in terms of schooling engineers. If that was the case, school leaders might decide to focus resources on the engineering curriculum. To do that, they might consider outsourcing the history department, getting those courses from some other school via DLT. Schools might focus on what they do best and outsource the rest, becoming both the provider and receiver of instruction through DLT. If such a scenario came true, it would lead to greater specialization among institutions.

Three research opportunities in the strategic use of DLT are (1) the strategies themselves, (2) the confusion over faculty recompense, and (3) the transformation of the process of instruction. First, each strategy bears watching, and interesting future case research would compare the success of schools that chose the same strategy. Second, the case research revealed policy on faculty recompense all over the board. It even varied from one college to another at the same school. Will a standard policy emerge? Finally, technology affects process in other organizations, and higher education institutions will be no different. Future research could explore the change in process in terms of the Zuboff and Scott Morton framework.

CONCLUSION

The central issues regarding DLT revolve not around the technology itself, but how it is used (or not used). Those schools that employ DLT must make effective choices in how they use it and address how the organization relates to it. Perhaps the best gauge of how schools may use DLT comes from what they do now. Do they focus on quality or creative instruction? Maybe they will follow the Guest Lecturer strategy. Do they have a history of outreach? They may pursue the Automated Correspondence Course strategy. Do they serve large numbers of students? Then they may consider the Large Lecture Hall strategy.

Schools may pursue any of the three strategies or some combination of them. What matters most is not the technology but the plan for using it. DLT use must conform to the larger mission of the school, and the school must also be aware of how others are using the same technology. To do less in either case is to put a school at a distinct competitive disadvantage.

REFERENCES

Albrecht, Robert & Bardsley, Gary (1994). Strategic planning and academic planning for distance education. Willis, Barry (Ed.), *Distance Education Strategy and Tools* (pp.67-86). Englewood Cliffs, NJ: Educational Technology Publications, Inc.

Baldwin, Lionel V. (1991, March). Higher-education partnerships in engineering and science. Vivian M. Horner & Linda G. Roberts (Eds.), *Annals of the American Academy of Political and Social Science: Electronic Links For Learning (514)* (pp. 76-91). Newbury Park, CA: Sage Publications.

Basinger, Julianne (1999, January 22). Former Michigan president seeks to turn higher education into a 'knowledge industry.' *The Chronicle of Higher Education*, A30.

Berge, Zane L., Collins, Mauri P., & Day, Michael. (1995). Introduction.

In Zane L. Berge & Mauri P. Collins (Eds.), *Volume one: Computer-mediated communication and the online classroom: Overview and perspectives*). Cresskill, NJ: Hampton Press, 1-10.

Biemiller, Lawrence (1998, October 9). U. of Utah president issues a pointed warning about virtual universities. *The Chronicle of Higher Education*, A32.

Biemiller, Lawrence & Young, Jeffrey R. (1997, November 7). EDUCOM notebook: Merger plans, high-tech colleges, and the death of the book. *The Chronicle of Higher Education*, A29.

Blumenstyk, Goldie (1998a, February 6). Western Governors U. takes shape as a new model for higher education. *The Chronicle of Higher Education*, A21.

Blumenstyk, Goldie (1998b, July 17). Museums collaborate to put images of thousands of their art treasures on line. *The Chronicle of Higher Education*, A29.

Carey, John. (1991, March). Plato at the keyboard: telecommunications technology and education policy. *Annals of the American Academy of Political and Social Science: Electronic Links For Learning (514)*, Vivian M. Horner & Linda G. Roberts (eds.), Sage Publications, Newbury Park, CA, 11-21.

Dede, Christopher J. (1991, March). Emerging technologies: Impacts on distance learning. *Annals of the American Academy of Political and Social Science: Electronic Links For Learning (514)*. Vivian M. Horner & Linda G. Roberts (eds.), Sage Publications, Newbury Park, CA. 146-158.

Deloughry, Thomas J. (1996, September 20). New school for social research bolsters flagging enrollment with 90 on-line courses. *The Chronicle of Higher Education*, A27-A28.

Fischetti, Mark, Anderson, John, Watrous, Malena, Tanz, Jason, & Gynne, Peter (1998). The march of Phoenix," *University Business*, 46-51.

Freeman, Laurie (1997, January). Bookstore contract boosts revenues. *School Planning and Management*, 20F(3).

Glassman, Bernard (1997, July/August). Oh pioneer! *On the Horizon*, 15-16.

Godbey, Galen. (1993, Spring). Beyond TQM: Competition and cooperation create the agile institution. *Educational Record (74:2)*, 37-42.

Gold, E. L. (1998, November 18). MSU center won't be on HCC campus. *Kentucky New Era*, pp. 1-2.

Gransden, Gregory. (1994, July 13). Bringing education to the remote expanses of Siberia. *The Chronicle of Higher Education,* A36.

Green, Kenneth C. (1997, November/December). Money, technology, and distance education. *On The Horizon.* 1-7.

Gubernick, Lisa & Ebeling, Ashlea (1997, June 16). I got my degree through e-mail," *Forbes,* 84.

Guernsey, Lisa (1997, December 19). Is the Internet becoming a bonanza for diploma mills? *The Chronicle of Higher Education,* 22.

Guernsey, Lisa (1998, May 8). Historians form new organization on technology in teaching and research. *The Chronicle of Higher Education,* A30.

Hawkins, Jan. (1991, March). Technology-mediated communities for learning: Designs and consequences. In Vivian M. Horner & Linda G. Roberts (Eds.), *Annals of the American Academy of Political and Social Science: Electronic Links For Learning (514),* 159-74). Newbury Park, CA: Sage Publications.

Ives, Blake & Jarvenpaa, Sirkka L. (1996 Spring). Will the Internet revolutionize business education and research? *Sloan Management Review,* 33-41.

Jacobson, Robert L. (1994a, July 6). Extending the reach of 'virtual' classrooms. *The Chronicle of Higher Education,* A19-A23.

Jacobson, Robert L. (1994b, July 6). 2-Way video praised by many educators; others question its benefits and costs. *The Chronicle of Higher Education,* A20.

Johnstone, Sally M. & Jones, Dennis (1997, November/December). New higher education trends reflected in the design of Western Governors University. *On the Horizon,* 8-11.

Jordahl, Gregory. (1995, January). Bringing schools closer with 'distance' learning. *Technology & Learning (15:4),* 16-19.

Keller, George (1997, May/June). Beyond bytes and bandwidth. *On the Horizon,* 14-15.

Kiernan, Vincent (1998, December 4). Escaping the chilly ballroom: Researchers to attend a biomedical conference on line. *The Chronicle of Higher Education,* A22.

King, Paul (1997a, July 7, 1997). Contractors give 'the old college try' in battle for university food dollars. *Nation's Restaurant News,* 57(4).

King, Paul (1997b, August 25). NACUFS [National Association of College and University Food Services] needs to settle contractor debate. *Nation's Restaurant News,* 34(1).

Lambert, Richard D. (1991, March). Distance education and foreign languages. *Annals of the American Academy of Political and Social Science: Electronic Links For Learning (514)*, Vivian M. Horner & Linda G. Roberts (eds.), Sage Publications, Newbury Park, CA, 35-48.

Lively, Kit & Blumenstyk, Goldie (1999, January 29). Sylvan Learning Systems to start a network of for-profit universities overseas. *The Chronicle of Higher Education*, A43.

Lord, Mary (1998, September 28). Sheepskin fleecers. *U.S. News & World Report*, 72-73.

Mangan, Katherine S. (1999, January 15). Top business schools seek to ride a bull market in on-line M.B.A.'s. *The Chronicle of Higher Education*, A27.

Monaghan, Peter (1998, June 19). U. of Washington professors decry governor's visions for technology. *The Chronicle of Higher Education*, A23.

Morrison, James L. (1997, March/April). Academic cybermalls. *On the Horizon*, 2-3.

Moses, Kurt D., Edgerton, David, Shaw, Willard E., & Grubb, Ralph. (1991, March). International case studies of distance learning. *Annals of the American Academy of Political and Social Science: Electronic Links For Learning (514)*, Vivian M. Horner & Linda G. Roberts (eds.), Sage Publications, Newbury Park, CA, 58-75.

Neal, Ed (1998, June 19). Using technology in teaching: We need to exercise healthy skepticism. *The Chronicle of Higher Education*, B4.

Nicklin, Julie L. (1997, November 21). Universities seek to cut costs by 'outsourcing' more operations. *The Chronicle of Higher Education*, A35(2).

Ohler, Jason. (1991, March). Why distance education? *Annals of the American Academy of Political and Social Science: Electronic Links For Learning (514)*, Vivian M. Horner & Linda G. Roberts (eds.), Sage Publication, Newbury Park, CA, 22-34.

Parisot, Arlene & Waring, Suzanne. (1994, March / April). At a distance. *Adult Learning (5:4)*, 10-11.

Porter, Michael E. (1980). *Competitive Strategy*, Free Press.

Rayburn, William (1997). Not what but how: The role of institutional and environmental factors in the use of distance learning technology for higher education. Southern Illinois University.

Robbin, L. Katherine (1996, November 11). Modern technology: A quantum leap forward on today's Christian college campuses. *Christianity Today*, 60.

Schmidt, Peter (1999, January 29). Concept of university centers has appeal in several states. *The Chronicle of Higher Education*, A41.

Scott Morton, Michael S (1991). Introduction. *The Corporation of the 1990s*, Michael S. Scott Morton (ed.), Oxford University Press, 3-23.

Selingo, Jeffrey (1999, February 5), Plan to reshape California State U. disturbs many faculty members. *The Chronicle of Higher Education*, A32.

Stair, Ralph M. & Reynolds, George W. (1998). *Principles of Information Systems: A Managerial Approach*, Course Technology.

Threlkeld, Robert & Brzoska, Karen. (1994). Research in distance education. *Distance Education Strategy and Tools*, Barry Willis (ed.), Educational Technology Publications, Inc., Englewood Cliffs, NJ, 41-66.

Vines, Diane, Thorpe, Barbara, & Threlkeld, Robert (1997, November/December). California higher education extends its reach. *On the Horizon*, 11-14.

Wallace, Bob (1997, June 30). More firms outsource remote support; IS hopes to cut big access bills. *Computerworld*, 49.

Watkins, Beverly T. (1994, August 10). Uniting North Dakota. *The Chronicle of Higher Education*, A17-A19.

Young, Jeffrey (1997, October 3). Canadian university promises it won't require professors to use technology, *The Chronicle of Higher Education*, A28.

Young, Jeffrey R. (1998, May 8). Skeptical academics see perils in information technology. *The Chronicle of Higher Education*, A29.

Zuboff, Shoshana. (1988). *In the Age of the Smart Machine*, Basic Books.

Chapter VI

Distance Learning Alliances in Higher Education

William E. Rayburn
Austin Peay State University

Arkalgud Ramaprasad
Southern Illinois University

INTRODUCTION

Consider the case of George Peabody College for Teachers and Vanderbilt University. The two private schools sat side by side in Nashville, Tennessee. Peabody trained generations of teachers across the United States. Vanderbilt was and remains a research university. For decades, the two schools maintained a partnership or *alliance*, and it functioned on many levels. Students at one school easily enrolled for classes at the other and transferred credits without trouble. The two schools shared library resources between themselves and a third, religious-oriented school. Athletes on Vanderbilt sports teams earned Peabody degrees. At times, Vanderbilt rented dormitory space from Peabody to house excess students. Separated only by a city street, the schools collaborated but remained distinct.

Then in the late 1970s, they announced a merger. Peabody would become part of Vanderbilt. By the early 1980s, the merger was complete. The change was wrenching for Peabody. Many faculty left or were laid off. Tuition increased to match that of Vanderbilt. Today Peabody survives only as the name of the College of Education within Vanderbilt (Dorn, 1996).

Peabody and Vanderbilt had an alliance, and it benefitted them both. At the same time though, that alliance affected the schools themselves and in the end erased the identity of the smaller or weaker member. Alliances have always dotted the higher education landscape, but today technology offers the promise (or threat) of new, expanded alliances.

The rise of distance learning technology (DLT) has attracted much notice from scholars and the press. Schools and for-profit firms are looking for creative ways to take advantage of DLT such as compressed video and Internet-based courses that have emerged over the last decade. Among the ways organizations try to take advantage of DLT is through alliances. DLT enables and fosters alliances which take diverse forms; they vary in level of involvement, structure, and the nature of the partners themselves. No one knows with certainty the long-term effect of distance learning alliances, but the subject is worthy of study.

This chapter examines distance learning alliances in detail. It begins with a review of the literature on alliances in distance learning, follows with a taxonomy of alliances used in higher education, discusses issues associated with alliances and concludes with ideas about future research. To complement the literature, the chapter cites findings from case study research conducted at a diverse group of higher education institutions (Rayburn, 1997).

BACKGROUND

Alliances are an outgrowth of strategy within higher education. Historically, schools have formed occasional, limited alliances with other institutions. Schools have collaborated on non-instructional needs such as purchasing insurance, hiring consultants, and sharing library access (Strosnider, 1998). Further, schools have let students from other colleges take certain classes by agreement (Strosnider, 1998). Most often partners have come from geographically close neighbors as was the case with Peabody and Vanderbilt. The literature discusses alliances such as a simple exchange as well as more formal partnerships. In simple exchanges, schools merely share certain courses to fill gaps in programs or to increase quality (Hajdu and Schreckengost, 1994; Moses, Edgerton, Shaw, and Grubb, 1991; Strosnider, 1998). Distance learning technology (DLT) makes alliances of any sort easier to form, and it promotes them beyond limitations of physical distance.

The literature also cites a more complex alliance or a consortium, a multi-school group that offers both courses and programs (Baldwin,

1991; Carey, 1991; Ferguson, 1994; Moses, Edgerton, Shaw, and Grubb, 1991). In a consortium, institutions may work with primary and secondary schools (Brownridge, 1993), junior colleges (Brownridge, 1993) and/or other universities (Baldwin, 1991). In advanced forms, the alliance itself becomes an entity with its own structure and personnel — a virtual university (Albrecht and Bardsley, 1994). One example is the Western Governors University (Johnstone and Jones, 1997). Here DLT does more than facilitate this form of alliance; without DLT, a virtual university could not exist. Indeed, many alliances such as Western Governors University would not exist but for DLT. An offshoot of the virtual university is the "university center," a central physical location which imports its instruction and degree programs from remote schools via DLT (Schmidt, 1999).

Our case study research on DLT usage concurs with the literature. The research on a diverse group of schools revealed at the least an awareness of alliances and at the most active participation in them. Examples of alliances ranged from the simple exchange of courses to formal partnerships that involved programs. At the lower end, the case study research revealed that one state university's Accounting Department exchanged courses with a sister school, taking advantage of special teaching resources unique to each school. In a more common example, schools in the case research reported full-scale partnerships with other entities such as other higher education institutions, for-profit concerns, and high schools. Although no virtual universities as such were encountered, school officers often cited the potential for them either as an outlet for that school or as a competitor.

The review of the literature and the case research yielded a working taxonomy of distance learning alliances in higher education. This taxonomy focuses on the individual school in an alliance. Attributes used to describe the school are depth, direction and nature of the other alliance members. Each attribute is considered in turn.

Depth of alliance

Depth describes the degree to which a school participates in an alliance, and the different depths also give name to the types of alliances. Three types or levels of alliance are: (1) the Simple Exchange, (2) the Partnership, and (3) the Virtual University. In the **Simple Exchange**, schools only exchange needed courses; the point is to fill specific gaps in the curriculum. On the next level, a **Partnership**, the relationship is more formal. Universities work with other schools or organizations such as to bring in a whole or partial program for students. Schools in a partnership retain their own identity; the focus remains on the individual institutions. Often the literature and schools themselves refer to such partnerships as consortia. Finally, a **Virtual University** draws on multiple sources to create a new entity; member schools provide instruction and perhaps other needed resources.

Direction of Alliance

Direction for an alliance member means whether the school is a provider or receiver of instruction or both. First, a school can provide instruction to another entity such as a high school, other higher education institution or private business (Godbey, 1993; Bigham, Kellogg, and Hodges, 1994). Second, a school can receive instruction from another school—that instruction can range from just a course to an entire program. One school in the case study research imported a health care concentration from another state school for its MBA program. Third of course, the same school can both provide and receive instruction. In one example, two nearby schools designed DLT classrooms in part to provide for a joint nursing program (Robbin, 1996).

Other Members of Alliance

Also of interest is the nature of the other members in a school's alliance. As mentioned before, the other alliance members can include primary and secondary schools, junior colleges, like institutions (four-year degree-granting) and for-profit concerns. Typically, schools would ally with the lower-level schools as providers of instruction to them. In the case research, one university provided instruction to area high schools in subjects such as advanced placement, mathematics, and foreign languages. Between four-year institutions, the role of a school more likely varies. The university in the case research that sent courses to high schools received courses from at least one other state school. Alliances with for-profit concerns appear more limited, but the case study research found one such case where the university and the for-profit business collaborated on a special program that the school could not have done on its own.

Alliances using DLT present a number of issues for the higher education environment. The next section examines issues that surround the rise of alliances.

MAIN THRUST OF THE CHAPTER

Alliances via distance learning technology (DLT) affect an institution whether it enters one or not; they affect the whole higher education environment. School leadership must decide whether to enter alliances and if so on what terms. Further, even if a school decides to pass on joining an alliance, its leadership must assess how others use alliances. Alliances using DLT can change curriculum, structure, finances, competition, and accreditation. Ultimately, alliances may affect the mission, identity, and perhaps even the survival of schools.

Curriculum

On the surface, the first thing that alliances change is the curriculum a school offers. An alliance can change scale, the number of students that instruction reach, or scope, the variety of instruction a school can provide students. A basic example of a change in both comes from the Simple Exchange alliance. In the case study research, one school sent a not-for-profit accounting class to a second school via compressed video. For the first school, the provider, the scale increased: the school provided the instruction to a larger number of students than before. For the second school, the receiver, the scope increased: the school received instruction in a topic for which it did not have faculty resources to supply.

In another example from the case research, a small private university entered a partnership with a for-profit business. Together, they provided continuing education courses. The courses bore the name of the university, and the school administered the program. Course development was shared with the for-profit concern. Through this alliance, the school reached students it would not otherwise with a group of courses it could not provide on its own.

Schools must consider their own needs and interests first before entering an alliance. If a school might provide instruction to another school, it should ask if both it and the other school have the means to deliver instruction in a quality acceptable to both. Further, does the provider school have adequate resources to avoid diluting its product? In another example from the case studies, one university considered carefully before "sharing" a graduate library degree with a second school. The university assessed both its own program and the resources at the second school. If a school receives instruction, it should consider what the imported course or program adds. As with the case study school that brought in a Health Care Administration concentration to its MBA program via DLT, schools should ask how or to what degree a new course or program enhances the current curriculum.

Structure

Structure matters as well when a school enters an alliance. Such concern often distills down to "nuts-and-bolts" issues. Two university officers in the case study research cited coordination problems to overcome. They detailed schedule problems that a provider and a receiver school must resolve before sharing instruction. Those problems include when the semester starts and ends, when class periods begin and end, how long the classes periods run, and what holidays and other break times each school observes. Schools must resolve these issues for instruction to run smoothly. At one case study school, an officer cited an instance where the university provided instruction to multiple area high schools, each with its own unique school term and class times. The more alliance members, the greater the challenge for coordinating schedules. At some point, schools must compromise on certain structural issues.

There are of course larger structural issues as well. These include the division of responsibility among alliance members as well as how the schools interface. Schools may interface between the units providing and receiving instruction, or they may coordinate activities through a central distance learning or continuing education organization. At one school in the case study, the continuing education unit handled most of the detail work on linking instruction from one school to another. At another school that merely pursued a simple exchange of courses, the academic unit involved largely handled the process. Among other problems, schools must resolve class size, coordination of offerings during each term and registration. One school may constrain class size below what another does, and another school may need certain special courses offered during certain terms. Finally, registration problems will likely surface: who gets "credit" for the students enrolled in a class off-campus? Providers and receivers of instruction must resolve this issue, and the ownership of head count links directly to the next issue, finances.

Finances

Perhaps even more so than registration, finances can raise thorny issues in an alliance. Boiled down to a simple question, who gets the tuition money and who gets the costs? Both provider and receiver can make a case for shares of the money: the provider supplies the needed instruction, and the receiver supplies the students. As with the structural issues, schools will likely compromise. If the alliance members are all public schools in the same state, some governing board might resolve money issues. Regardless, schools will likely negotiate toward their own advantage on structural and especially money issues.

Virtual universities pose added problems for both structure and finances. The virtual university by nature is its own entity, but it relies on the resources of member institutions. The Western Governors University is one example (Blumenstyk, 1998). Again, schedules and terms need resolution; and as with a more traditional alliance, splitting revenues and costs may require negotiation. Where the virtual university and its alliance members make matters more complex is the relationship of resources. All parties have to agree where one organization leaves off and another begins. Further, members must define which organization employs which personnel or how the virtual university draws staff and especially faculty.

Competition

An issue somewhat related to structure and money is competition. DLT changes the competitive environment in general, and the dynamics of competition change further with the presence of alliances. For many state schools, geographic neighbors have been their strongest rivals for decades. Now with the possibility of alliances via DLT, these rivals may join together for certain courses or programs. The somewhat odd situation arises that two or more schools who have competed in many areas may continue to do so but at the same time collaborate in one or more special areas. Such a mix of competition and collaboration complicates a relationship. In at least four instances among the case study schools, schools allied themselves with other schools that they had traditionally competed with for students. These competitors / allies ranged from two-year schools to other four-year institutions. As with finances and structure, a state governing board may mediate between schools.

Virtual universities may impact competition but more likely that is a future issue. For present, the focus appears to be on reaching students who would not otherwise attend a member institution. Among its stated aims, the Western Governors University plans to reach students cut off from traditional schools by distance or time constraints (Blumenstyk, 1998).

Accreditation

A final issue involves accreditation. Traditional accrediting methods and bodies have not fully accounted for changes in distance education. Accrediting concerns appear to focus mainly on the quality of instruction; schools would need to verify that instruction sent or received through an alliance would match the school's internal standards (McCollum, 1998). In the long run accreditation will adjust if alliances using DLT prove acceptable; in the short run it may challenge a school's efforts.

The short term poses a range of problems for schools. Most, like schedules and money, center on tasks or roadblocks to deal with on the way to making an alliance function. A few longer-term or deeper issues range beyond those current ones. The next section looks at the future and also suggests research opportunities.

FUTURE TRENDS

In a longer view, alliances will begin to affect schools on both the inside and the outside. For schools on the outside of a particular alliance, the alliance of course affects the competitive environment. Alliances introduce an added competition and change the dynamics of that competition. An alliance through DLT may enter markets that individual member schools could not. Most likely, those markets would be geographic in nature and attractive in potential students. Alliance members previously cut off from an under-served growth area could use their combined strength to enter that local market. Existing schools in such a market would feel pressure on their own enrollment.

Alliances, if successful, would affect member schools in more profound and subtle ways. Three ways an alliance could affect a member school are (1) it could constrain or control the school's resources, (2) it could force the school to redefine its mission - what it does and how it functions, and (3) it could affect the identity or even threaten the survival of the school as its own entity.

Constraint and Control

First, a successful alliance will likely assume a larger role in instruction at the same time as it may limit the prospects of a member school. Political boundaries would make a difference here. For instance, an alliance among public universities all contained within the same state may constrain member schools much more than an alliance that crosses state lines. For an alliance contained within one state, a board or some other government entity would exert influence and control over all member schools. Alliances in the long-term could strengthen a central authority, weaken member schools or in some way change the terms of how they related to each other.

When alliance membership crossed state borders on the other hand, two or more governing bodies would enter the picture. Member schools in that setting might retain greater control. An alliance might more closely adhere to its original purpose and limits. Expansion of the mission of such an alliance would face stronger scrutiny from more parties.

Do alliances open the door to changes within member schools? Logic suggests they do. An alliance makes new demands on funding and other limited resources a school has. For state public schools, a DLT-enabled alliance means another budget item that competes for state dollars, and an alliance via DLT at least on paper provides a fresh, attractive way to spend money in higher education.

With any degree of perceived success, an alliance might limit future expansion at traditional universities. For instance, an argument against plans for a new graduate nursing program at School A would be that School B already has one and since they both are in a DLT-enabled alliance, School B should share its program with School A. On a smaller scale, an alliance might even affect hiring new faculty. The needs of the alliance could dictate who got hired and what skills the position required.

Redefinition

Second, beyond conflict over the control of resources, an alliance could push a member school to redefine its purpose. Prahalad and Hamel (1990) suggested the idea of core competencies - very roughly what an organization does best. Businesses have core competencies; schools certainly do too. A growth in alliances could prompt schools to examine what they do best - and outsource the rest! Outsourcing services is not new; schools have done that with computer systems and services (Wallace, 1997), bookstores (Freeman, 1997), security, and custodial services (Nicklin, 1997). A typical reason given is that cost pressures force administrators to look elsewhere and that outsourcing allows the institution to focus on its core function: instruction. Instruction has been defined *in general terms* thus far (Nicklin, 1997). What happens though when the core function of the university is defined as instruction *in more specific terms*? For example, if an engineering school determines that its core competency or function is strictly in engineering and related areas, it could seek a partner via DLT to provide the history and language courses it needs to round out a student's curriculum. Outsourcing some instruction would permit the school to redeploy resources to its premier programs. Taking the idea a step further, the school would position itself so it could export its strength - engineering or other technical instruction - to other schools via DLT. Indeed, some have already speculated that technology could lead to greater specialization (Morrison, 1998). Before administrators outsourced a school's instruction, they would need to answer a number of questions such as how well the provider's courses matched the school's needs academically and economically, how easy it would be to end an outsourcing alliance and how the school would benefit from outsourcing. Administrators may one day ask themselves not only what instruction they should "buy" but also what instruction they can "sell."

Identity

Third, beyond even redefinition, members of an alliance may "suffer an identity crisis." The beginning of this concern is whose name goes on the diploma a student gets. Does the diploma come from the school that provides the instruction, the one that receives it, some new title tied to the alliance itself, or whatever the best "brand name" is? Regardless of the name, this question is but a symptom of a larger issue: how the alliance and its members relate over time. One school might at the least subvert its name and at the most surrender its identity and control totally to the alliance itself or to a larger, more powerful member school. Bleeke and Ernst (1995), in their analysis of strategic alliances in business, warned that most alliances they observed ended with merger in one form or another. Could that pattern of alliance-to-merger repeat itself in higher education, enabled by DLT? As seen with Peabody and Vanderbilt, it has already happened even without technology as a catalyst.

Future research into distance learning alliances would shed light not only on their prospects but also on how they affect member schools. Longitudinal studies on alliances would chart how they evolve and what happens to member schools. Multi-subject case studies based on a taxonomy like that presented here would contrast different methods and environments.

Distance learning alliances raise issues both short-term and long-term. The last section closes the discussion with some final thoughts about technology, alliances and decision making.

CONCLUSION

Distance learning technology (DLT) has attracted great attention in higher education, but what matters most is how schools choose to use that technology. Technology of all sorts has served as a catalyst for change, and DLT will do the same. One option many schools are now considering or facing is an alliance of schools spawned by DLT. Although the outcome is uncertain, the use of DLT in diverse organizational forms proceeds, and schools must address a number of issues both short-term and long-term. Even if a school rejects membership in a DLT-enabled alliance, administrators must recognize how alliances could alter the competitive landscape.

Schools must look at alliances in both a short-term or tactical light as well as in a longer-term or strategic light. In the short-term, those issues concern how to start an alliance and how to make it function. If successful, the alliance opens a new array of future concerns. These future concerns revolve around not just the relationship between alliance members but also the mission, identity and survival of the individual school. Taking actions such as joining an alliance without a clear view of the implications can hurt the organization and may one day end it. Rash choices today limit options tomorrow.

REFERENCES

Albrecht, Robert & Bardsley, Gary (1994). Strategic planning and academic planning for distance education. Willis, Barry (Ed.), *Distance Education Strategy and Tools.* . Englewood Cliffs, NJ: Educational Technology Publications, Inc., 67-86.

Baldwin, Lionel V. (1991, March). Higher-education partnerships in engineering and science. Vivian M. Horner & Linda G. Roberts (Eds.), *Annals of the American Academy of Political and Social Science: Electronic Links For Learning (514),* Newbury Park, CA: Sage Publications, 76-91.

Bigham, Sandi, Kellogg, Jane, & Hodges, Jimmy. (1994). *Telecommunications Technology Planning Manual*, South Central Bell.

Bleeke, Joel & Ernst, David. (1995, January-February). Is your strategic alliance really a sale? *Harvard Business Review*, 97-105.

Blumenstyk, Goldie (1998, February 6). Western Governors U. takes shape as a new model for higher education. *The Chronicle of Higher Education*, A21.

Brownridge, Ina C. (1993). Distance learning partnership *Education* (113:3), 353-55.

Carey, John. (1991, March). Plato at the keyboard: telecommunications technology and education policy. *Annals of the American Academy of Political and Social Science: Electronic Links For Learning (514)*, Vivian M. Horner & Linda G. Roberts (eds.), Sage Publications, Newbury Park, CA, 11-21.

Dorn, Sherman (1996). *A brief history of Peabody College.* Peabody College of Vanderbilt University.

Ferguson, Carl E., Jr. (Fall 1994). Classroom without walls. *Focus,* University of Alabama, College of Commerce and Business Administration, 5-8.

Freeman, Laurie (1997, January). Bookstore contract boosts revenues. *School Planning and Management*, 20F(3).

Godbey, Galen. (1993, Spring). Beyond TQM: Competition and cooperation create the agile institution. *Educational Record (74:2)*, 37-42.

Hajdu, Dorothy L. & Schreckengost, Deborah L. (1994). Distance learning. Charles E. Greenawalt II (Ed.), *Educational innovation: An agenda to frame the future, The Commonwealth Foundation for Public Policy Alternatives*. University Press of America, 285-307.

Johnstone, Sally M. & Jones, Dennis (1997, November/December). New higher education trends reflected in the design of Western Governors University. *On the Horizon*, 8-11.

McCollum, Kelly (1998, May 15). Accreditors are urged to prepare to evaluate distance learning. *The Chronicle of Higher Education*, A34.

Morrison, James L. (1998, January/February). Technology and education: An interview with William H. Graves. *On the Horizon*, 2-4.

Moses, Kurt D., Edgerton, David, Shaw, Willard E., & Grubb, Ralph. (1991, March). International case studies of distance learning. *Annals of the American Academy of Political and Social Science: Electronic Links For Learning (514)*, Vivian M. Horner & Linda G. Roberts (eds.), Sage Publications, Newbury Park, CA, 58-75.

Nicklin, Julie L. (1997, November 21). Universities seek to cut costs by 'outsourcing' more operations. *The Chronicle of Higher Education*, A35(2).

Prahalad, C. K. & Hamel, Gary. (1990, May/June). The core competence of the corporation. *Harvard Business Review*, 79-91.

Rayburn, William (1997). Not what but how: The role of institutional and environmental factors in the use of distance learning technology for higher education. Southern Illinois University.

Robbin, L. Katherine (1996, November 11). Modern technology: A quantum leap forward on today's Christian college campuses. *Christianity Today*, 60.

Schmidt, Peter (1999, January 29). Illinois considers a new model for providing higher education. *The Chronicle of Higher Education*, A40.

Strosnider, Kim (1998, May 29). Private colleges in Ohio are collaborating to cut costs. *The Chronicle of Higher Education*, A41.

Wallace, Bob (1997, June 30). More firms outsource remote support; IS hopes to cut big access bills. *Computerworld*, 49.

Chapter VII

Elements of a Successful Distributed Learning Program

Lore Meyer-Peyton
Department of Defense Education Activity

INTRODUCTION

Global connectivity has opened up a new dimension in education, namely, the concept of delivering education via technology to students who may never see their classmates or their instructor face to face. The typical school with its traditional classrooms does not exist in this new scenario, and many of the professionals responsible for developing distributed learning courses are new to the task. This chapter will guide the reader through the process of planning and implementing a distributed learning program.

The model for this chapter is the distributed learning program provided by the Department of Defense Education Activity to schools serving the family members of U.S. military personnel at home and abroad. The DoDEA Electronic School (DES) offers sixteen courses to over six hundred students at 56 high schools in fourteen countries, spanning twelve time zones. The program has been in existence for over twelve years, evolving from a two-teacher program to a worldwide school headed by an administrative staff and employing 23 instructors and four technical support staff members. Courses currently available through the DES include seven advanced placement courses (Calculus AB and BC, Physics B, German, United States History, and Computer Science A and AB); five computer programming courses (Pascal I and II, Q-BASIC, Visual BASIC, and C++); economics; health; humanities; and science research seminar.

In addition to offering student courses, the DES is in the process of adding an extensive staff development component. With teachers and staff based worldwide, the system can save a significant amount of travel money by providing staff development opportunities that are accessible at the local site.

The DoDEA Electronic School grew up with technology. During those first years, students used an acoustic coupler and a telephone to call a central computer in the United States, where they accessed a text based conferencing program to communicate with their classmates and instructors. Today's DES instructors develop their courses in Lotus Notes, and students can use either the Lotus Notes client or a Web browser. Domino servers at each school send and receive information via the Internet, resulting in efficient transfer of data.

In today's environment, rich with technology but short on hours in the day, there is no time afforded for the luxury of "evolving." Professionals tasked with developing distributed learning programs for their organizations are given a staff, a budget and a mandate—and certainly a challenge. The goal of this chapter is to help those professionals meet the challenge by examining the key elements of a successful distributed learning program.

ELEMENT 1: THE PROGRAM HAS A CLEAR PLAN.

Planning a distributed learning program begins with determining the goals of the program. Start with a description of the potential audience. For example, what level of education does the program intend to offer, and to what age group? Will it be a degree program? What will be the geographical spread of the students? The answers to these questions will influence some of the most important planning considerations, such as the courses themselves, the method of delivery, and the delivery platform.

One of the main goals of the DoDEA Electronic School, for example, is to deliver courses to students whose schools are too small to offer a wide range of choices, thus giving these students the same opportunities that they would have at a larger school. Accordingly, advanced placement and computer programming courses were the first courses offered by the DES. Although the mandate is still the same, the target audience has been expanded to include students at a variety of levels.

Once the audience has been identified, the next step is to map out the courses and the time schedule for offering the courses. For example, will the school offer all courses the first time it opens its virtual doors, or will courses be added gradually?

Each course should be described in detail, including the goals and objectives, course content, instructional methodology, materials needed, and performance standards for success.

ELEMENT 2: THE DELIVERY PLATFORM ENABLES THE IMPLEMENTATION OF THE COURSE GOALS AND STRUCTURE.

The delivery platform must support the course content and methodology. How does the instructor plan to design the course? Will class discussions and projects play an important role? If so, the platform must support conferencing and not just the exchange of data. Does the course rely on multimedia? If the answer is yes, the delivery platform must be robust enough to support multimedia, preferably across multiple operating systems.

When choosing a delivery platform, it is vital to note that the technology should not drive the course — the technology should be the vehicle for the course.

Perhaps the most important decision to be made regarding the delivery method is the choice between delivering the course synchronously or asynchronously. For the DoDEA Electronic School, the choice was a foregone conclusion. Since the students are based in several different time zones, delivery is, for the most part, asynchronous. However, the DES is exploring the use of synchronous technologies to augment the asynchronous platform.

In self-contained districts, distributed learning courses are often delivered synchronously by an instructor at a central site who interacts with groups of students at remote sites. Each group meets in a room at the local school; the students watch the instructor on video (real time) and speak with the instructor and other students via an 800 line.

Regardless of whether the program uses synchronous or asynchronous technology, the delivery site or platform must be readily accessible to the audience. If the students must travel to a specific location, that location must be within a reasonable commuting distance. If participants regularly work from home or other remote sites, it is imperative that the course be easily and reliably accessible from remote computers.

Implementation costs for the platforms under consideration must be researched and compared. Costs include equipment, such as video conferencing equipment and servers, and software licensing. Often additional support staff must be hired.

The most important point to remember when considering delivery platforms is that if the students experience frustration with the technology, they will drop out. It is imperative that the platform be easy to learn, convenient to access, reliable, and user friendly. If the students cannot get past the technology, they will not take the courses.

ELEMENT 3: THE EQUIPMENT AND INFRASTRUCTURE ARE RELIABLE AND ROBUST.

Since distributed learning relies so heavily on technology, the equipment — workstations, servers, video conferencing equipment — must be reliable, and the infrastructure — network, Internet connection, phone lines — must be robust. When a key component is down, the students lose productivity time — a situation that is simply not acceptable.

When buying equipment, a good policy is to allow for more than the minimum configuration and then budget for future upgrades. If your system relies on another system, be sure that the technicians for that system understand the relationship — and the importance of a reliable network to your organization.

In order to minimize down time, plan redundancy into the system. For example, the DES has a Domino server and Lotus Notes clients, both running on Windows NT 4.0 computers, at every site. The students work locally, while data exchange, or replication, is accomplished via the Internet. If the Internet is down, backup phone lines are used for replication.

If the site server goes down, the students can easily access servers at other sites by simply creating an Internet connection to another server. Alternatively, the students can access their courses via the Web, using Netscape or Internet Explorer. With this built-in redundancy, the entire school network would have to fail for a student to miss a day of work. Even then, the students can work from home or from the community library.

ELEMENT 4: WHEN PROBLEMS DO OCCUR, TECH SUPPORT IS IMMEDIATE.

What happens when a technical problem occurs? Since technical problems are inevitable, the program must have a technical support team tasked with keeping the infrastructure up and running.

If the distributed learning program is based at more than one site, it is time and money well spent to send the tech support team to each site to set up the equipment, map out and document the configuration, meet with the local support personnel, and train users. When a problem occurs, the support team will have instant access to site information, as well as a rapport with the local technologists. In addition, the team members should meet with administrative personnel (principals and counselors at the secondary level, for example) to establish lines of communication and to answer questions about the program.

After the initial installation, it is wise to budget for annual visits to each site by a member of the tech support team for preventive maintenance, upgrades, and training.

Building trust with the users "in the field" — students, local support personnel, administrators — is a vital part of tech support. Users need to know that tech support is available and responsive. To that end, tech support should be accessible in several ways: phone, e-mail, and a help area on the Web site. Even if the tech support person is unable to solve the problem immediately, he or she should keep the user informed about the status of the help request.

With reliable tech support, the infrastructure stays up and running - and the users stay enrolled in their courses.

ELEMENT 5: THE INSTRUCTORS ARE DEDICATED TO THE CONCEPT OF DISTRIBUTED LEARNING AND VERSED IN DISTRIBUTED LEARNING PEDAGOGY.

The instructors are, of course, key players in any distributed learning program. They must be truly dedicated to the success of the program, because they invariably spend long hours responding to students, planning lessons and video presentations, and researching the best methods for course delivery. Teaching a distributed learning course is very labor intensive, especially if the course is taught asynchronously. Each question has to be answered in writing; each assignment has to be graded, with comments made in writing; each lesson has to be written out in its entirety.

The intensity of the work begins long before the course reaches the students. Distributed learning courses don't just "happen" — they have to be carefully and thoughtfully designed. The instructors must "translate" a traditional course into a distributed learning environment, using effective and varied methods to impart the material to the students, while keeping within the parameters of the delivery platform. The DoDEA Electronic School instructors develop their own courses in Lotus Notes, with the assistance of two support staff members.

Before an instructor starts designing a course, consider sending the instructor to training in distributed learning pedagogy. A distributed learning course does not have to be — and should not be — a "correspondence school." With thought and planning, techniques such as collaborative learning can certainly be applied to distributed learning courses. Discussions and projects become a vital part of the course. In a distributed learning course conducted asynchronously, the bell never rings before a student has the opportunity to contribute.

ELEMENT 6: THE INSTRUCTORS ARE COMFORTABLE WITH THE TECHNOLOGY.

The instructors should be trained during the planning and design phases so that they feel comfortable with the technology. They should also receive training at regular intervals during the implementation.

Time spent training the instructors will save problems in the long run. The instructors are for the most part curriculum experts, not technology experts. If they have agreed to design and teach a distributed learning course, they are obviously willing to learn the technology — but they do have to be taught at the outset and provided with ongoing assistance as problems and questions arise.

The DoDEA Electronic School brings the entire staff together at the end of each school year for two weeks. The instructors refine their Lotus Notes databases and update the curriculum for the following year, while the tech support team members explore new products and techniques for improving the infrastructure.

These meetings help develop team spirit and camaraderie, with the result that the staff is extremely close, although geographically far-flung. Staff members communicate regularly via e-mail, over the phone, and on-line in the open staff forum. Instructors teaching the same course often team teach, and staff members help each other with design and curricular issues. The tech support team considers the instructors the top priority.

ELEMENT 7: THE INSTRUCTIONAL MODEL INCORPORATES A VARIETY OF TECHNIQUES.

Distributed learning students have in effect taken on the responsibility for their own learning. There is no instructor in front of the classroom — in fact, there may not be a classroom!

The instruction is resource based, in that the students have at their sites everything they need to be successful: materials, the course syllabus, access to the technology, and access to the instructor via computer or telephone. The instructor ceases to be the "sage on the stage," assuming instead the role of facilitator, or "guide on the side."

This instructional model incorporates student — student as well as student — instructor interaction. Students are encouraged to learn from each other and to work together to solve problems. Collaborative activities — not just discussions — are built into the curriculum.

Collaborative work is done in open forums, sometimes accessible only to group members and the instructor, sometimes accessible to the entire class.

As in a traditional classroom, the instructor incorporates several types of instruction in order to address student learning styles.

An advantage of distributed learning is that every student has center stage when the instructor is responding to him or her, whether via the computer or on the telephone. DES instructors report that they often develop close relationships with their students, even though they have never met the students face to face.

Distributed learning students who are quiet in "live" classes often blossom in distributed learning classes, becoming discussion leaders and group facilitators. Local teachers are often astounded when the class wallflower becomes the mover and shaker in a distributed learning course.

ELEMENT 8: LOCAL PERSONNEL ASSIST WITH ON SITE FACILITATING AND SUPPORT.

If the students are based at several sites, such as secondary schools, it is vital that local personnel assist with the distributed learning program. For example, the administrators and counselors are generally responsible for advertising the courses and enrolling students.

However, the key player at schools served by the DES is the "local facilitator," who serves as a liaison between the students and the distributed learning instructors. At the beginning of each semester, the local facilitator registers the students with the DES, ensures that the students have access to the network and the platform, and helps the students learn the platform. In addition, the local facilitator provides the students with a quiet place to work, computers, and course materials. The facilitator monitors the students regularly and reports problems to the distributed learning instructor. In short, the local facilitator mentors the students and can make or break the program at the site.

Other instructors at a site can often provide important support for the distributed learning program. For example, a science instructor may be able to help a struggling AP Physics student with an immediate question. The DES is planning to establish a mentoring program in order to identify local staff and community members who are willing to provide assistance.

ELEMENT 9: THE PROGRAM IS CONSTANTLY MONITORED AND EVALUATED FOR EFFECTIVENESS.

It is important to evaluate the program on an ongoing basis so that the instructor stays in tune with how the students are doing with both the course and the technology.

The ubiquitous end-of-course evaluations do not help the current students. If the instructor sets up a way for the students to communicate their thoughts and concerns on an ongoing basis, the instructor can make improvements as the course moves forward.

Both cognitive and affective student outcomes are taken into consideration. Cognitive outcomes are measured relative to the goals and objectives of each course, generally by some type of assessment.

Affective outcomes can be measured by less formal means, such as journals, discussions in open forums and private discussions with the instructor.

CONCLUSION

This chapter has attempted to acquaint the reader with the key elements of a successful distributed learning program and assist with the planning phase of a new program.

Gearing up for a distributed learning program is both an exciting and formidable undertaking. In order for the program to succeed, all of the elements must be in place: a comprehensive plan, a robust platform with a reliable infrastructure, capable tech support, dedicated instructors, well-designed courses and dependable local support.

While not pretending to replace traditional education, distributed learning programs offer another dimension of opportunity to students who are better served by flexible schedules and workplaces. Gone are the days when distributed learning was a small, somewhat maverick, operation in a few pioneering organizations. In today's networked world, distributed learning has taken its place in the education mainstream.

Chapter VIII

Online Teaching and Learning: Essential Conditions for Success!

Lynne Schrum
University of Georgia

INTRODUCTION

Today the global education community is faced with a unique problem. Learners in every location must acquire new skills, be literate, and understand constantly changing dynamics. The challenge has always been to balance the need for intense and personal interaction to learn conceptual information with the reality of limited financial resources. Distance education has been viewed as a way in which to offer lifelong learning to those who are geographically separated from traditional institutions, have obligations that limit their ability to attend regular courses or have other exceptional challenges.

Distance learning in various forms has been around for a long time. Traditional distance learning environments were based on correspondence through passive media (paper, audio and video broadcast). Now, developments in network and communication technologies have provided the ability to offer online courses to large numbers of individuals. With the changes in electronic communications, and the resulting transformed model of distance learning, individuals expect interactivity and close to "traditional" classroom-based education.

This shift means that distance education is now seen as a viable alternative for a myriad of "just in time" professional development and lifelong learning opportunities. These include informal courses, professional development tutorials, and even full degree programs; however, we are still uncertain about the conditions that are essential to create a successful venture. The growth of online courses, enhanced by the ease of access, media attention, and interest from the private sector, has increased demand, and efforts are underway to respond with various online learning activities. Thus, it is timely to study these courses since it is essential that institutions take the lead to ensure that courses are pedagogically sound, organizationally strong and institutionally supported. Frequently, however, institutions are unsure about where to begin and what issues to consider as they make this transition (Ehrman, 1995).

The purpose of this chapter is to discuss online education from the perspective of potential course developers, and to offer a view of the issues necessary to consider for success for the institution and for the learners. The author has many years of experience in researching and teaching various types of distance learning as well as having designed and taught online courses. The ideas in this paper draw upon those experiences, reviews of pertinent literature, and on interviews with instructors, potential instructors and students of online courses.

PERSPECTIVES

Examples of traditional courses being offered using a variety of telecommunications methods (electronic mail, computer conferencing, two-way audio/video, satellite delivery) have been widely discussed in the literature (Harasim, 1993; Hiltz, 1990; Rice-Lively, 1994; Schrum, 1992; Sproull & Kiesler, 1991). Results of studies have concluded that this form of education is effective for well-motivated students. More importantly, it is clear that one should not simply take a traditional course and place it on any form of educational network (Schrum, 1998; Wagner, 1993).

The growth in the practice of lifelong learning is reflected in large numbers of students who are nontraditional in age and responsibilities. These individuals frequently must overcome concerns about time, distance and money that traditional students do not have. Online and independent learning offers one potential solution to these issues and now military, business, and nontraditional educational providers have begun to investigate its potential. As the number and types of online courses have grown, many educational institutions have expanded their programs to include traditional and nontraditional courses, partially or entirely online, and other entities are considering implementing such courses. For example, institutions are feeling particularly vulnerable because the advantage of location no longer ensures them a market based on geography. Institutions that offer a traditional MBA now must compete with the true giants in the field which offer that degree online (Business Week, 1997).

Traditionally distance learning courses were frequently conducted as independent experiences, with each learner corresponding only with the instructor. Recent developments in technology and access have offered the opportunity to improve these environments through increased communication, interactivity among participants, and incorporation of collaborative pedagogical models. Other advantages to using this type of distance learning include:

- instantaneous (synchronous) and delayed (asynchronous) communication modes.
- access to and from geographically isolated communities.
- multiple and collaborative participation among widely dispersed individuals.
- ultimate convenience, when and where you choose
- interaction with and among individuals from diverse cultures, and
- ability to focus on participants' ideas, without knowledge of age, race, gender, or background.

Harasim (1990) summarized the characteristics of online courses as place and time independent, many-to-many communication that fosters real collaborative learning and dependence on text-based communications to promote thoughtful and reflective commentary.

It has become clear that communication through technology has the potential to change the way in which people behave, according to Lea and Spears (1991). They identified a change in informal and formal talk, and individuals' loss of identity and de-individuation. Tatar, Foster and Bobrow suggest consideration for what group work really means. It is not just individuals working at computers at the same time, but it means "giving participants the ability to judge when it is appropriate to overlap, just as they judge the efficacy" of adding to verbal conversations (1991, p. 77). It is necessary that group members have support to learn and act out their roles in these situations (Olson & Bly, 1991).

The literature reports an increasing number of courses and degrees delivered entirely or partially through digital networks. Some of these courses are traditional subject matter courses, often undergraduate, while others are more geared to ongoing professional work activities. In some circumstances the technology is only a repository and merely holds materials (Boston, 1992; Schrum, 1995), and in others there is evidence that the technology itself assists in a paradigm shift so that it becomes the environment for learning (Dede, 1995).

Development of an online educational environment is not a trivial task. Wiesenberg and Hutton (1996) identified three major challenges for the designer to consider: increased time for developing and delivering the course (they estimate two or three times what is necessary for a traditional course), creating a community online, and encouraging students to become independent learners. They also reported fewer interactions than expected from participants of an online course.

Reid and Woolf (1997) discuss the benefits of integrating online components into traditional classes, such as accessibility, learner control, heightened communication, access to worldwide resources, and the potential for a student centered environment. Heeren and Lewis (1997) suggest matching the media with the task, to keep lean media for tasks that do not require much interaction, for example, electronic mail, and reserve rich media for things that require more interaction and broader spectrum of activity (face to face).

Learners report greater control and responsibility toward their learning; students also find that the act of writing demands greater reflection than speaking (Harasim, 1990; Rohfeld & Hiemstra, 1994). Several research and anecdotal studies have looked at online components of traditional courses and have concluded that these components substantially increase the communication between the teacher and the students, and among the students, when compared with similar classes without the computer communication component (Hartman, Neuwirth, Kiesler, Sproull, Cochran, Palmquist, & Zubrow, 1994; Hiltz, 1990; Schrum, 1995; Schrum & Lamb, 1997).

Groupware is a new class of software that has contributed to the development of online learning. The name refers to software that supports and augments group work. However, most investigations have focused on those capabilities useful in business settings, particularly among co-located populations who used the software synchronously, often in group decision activities (Valacich, Dennis, & Nunamaker, Jr., 1991). The literature is now beginning to expand the conceptualization of the use of groupware to include asynchronous and geographically distant activities.

ISSUES TO CONSIDER IN DESIGNING SUCCESSFUL ONLINE INSTRUCTION

Historically, good teachers in the place-based classroom responded to students in a variety of ways. Without thinking about it, if glazed looks appeared on students' faces, an experienced teacher would have developed strategies to remediate the situation, often as tacit knowledge. It is possible that many teachers adapt to the online environment with similar automatic reactions. To the extent a method or activity works or does not, the online teacher adjusts accordingly. How do we explicate, discuss and share that which we do in the online environment? Laurillard (1996) describes a "Conversational Framework" for academic learning and differentiates between the "discursive level" (where the teacher articulates the subject matter and the student joins the dialogue) and the "interactive level" which she says is

> …the level of practice, representing the way the student acts in the world, or at least in a world constructed by the teacher such that their interactive activities will give them experience of the theory in action. Here the teacher sets a task, the student acts, the world responds to their action, and the student can modify their action in order to better achieve the goal of the task. (Laurillard, 1996, N. P.)

Principles of instructional design indicate a need for alignment among the content of a course, the instructional goals and objectives, the evaluation and the practice activities in which students are encouraged to engage (Yelon & Berge, 1988). Given this framework, it becomes important that the designer/teacher use instructional methods and strategies that promote student activity that corresponds to the goals for each course.

The data gathered from personal experience and interviews have provided two significant results. First, the author has been able to identify student characteristics that indicate success with this type of delivery. Students identify themselves as successful when: they had strong reasons for signing up for this type of course, moved through the lessons fairly rapidly, had support from their family, were independent learners, and began with a certain level of technological knowledge and experience. It is also reported that the ongoing change in practice and continued use of information technology is dependent on the ease and cost of access, time available for practice and experimentation, and support for risk-taking. These characteristics must be taken into consideration when designing an online educational experience (Schrum, 1995; 1996). Second, it is evident that certain pedagogical, organizational, and institutional issues must be considered before beginning to teach an online course. The characteristics and questions that emerge from these two results can be used to help construct guidelines for making decisions about the creation of courses.

Pedagogical Concerns

Before decisions can be made about delivery or models, an instructor must make pedagogical decisions about the fundamental goals of a course. The salient questions when creating an educational experience have always been, "What are the instructional and personal goals of this course for all students?" "What is the purpose of this course?" These are questions that all educators must ask themselves when designing courses, and in general, they have become comfortable and adept at doing this.

Duchastel (1996-97) suggests a continuum that helps an instructor rethink the traditional classroom model to one more fitting the electronic processes and global resources. He argues for moving from:

static content to specifying goals to pursue;
one answer to accepting a diversity of outcomes;
representing knowledge to requesting production of knowledge;
evaluating at the product level to looking to the task level;
individual efforts to building learning teams;
one classroom to encouraging global communities. (p. 224)

The structure of the course, the planning for educational and personal needs, and the teacher's role must all be reconceptualized. It is clear that active and independent learning must take place. The designer will have to determine what actions will promote this type of learning. Further, from adult learning theory we know that authentic learning, relevant materials, and negotiated assignments are required to ensure participation and involvement necessary to meet these goals. This is an ideal opportunity to create a Development Team, composed of a Subject Matter Expert (SME), an instructional designer, and at least one person with experience in distance education.

One way to begin might include taking an assignment that has proven useful and authentic in traditional classroom use. This might be creating a small project, identifying specific content, or synthesizing activities. Now the instructor must consider how this could work in an online experience. Would certain materials be available to each student, with the students then required to work together? Would the activity require students to work independently, to gather resources, and then to present them online to the rest of the class? Should students take turns having the responsibility for organizing and leading a discussion? Perhaps the most significant challenge is one for instructors. They must give themselves permission to go through trial and error before feeling satisfied with the results. It would not be unusual for this to require a few iterations and certainly the feedback from the learners would be important in this process.

The nature of online teaching requires the instructor to rethink the evaluation process as well. The evaluation component must be ongoing and continual, just leaving everything to one midterm and a final paper would put everyone at a disadvantage. It is important that the instructor become familiar with each student's work, and the only way to accomplish that is through many instructional activities. Additionally, without visual cues the instructor might not be aware of a student's confusion or total misunderstanding of subject matter or what is required. The feedback loop is also essential, so perhaps it is wise to include specific times during the term when students fill out an anonymous questionnaire regarding the progress of the course. Some faculty members have included one question each week that requires students to consider various aspects of the content, interaction, and affective reaction to the online environment.

Organizational Issues

Once the pedagogical questions are answered, the instructor can turn to the organizational questions. First, a decision must be made to determine how much of the course will be online. In other words, is this to be a web-enhanced course or a web-only course? The online component may range from occasional electronic assignments that supplement traditional class meetings, to a course that is basically online with two or three physical class meetings, to a course that is entirely online. Obviously many factors may be predetermined and out of the instructor's control; for example, if the course is intended for a geographically dispersed audience then meeting face to face may not be an option.

Another organizational determination must be made as to the type of assignments and interactions that are to be included. These may range from group projects, created and delivered online, using process writing and interactions, or completely individual assignments. If everyone is moving through the course at the same time, could the interaction be enhanced by one or more synchronous activities, when all students are online at the same time? As research has demonstrated, even in the case of having independent online lessons, it is useful to add a component that requires students to interact with their colleagues in some way (Dehler & Poirras-Hernandez, 1998; Schrum, 1992).

Other organizational issues must be considered. Group size may influence the communications patterns, but it also may significantly impact the life of the teacher. Teaching online courses requires a great deal of time — to answer mail, manage the data, and respond to postings. Students have come to expect instant responses that arrive seven days a week and 24 hours a day! It has been suggested that 15 to 20 individuals are a manageable number for interaction. However, some institutions believe that online courses could handle a large number of students at one time. The instructor might ask if extra tutors are available to assist. Or perhaps it is possible to team-teach this type of course.

In addition, some mention must be made of the prerequisite skills that are expected of the students. Individuals who do not have experience with computers are found to be less able to learn from online courses since they spend enormous amounts of time just completing the most basic of word processing tasks (Gibbs, 1998).

Although some educators prefer to determine their curriculum and activities as a course evolves, in this environment it is especially important that students be given a list of readings, assignments, and expectations at the beginning of the course. The course must be well organized and introductory activities must be appropriate for novices and experts alike; collegial interaction must be fostered in some way. Rules for using any online environment need to be established among the group, for whichever configuration is ultimately chosen.

Finally, the instructor is going to need to decide whether to have the course interactions occur at the same time (synchronously) or in the time/place independent manner (asynchronously). Each has advantages and disadvantages, but for most tasks that require thought and reflection, the synchronous model may not be very useful. Individuals report frustration in keeping track of what others are typing and also being able to type their own contributions. Frequently, one person who can type very rapidly is able to dominate the conversation. Also, the timing may not be viable for all participants. If this model is chosen, then very careful structures, advanced organizers, and monitoring are essential.

Creating Interactivity. A special question bridges both pedagogical and organizational issues. It is the question of creating interaction within the course. Interaction is now supported and facilitated in new ways. Everyone is likely aware that the amount of interactivity might vary widely in a traditional course. Consider that learners interact with the content, the instructor and with other learners (Moore, 1989). The online environment offers some ways in which desirable interaction might occur within these categories.

It is easy to consider how students can interact with the content in a variety of ways. However, as in most areas of learning, self-regulation and active participation are essential. The instructor might require discussion on topics of the course, or have students post comments upon various readings for others and provide information about global resources that have been investigated. Having access to the instructor's personal notes and pertinent questions can often focus the readings. Students can also post other artifacts of their work (drawings, web pages, and slides) that demonstrate their conceptualizations.

The instructor and each individual student are likely to create their own preferences for how interaction occurs. Electronic mail has supported interaction for some time, but the instructor might improve the use of e-mail through considering the suggestions of Laurillard (1993). She describes four ways of supporting interaction with learners in an electronic environment. These include a need for discursive language in order to understand each other's conceptions; adopting an adaptive perspective, so that the focus shifts as each student's needs shift; authentic activities for students to demonstrate their understandings, and reflection on the student's work.

Student to student work that is collaborative in nature requires another level of consideration (Schrum & Berge, 1998). A learning activity may be designed to support the learning objectives, such as groups of learners solving a problem, creating a simulation for others, designing a product or completing a task (Blumenfeld, Marx, Soloway, & Krajcik,1996). These activities may or may not carry a mandatory requirement and the groups may be self-selecting or may be created by the instructor. Some instructors have each member of the class post the type of project they would like to do, and also list something about their work style. For example, individuals who are comfortable finishing at the very last minute may not work well with those who wish to be finished a week ahead of time. Similarly, students who wish to talk about a project only after midnight might clash with those who prefer to work at 6 AM.

Historically, teachers and designers have emphasized the need to create interactivity between student and content and between students and the instructor. Use of such techniques as study questions to help guide textbook readings, and impromptu questioning during lectures have been effective to varying degrees as incentives for students to interact with content and teacher. The technologies used today in the online classroom promote an emphasis on discussion and interaction among students as well.

Institutional Issues

Institutional issues must be considered and discussed as an educational organization begins to focus on online education (Phelps, Wells, Ashworth, & Hahn, 1991). Foremost must be recognition (perhaps in the promotion and tenure process) for faculty, but others might be by offering release time and assistance. Institutional support for innovative practices is essential, but it requires that time be allowed for design and development. While acceptance of this type of learning experience is growing, the reality is that at many organizations online courses do not count as part of an instructor's teaching load and further, the time necessary to prepare is not available prior to implementation. The resolution of these issues needs to be established before creation of any course.

Other institutional issues concern the amount and type of credit offered for online courses, and the students' ability to use the credit for postgraduate or graduate degrees, for salary increments or certification. Will the students of a distance course be supported in registration, transcripts, etc., in the same ways as traditional on-campus students? Who will bear the expense of additional access and connections associated with online courses? Will modems or computers be loaned to students who cannot afford them? Will students be given access to the networks and other resources? How do students at a geographic distance gain access to materials on campus? Many of the access questions can now be answered more easily by archiving resources online using the Internet.

Last, it is essential that an evaluative component be included for every course. Is the course pedagogically sound? Has the course accomplished its educational goals? Is the organizational structure appropriate and equitable? Did the institution offer the support necessary for students and for the educator? Did unique problems arise from the nature of the online course or components? Another issue concerns evaluation of the instructor. Currently students evaluate most instructors, however, in an online environment the love of subject, commitment to students, sense of humor, and willingness to adapt might not come through. This calls for a more substantial and perhaps collaborative evaluation of the instructor by all stakeholders.

ENSURING STUDENT SUCCESS IN THE ONLINE ENVIRONMENT

Students who are considering taking an online course might well be counseled about this choice because rates of noncompletion in all types of distance learning courses are far higher than those of face to face classes. They will need to be aware of the prerequisites for taking the course, but the following types of suggestions might also assist them. These suggestions are based on students' understanding of

If you prefer or enjoy:	Try a course that includes:
Face to face interaction	A combined format course, with several face to face meetings
Lots of interaction with the instructor	One-to-one online independent study course
Immediate feedback on assignments	A plan of feedback, and assurance of multiple communication channels
Deadlines for work assignments	Traditional timing (following a school schedule)
Hands-on technical support	A locally offered online course, with contact information for assistance
Discussions with class members	A well functioning threaded discussion that is easy to follow, plus an occasional face to face meeting
To complete the course quickly, on your own	Completely online course, regardless of geographic location; ability to move ahead on your own
Ongoing support for your work	An instructor willing to engage in dialogue
Authentic assignments	An instructor with an open-ended syllabus and flexibility
Help staying on task	Pick a course that someone you know will take too

their own learning preferences.

To the student: You may want to pay attention to the features of each course you consider taking, to make the most of the environment for your style and needs. Here are a few examples:

CONCLUSION

This chapter provided an overview and introduction to the issues surrounding the emerging area of online education. The growth in the number of organizations involved in online education will impact the entire educational community as well as individual stakeholders. The challenge is to put together a well-articulated plan of implementation, one that begins with needs assessment and goal setting. It is important to select a topic and audience that will succeed.

From years of interaction with online educators, students and administrators, it is obvious that all entities are struggling with balancing goals, needs and support but clearly the desire exists to create positive educational opportunities. It is also clear that some conclusions may assist those beginning this journey. The following are offered in that spirit.

1. Create a team of developers that includes a technical person, subject matter expert, and instructional designer.
2. Allow time for this team to fully explore, experiment, and evaluate their activity.
3. Begin with a small number of courses or projects and grow those efforts. Reward the early innovators for their willingness to take risks.

Educators, course designers and institutional planners must consider pedagogical, policy and support issues before plunging into offering online courses. Further, as a community of scholars and educators, we must create more avenues for sharing of experiences and research among all the international players, be willing to describe difficulties, and take feedback from learners. The challenges are substantial, but the potential rewards are worth the efforts.

Suggestions for Student Success

Questions and Strategies for the learner to consider

There are many questions potential learners may want to ask before enrolling in an online course. First, think about the organizational issues.

- How is the course structured – does it conform to the timeline of an institution or can you work at your own speed?
- Will you meet face to face during the term?
- Does the instructor have a time set aside for his/her distance students (so you can be sure to reach the instructor by phone)?
- Are some of the requirements dependent on other students, and is there an easy way to accomplish this?
- What are the recommended prerequisites for the course (technological, pedagogical and time commitments)?

NOTE: Independent courses give you greater freedom to schedule your work, but they also require more self-discipline.

Second, think about institutional issues and questions that relate to this area. For example,

- Is the instructor doing this as an "extra job" in addition to his/her regular work? (She/he may have less time for interaction or providing timely feedback.)
- If you are interested in a degree program, what are the total costs of that degree?
- Can you talk to other students who have finished the program or course?
- What type of evaluation has the institution done on the courses?
- What kind of support does the institution give to remote students? Will you have access to library resources or materials?
- What technical support do they have for the system?

REFERENCES

Blumenfeld, P. C., Marx, R. W., Soloway, E., & Krajcik, J. (1996). Learning with peers: From small group cooperation to collaborative communities. *Educational Researcher, 25*(8), 37-40.

Boston, R. L. (1992). Remote delivery of instruction via the PC and modem: What have we learned? *The American Journal of Distance Education, 6*(3), 45-57.

Dede, C. (1995, July). *The transformation of distance education to distributed learning. InTRO [On-line],* Available: http://129.7.160.78/InTRO.html.

Dehler, C., & Poirras-Hernandez, L. H. (1998). Using computer mediated communication (CMC) to promote experiential learning in graduate studies. *Educational Technology, 38*(5), 52-55.

Duchastel, P. (1996-97). A web-based model for university instruction. *Journal of Educational Technology Systems, 25*(3), 221-228.

Ehrmann, S. C. (1995). Asking the right questions: What does research tell us about technology and higher learning? *Change: The Magazine of Higher Learning, 27*(2), 20-27.

Gibbs, W. J. (1998). Implementing online learning environments. *Journal of Computers in Higher Education, 10*(1), 16-37.

Harasim, L. M. (Ed.). (1990). *Online education: Perspectives on a new environment.* New York: Praeger.

Harasim, L. M. (Ed.). (1993). *Global networks: Computers and interna-*

tional communication. Cambridge, MA: The MIT Press.

Hartman, K., Neuwirth, C. M., Kiesler, S., Sproull, L., Cochran, C., Palmquist, M., & Zubrow, D. (1994). Patterns of social interaction and learning to write: Some effects of network technologies. In Z. L. Berge & M. P. Collins (Eds.), *Computer Mediated Communication and the Online Classroom,* (pp. 47-78). Cresskill, NY: Hampton Press, Inc.

Heeren, E., & Lewis, R. (1997). Selecting communication media for distributed communities. *Journal of Computer Assisted Learning, 13*(2), 85-98.

Hiltz, R. S. (1990). Evaluating the virtual classroom. In L. Harasim (Ed.), *Online education: Perspectives on a new environment,* (pp. 133-184). New York: Praeger.

Laurillard, D. (1993). *Rethinking university teaching: A framework for the effective use of educational technology.* London: Routledge.

Laurillard, D. (1996). *The changing university.* [Online.] http://tecfa.unige.ch/Hypernews/get/forums/staf15-forum/4.html

Lea, M. & Spears, R. (1991). Computer mediated communication, de-individuation and group decision-making. In S. Greenberg (Ed.), *Computer supported collaborative work and groupware .* San Diego, CA: Academic Press, Inc., 155-173

Moore, M. G. (1989). Distance education: A learner's system. *Lifelong Learning, 12*(8), 8-11.

Olson, M. H., & Bly, S. A. (1991). The Portland experience: A report on a distributed research group. In S. Greenberg (Ed.), *Computer supported cooperative work and groupware,* (pp. 81-98). San Diego: Academic Press Limited.

Phelps, R. H., Wells, R. A., Ashworth, R. L., & Hahn, H. A. (1991). Effectiveness and costs of distance education using computer-mediated communication. *The American Journal of Distance Education, 5*(3), 7-19.

Reid, J. E. & Woolf, P. (1996). *Online curriculum development at shorter college: A report from the field.* Available online: http://www.caso.com/iu/articles/reid02.html.

Rice-Lively, M. L. (1994). Wired warp and woof: An ethnographic study of a networking class. *Internet Research, 4*(4), 20-35.

Rohfeld, R. W., & Hiemstra, R. (1994). Moderating discussions in the electronic classroom. In Z. L. Berge & M. P. Collins (Eds.), *Computer Mediated Communication and the online classroom.* Cresskill, NJ: Hampton Press, Inc., 91-104

Schrum, L. (1992). Professional development in the information age: An online experience. *Educational Technology, 32*(12), 49-53.

Schrum, L. (1995). Educators and the Internet: A case study of professional development. *Computers and Education, 24*(3), 221-228.

Schrum, L. (1996). Teaching at a distance: Strategies for successful planning and development. *Learning and Leading with Technology, 23*(6), 30-33.

Schrum, L. (1998). Online education in the information age: A study of emerging pedagogy. In B. Cahoon (Ed.), *Adult learning and the Internet*, (pp. 53-61). San Francisco: Jossey-Bass, Inc. Publishers.

Schrum, L., & Berge, Z. L. (1998). Creating student interaction within the educational experience: A challenge for online teachers. *Canadian Journal of Educational Communication, 26*(3), 133-144.

Schrum, L., & Lamb, T. (1997). Computer networks as instructional and collaborative distance learning environments. *Educational Technology, 37*(4), 26-28.

Sproull, L., & Kiesler, S. (1991). *Connections: New ways of working in the networked organization.* Cambridge, MA: MIT Press.

Tatar, D. G., Foster, G., & Bobrow, D. G. (1991). Design for conversation: Lessons from Cognoter. In S. Greenberg (Ed.), *Computer-supported cooperative work and groupware.* San Diego: Academic Press, Inc., 55-80.

Valacich, J. S., Dennis, A. R., & Nunamaker, J. F. (1991). Electronic meeting support: The GroupSystems concept. In S. Greenberg (Ed.), *Computer-supported cooperative work and groupware.* San Diego: Academic Press, Inc., 133-154.

Wagner, E. D. (1993). Variables affecting distance educational program success. *Educational Technology, 33*(4), 28-32.

Wiesenberg, F., & Hutton, S. (1996). Teaching a graduate program using computer-mediated conferencing software. *Journal of Distance Education, 11*(1), 83-100.

Yelon, S. & Berge, Z. L. (1988). The secret of instructional design. *Performance and Instruction.* January, 11-13.

Chapter IX

Developing a Learning Environment: Applying Technology and TQM to Distance Learning

C. Mitchell Adrian
Longwood College

INTRODUCTION

It is known that good classroom management techniques help promote a suitable learning environment, an environment in which students are interested and participate as a community of learners (Brophy & Alleman, 1998). In this type of environment, learning occurs when faculty develop and encourage discussion through the use of social interaction (Brophy & Alleman, 1998). The problem in applying these concepts to a distance education program is "how to develop or maintain an environment of social interaction?"

To contribute to the learning environment in a distance education program, a combination of new and readily available electronic communication technologies can be combined with concepts taken from Total Quality Management (TQM). The term "distance education" covers a wide range of educational practices, ranging from the traditional correspondence course to synchronous teleconferencing via multiple classrooms. The techniques discussed here are designed primarily for a distance environment that allows for some degree of student-faculty interaction.

Regardless of the learning methods used, a distance education program is dependent upon student commitment and the TQM approach gives students a high degree of ownership of the learning process. Likewise, electronic communication technology allows faculty to assess student progress and provide feedback in a timely fashion – regardless of the geographic distance between the student and the faculty member.

Changes in Academia

Academia in America has felt profound change while progressing from the 20th to the 21st centuries. Society no longer accepts the "ivory tower" premise and is beginning to value teaching efforts as much as research. In summary, social pressures are demanding university accountability for student learning (Hill, 1997). These pressures reach state-funded campuses in the form of financial incentives (or disincentives) from state legislators, who seek quantifiable results of educational contributions to society. Reacting to these pressures, institutions of higher education have pushed faculty to focus efforts on enhancing the student's learning process (Hill, 1997).

The Growth of Distance Education

As an outgrowth of the increased focus on quantifiable contributions to society, higher education has attempted to "reach out" to an increasingly larger population of potential students. Many schools are attempting to reach these students through what is hoped to be a cost-effective method of distance education (Noon, 1996). As a result, a 1999 study indicated that 58% of two-year and 62% of four-year public colleges offer courses through the Internet (Hodgson, 1999).

The concept of distance education and distance learning has gone through many changes over the past few decades inspired mostly by advancements in technology. Once relegated to the level of a "correspondence course," electronic communications technology now allows a distance learning course to function much more like a traditional course, including "real-time" lectures and discussions.

The downside to advances in electronic technology is that developments have progressed faster than faculty can learn to apply the new technologies. This growth of electronic and communications technology has forced many faculty to question how to apply this technology to student education (Black, 1997). Faculty are now expected to be masters of technology and delivery management as well as experts in their subject (Laird, 1999). In order to make distance education an effective learning tool, the role of the teacher will be essential in using technology to its best advantage (Bayram, 1999). Therefore, to develop an effective learning environment in distance education we must first understand a few basic concepts of learning theory.

Learning Theory

Efforts focused on understanding how we learn have lead to a broad range of learning theories. If we focus on learning in higher education and theories regarding adult learners then a few basic foundations for learning can be found. Primarily, adults learn best through high levels of immersion (or hands-on practice) and teacher-student dialog. For instance, in the "holistic" learning theory it is believed that all facets of a student's life are part of their total learning (immersion). The role of the faculty member is to assist students at interpreting and comprehending various inputs from the world around them (Argyris, 1997). In addition, collaborative activities by students help participants learn from each other, suggesting that active participation is more important than passive listening (Pike & Mansfield, 1996). In a concept called productive constructivism, the teacher's job is to fuse students' knowledge with what experts know, typically accomplished through teacher-student dialogue (Zahorik, 1997). Discussion allows students to refute traditional concepts while at the same time incorporating new ideas.

What these theories have in common is that learning centers on student immersion and faculty-student dialog. While we may take the existence of dialog for granted in a traditional classroom environment, specific efforts must be made to effectively utilize faculty-student dialog in the application of a distance learning course. In addition, distance learning on the Web has the potential to offer a greater level of student immersion than traditional courses (Mirabito, 1996).

APPLICATIONS OF DISTANCE LEARNING AND ELECTRONIC TECHNOLOGY: A THREE STEP APPROACH

The first question that most faculty face when considering a distance learning program and the use of new technologies for their educational efforts is "how to do it." Some faculty fear potential problems of having to learn to apply new electronic technologies, while others embrace the idea and make great efforts to incorporate electronic technologies to the classroom environment. In either instance, however, we must constantly remind ourselves that distance does not necessitate reduced communication and that new technologies are tools rather than ends in themselves. Educators, like professionals in many other fields, become swept up by the "bells and whistles" that are offered with various technological packages and often lose sight of their original objectives.

What are arguably the most important educational criteria for all faculty to remember are that of *organization* and *clarity*. Whether a traditional course or a distance learning course, organization and clarity may be the two most important factors in student understanding and comprehension of the tasks and materials. This is compounded in courses that are heavily dependent on electronic communications (as are most distance learning courses). If organization and clarity are not present, the electronic communication tools tend to make these deficiencies even more prominent. For that reason, a three-step course development and implementation process has been established.

Step 1: Design Course Objectives

Just as with traditional courses, a faculty member's first step is to determine the primary course objectives. This is an even greater priority in a distance learning course and courses using electronic and communications technology. Not only should the contextual learning objectives be defined, but also the more general and overriding objectives regarding course design. For instance, it is assumed here that the primary objective will always be student learning and that faculty will want to create a sense of "enjoyment" regarding learning to encourage students to become lifelong learners.

The course design must contribute to the development of a learning environment, even in a distance learning program. Again, one essential ingredient for developing this learning environment is teacher-student dialogue (Pike & Mansfield, 1996; Zahorik, 1997).

Step 2: Design the Course Structure

Even more than a traditional class, success in a distance learning environment is more dependent upon a beneficial melding of synchronous and asynchronous teaching. Typically we think of most traditional courses as focusing on synchronous techniques and most distance courses as focusing on asynchronous techniques. However, electronic technologies allow us to deviate from this traditional model. Each technique has advantages and disadvantages, but building a strong distance learning program may depend upon the degree of synchronous learning that can be effectively incorporated into the program.

In order to design a distance learning course that provides an adequate mix of synchronous and asynchronous learning, philosophies from Total Quality Management can be mated to electronic technology to work in tandem. Following a quality initiative may be an effective way to motivate students to learn (Chen & Rogers, 1995; Bonser, 1992; Del Valle, 1994; Hequet, 1995; Harvard Business Review, 1991; Peak, 1995) and may thus be a logical foundation for a distance learning environment.

Transferring the Quality Philosophy to the Distance Classroom

To establish a foundation for applying concepts of quality management to education, insights from leading writers in the field can be combined into the key elements of quality (Brocka & Brocka, 1992). Most notable of these elements are: (1) knowing and satisfying the customer, (2) empowering employees, and (3) having managers function as leaders. (Beaver, 1994; Brocka & Brocka, 1992).

Several of the basic tenets from TQM can be applied to the classroom to establish a system of Total Quality Education (TQE) and, thus, enhance the learning environment. However, one dilemma is that not all of the principles of TQM seem applicable to the classroom setting (Arnold, 1994). For that reason, a specific set of assumptions and procedures should be developed for educational purposes.

Assumptions

Students should be viewed as the employee/product.

While some may argue that students are the customer (e.g., Beaver, 1994; Froiland, 1993; Knappenberger, 1995), it is more appropriate to consider other instructors as internal customers and businesses that hire new graduates as external customers (Arnold, 1994). Thus, the student is viewed as both product and employee. To improve the product (the student), we must examine and adjust the learning process. Inputs are the body of knowledge pertinent to the course. The instructor serves as the manager, students serve as employees (or processors), and the resulting knowledge and skills possessed by students is the output (Arnold, 1994).

Colleges and Universities are Suppliers

Internally, students completing a basic course are supplied to later courses which base their content on previously learned information. Externally, colleges are suppliers to employers. The products offered are graduates who possess the knowledge and skills required by industry (Arnold, 1994).

The Majority of Students are Capable of Performing at a Quality Level

If students do not perform at acceptable quality levels, instructors must analyze the entire learning process to determine what barriers are hindering performance. Deming (1986) states that most assignable variation is caused by problems in the process. Thus, it is dangerous for faculty to begin with the assumption that students do not perform at acceptable quality levels because they are defective inputs (Arnold, 1994). This assumption erroneously focuses attention on a defective input and away from problems in the learning system which may be preventing quality performance.

Instruction Does Not Necessarily Equal Learning

As managers, instructors must create an environment that allows employees (students), to produce a quality product (themselves). The more traditional thought in higher education is that it is the instructor's job to "profess" and the students' job to learn (Arnold, 1994). However, this allows the manager to avoid all responsibility for unacceptable quality. We must create a classroom situation that facilitates the learning process. Students, as employees who build the product, are responsible for their learning with faculty serving as the mangers who are responsible for providing students the tools they need to accomplish the task of learning. (Arnold, 1994).

Applying a Quality Philosophy

When applying quality concepts in the classroom, the initial difficulty is in translating concepts designed for the production pro-

Table 1: Parameters for Course Design

a. Limit lecture.
b. Apply a variety of learning experiences.
c. Use written learning experiences.
d. Use oral learning experiences.
e. At least one performance must be a team activity.
f. Participation is part of the quality imperative.
g. Tests are mandatory; use subjective tests when possible.

cess to an educational environment. In the original experiments attempted by Arnold (1994) and later by the author, it was found that a specific set of guidelines can be used for implementing Total Quality Education.

Quality Output is Required

To achieve quality performance, the employee (students) must understand how quality is defined and determined within their environment. The manager/instructor must emphasize the expectation of high performance. The instructor must also emphasize how he/she will provide the tools necessary for students to achieve this level of performance (Arnold, 1994).

Emphasize the Entire Learning Process

The learning process, the sum of all educational experiences, results in some level of quality. Consequently, improving quality depends on adding, modifying, improving, or replacing segments of the learning processes (Arnold, 1994). To better design the learning process in distance education, a non-inclusive set of parameters for course design has been established (Table 1). It must be remembered that the learning process includes the student's "out of class" study activities. To better facilitate learning, a non-inclusive list of suggested learning experience ideas are provided in Table 2.

Customer Satisfaction

Customer satisfaction is the most relevant measure of the quality of our product. Employers and future instructors receiving our students are viewed as the relevant customers. A survey of employers provides the best indication of external market satisfaction with product quality (graduates). In lieu of a survey, general market

Table 2: Distance Learning Experience Alternatives

Lecture by Instructor (limited)	Group discussions
Presentation of Chapter Material	Studying for Written Exams
Writing an Original Case	Case Analysis (individual or team)
Problem/Case Solutions	Video Tapes
Term Papers	Internet Exercises
Business Simulation	Chapter Summary
Computer Games	Viewing and Analyzing Existing Business
Role Playing	Term Paper
Preparing Test Questions	Library
Presentations	Analysis of Business
Written Assignments	

indexes can be used by examining the knowledge, skills and abilities reported as desirable by most firms.

Empowerment

Empowerment involves delegating power or authority to employees. Since students are viewed as employees in the classroom situation, the students must be empowered (Arnold, 1994). A key method of empowering students is to give them ownership of as many tasks as possible. While it is the instructor's role to determine primary goals and objectives of the course, students should be empowered to develop intermediate goals and the processes by which they will achieve those goals. Note that empowerment does not imply a democracy or complete freedom. Instead, empowerment must occur within specific parameters established by management (Arnold, 1994). Empowerment may be the key to applying TQE in distance learning. Geographic separation forces students in distant locals to take increased responsibility for their learning. By formalizing the process and empowering these students their motivation level is increased.

As stated, empowerment, or allowing employees the authority to develop production goals and procedures is a foundation of the quality initiative. Traditionally, academic expectation is defined as the level of achievement that students must reach in order to satisfy a standard established by the teacher. Unlike academic expectations, goal setting is a target to aim for rather than a standard that must be reached (Madden, 1997). Schunk (1984) states that goal setting for the learner involves the establishment of an objective to serve as the aim of one's actions. Punnett (1986) says that the perceived ability of the learner to achieve the goal is necessary for successful goal setting. Consequently, individual goals are more effective than one goal for all students. Motivation is the desire to achieve a goal that has value for the individual (Linskie, 1977). Motivation is a process that leads students into experiences in which they can learn, that keeps them focused on a specific task, and which helps fulfill their needs for immediate achievement and a sense of moving toward larger goals (Madden, 1997). As a result, students are interested in the things which they plan themselves. They work much harder on self-made goals than they ever would on the expectations of someone else.

Leadership

With the instructor in the role of manager, he/she is responsible for providing leadership. This is especially important in a distance learning environment. The instructor must design and articulate the quality approach while implementing and sustaining it throughout the semester (Arnold, 1994). The instructor must demonstrate a commitment to quality and continuous improvement in every aspect of the course (Arnold, 1994).

Cross Functional Management

This concept is normally implemented in business by eliminating barriers between various functional areas. In a distance learning program, this is interpreted to mean that students should be involved in some type of team assignments (Arnold, 1994). One very useful team is to group volunteer students together in Quality Control Circles (or QC groups) that will meet regularly to help each prepare assignments, review performance of group members, receive feedback from the instructor and provide feedback to the instructor.

The use of a modified QC group can be particularly useful in a distance learning program. QC members can meet either in person or electronically as required by their geographic dispersion. Their task is to learn from other class members what processes students feel are working correctly and what processes need improvement. By communicating these ideas to the faculty member and other QC members, they can develop plans for improvement. In this role, QC members function as a communication link between students and faculty and focus on developing ideas for improving the learning process.

Continuous Improvement

Continuous improvement applies to processes, products/services, and people. An important difference between a quality approach and a traditional teaching approach is the commitment to change as a means of achieving improvement. If a process is not working as envisioned or a better method arises, the instructor must be committed to making the necessary change immediately, not at the end of the semester (Arnold, 1994). To facilitate continuous improvement, work with QC member to discuss class processes and relay information from instructor to students (Arnold, 1994).

Continuous Information

Continuous improvement requires continuous information. This means frequent feedback. For the manager/instructor, frequent information can be provided by the Quality Team. For the students/workers, frequent information requires frequent feedback on their performances (Arnold, 1994). Defective work (inadequate learning) should be detected and corrected quickly. Therefore, tests should be given frequently and cover relatively small amounts of material (Arnold, 1994).

Drive Out Fear

Students' fears seem to be associated with low grades and test taking. In a distance learning program, there are additional fears associated with application of new technologies and a somewhat unorthodox learning environment (Bayram, 1999). Fear can be eliminated through several steps. The instructor should be able to tell students exactly what he/she wants them to know about the course material and what constitutes quality performance (Arnold, 1994). In addition, technology can be used to eliminate some fears normally felt by students.

Applying Electronic Technology

Given the objective of student learning through the use of a total learning environment, Quality Management concepts serve as a template for the application of electronic technologies and distance learning. Rather than having technology determine the direction and function of the class, technology serves as the tool to support the

Figure 1

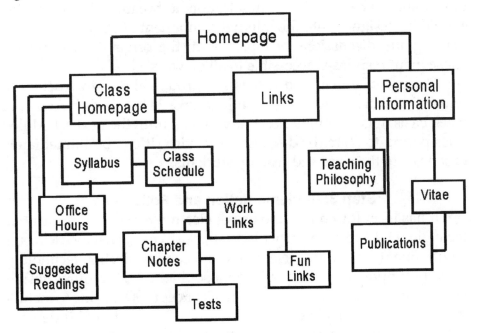

desired structure for student learning. In general, the electronic components assumed here are the Internet (including course material and on-line testing), e-mail, bulletin boards, chat, audio/video conferencing and in-class presentation material.

To develop the Internet portion of the course, a storyboard method should be used to map out the desired content and determine levels of access and linkage (Figure 1). In this example of a storyboard, this portion of the course provides continuous information to the students and revolves around the professor's homepage. A multilayered approach links class homepages and various other materials to the professor's homepage. From the class homepage, chapter notes, discussion areas and online testing can be reached.

In addition to the Internet components, communication is increased using e-mail and discussion groups. What must be remembered is that electronic communications have yet to fully replace the intricacies involved in face-to-face communication (Bayram, 1999; Jones, et. al. 1998) and were never intended as a replacement for classroom interaction. However, electronic communications are a beneficial supplement to face-to-face verbal communication. E-mail allows students and instructors to communicate one-on-one in a timely and efficient manner. In addition, a threaded discussion list should be designed into the Internet component of the course allowing ongoing discussions of topics, with the original idea and it's subsequent responses accessible to all viewers.

The use of e-mail and discussion groups allows instructors to remain in relative contact with students on a 24 hour a day, 7-day per week basis. It is no longer necessary to wait until the next scheduled class period to share or discuss a new idea. It can be immediately broadcast to the class and read by students.

Step 3: Implementation and Follow-Up

It has been found that the use of electronic and communication technologies have been particularly supportive of a distance learning environment. In addition, electronic and communication technology are very supportive of the quality philosophies used for course design. For instance, students can expand their concepts of learning to include more activities outside of the classroom. The ability of students to easily communicate at their leisure greatly increases the level and intensity of spontaneous academic interaction and provides an emphasis on the entire learning process.

Student empowerment is supported by the increased availability of contextual resources. Increased resources and increased communication facilitate the decision-making process of an empowered student body. This results largely from the continuous information provided by numerous "online" tests and quizzes, each with instant feedback of student performance. Increased feedback allows for continuous improvement efforts. Students can discover the errors in their performance while the subject is still fresh in their minds. However, to make such efforts work, true leadership is required on the part of the instructor. Some specific ideas for linking technology and TQM can include:

Emphasize the Entire Learning Process

This is undoubtedly the most taxing and most enjoyable portion of implementing a quality distance learning environment. Internet-based activities (class web pages, etc.), management simulations, group activities, etc. can be used. The number and type of these activities is limited only by the imagination.

Empowerment

Empowering students has often proven to be a challenge. Deming (1986) states that workers know how to do their job and should be allowed to do it unhindered. Unfortunately, most students do not yet have enough experience in information delivery formats to know what will help them learn. For this reason, instructors should suggest new instructional methods such as group discussion, group chat, student presentation of chapter material via PowerPoint™ saved in HTML format, etc., and encourage students to experiment with these techniques. As students gain experience in various learning techniques they will be better equipped to design their own learning program.

Continuous Information

It is generally supported by most learning theories that testing has distinct advantages for learning. When using multiple choice type tests combined with commercial Internet-based testing software, grading and performance feedback can be done instantly. However, there are also problems associated with testing in a distance learning environment. One recommended use of today's technology is to develop substantial practice tests. Most online testing programs contain a feature in which the student must pass test X before being allowed access to test Y. In addition, most will create tests from a bank of questions established by the instructor. Thus, a student can take a practice test that must be passed before attempting the graded test. If the student fails the practice test, they can retake a test on the same material with a new list of questions. This utilizes technology to reduce test-taking fears while immersing students in the material until they have demonstrated the ability to perform at a quality level.

Maintaining Dialog

Ironically, what has developed as the single most significant result of the adoption of electronic and communication technologies to a TQM approach to distance learning is the improvement of dialog with students. The addition of student dialog through electronic communications serves as a primer for class discussions utilizing teleconferencing and group chat sessions. Based on previous electronic discussions, students often enter real-time discussions with a topic they wish to explore. The net result can be an undergraduate level class that performs at a near-graduate level, particularly in regards to topic discussions.

The Next Step: Continuous Improvement

Constructing knowledge is a constant, naturally occurring process as students view new information in terms of their prior knowledge (Zahorik, 1997). It is the responsibility of instructors to nurture this process. While it is not claimed that the instructional methods described above are the final answer, the guiding philosophy may be a step forward in creating a better process for management/business education, especially in a distance learning environment. Student responses to the processes mentioned have to be overwhelmingly good. While many students are apprehensive of a new process at first, they tend to quickly adapt.

SUMMARY - BENEFITS OF THIS APPROACH

To recap and summarize the process, the implementation of a distance learning program differs little from traditional courses in that there are three basic steps to course design. *Step1: Design Course Objectives. Step 2: Design Course Structure, and Step 3: Implement the Process and Follow-Up on Performance.* When applying the quality philosophy to distance learning, remember that 1) *Quality output is required,* 2) *The entire learning process should be emphasized,* 3) *Customer satisfaction must guide goal formation,* 4) *Students must be empowered to influence the learning process,* 5) *Faculty must serve in the leadership role,* and 6) *There must be efforts for continuous improvement through continuous information, feedback and teamwork.* To make technology work, faculty must A) *Design the course, then apply the technology,* B) *Use technology in its fullest regarding faculty/student and student/student dialog,* and C) *Be creative in finding ways for technology to help accomplish various learning experiences.*

The application of Quality Philosophies to the distance education process typically results in students' feeling a greater amount of freedom in regards to the learning process. Student development of the learning process and goals increases the level of students' perception of course organization and clarity.

The use of Internet and e-mail technology has opened new doors for communication links between faculty and students. The procedures outlined above have resulted in students becoming more involved in discussion of course material in both synchronous and asynchronous environments. As the level of discussion increases, students become interested not only in the topic but also in learning in general.

The technologies used in this process are readily available to most institutions of higher education. As stated earlier, the primary tools are the Internet and e-mail, and this technology is now quite common. The TQM techniques used are not new although their application in education is not yet widespread. Overall, the methods discussed here focus on the learning process and how applied Quality Philosophies combined with technology can assist learning. Once applied, students become interested and active learners while faculty gain more freedom to explore and discuss issues in their field of interest.

REFERENCES

Adrian, C. M., McWee, W., and Palmer, D. (1997a). Moving from total quality management to total quality education. *SAM International Management Proceedings*, (March), 283-289.

Adrian, C. M., McWee, W., and Palmer, D. (1997b). Total quality education: Expanding the educational experience. *American Society of Business and Behavioral Sciences*, (Feb.), 6-12.

Argyris, C. (1997). Initiating change that perseveres. *American Behavioral Scientist*, 40, 3, 299-310.

Arnold, D. R. (1994). *TQM in the Classroom*. Unpublished Manuscript.

Bayram, S. (1999). Internet learning initiatives: How well do Turkish virtual classrooms work? *T H E Journal (Technological Horizons In Education)*, 26, 10, (May), 65.

Bayram, S. and Uzuncarsill, U. (1998). Virtual classrooms on the web: Problems and solution in Turkey. presented at the *Conference of the European Educational Research Association, Scottish Council for Research in Education (SCRE) and European Conference on Educational Research*, (September 17-28), Ljubjana, Slovenia.

Beaver, W. (1994). Is TQM appropriate for the classroom? *College Teaching*, 42, 3, 111-114.

Black, J. (1997). Technical difficulties. *CNET News.com*, [Online] February 28, 5:30 p.m. PT, Available WWW: http://www.news.com/

SpecialFeatures/0,5,8354,00.html.

Bonser, C. F. (1992). Total quality education? *Public Administration Review*, 52, 504-512.

Brocka, B. and Brocka, M. S. (1992). *Quality Management: Implementing the Best Ideas of the Masters*, Homewood, Ill; Richard D. Irwin Inc.

Brophy, J. and Alleman, J. (1998). Classroom management in a social studies learning community. *Social Education*, 62, 1, (Jan.), 56-58.

Chen, A. Y. S. and Rodgers, J. L. (1995). Teaching the teachers TQM. *Management Accounting*, (May), 42-46.

Del Valle, C. (1994). Total quality management: Now, it's a class act. *Business Week*, (October 31), 72.

Deming, E. W. (1986). *Out of Crisis*, Cambridge, Mass.: Center for Advanced Engineering study, MIT Press.

Duis, M. (1996). Using schema theory to teach American History. *Social Education*, 60, 3, 144-146.

Froiland, P. (1993). TQM invades business schools. *Training*, (July), 52-56.

Harvard Business Review. (1991). An open letter: TQM on the campus. (Nov.-Dec.), 94-95.

Hequet, M. (1995). Quality goes to school. *Training*, 32, (September), 47-52.

Hill, R. P. (1997). The future of business education's functional areas. *Marketing Educator*, 16, (Winter), 1, 7.

Hodgson. P. (1999). How to teach in cyberspace. *Techniques*, 74, 5 (May), 34.

Jones, G.R, George, J. M., and Hill, C. W. (1998). *Contemporary Management*. Boston Mass.: Irwin McGraw-Hill.

Knappenberger, J. A. (1995). Total quality management. *Business Education Forum*, (Feb.), 5-8.

Laird, Ellen (1999). Distance-learning instructors: watch out for the cutting edge. *The Chronicle of Higher Education*, 45, 38, (May 28), B6.

Leinhardt, G. (1992). What research on learning tells us about teaching. *Educational Leadership* 49, 20-25.

Linskie, R. (1977). *The Learning Process: Theory and Practice*. New York: D. Van Nostrand Company.

Loughlin, K. (1994). GED teaching and adult learning theory: Practical approaches. *Adult Learning*, 6, 2, (Nov-Dec), 13-14.

Madden, L. E. (1997). Motivating students to learn better through own goal-setting. *Education*, 117, 3, (Spring), 411-414.

Mirabito, M. (1996). Establishing an online educational program. *T.H.E. Journal*, 24, I, 57-60.

Noon, J. (1996). Publisher 's corner. *Syllabus*, 9, 9, 4.

Peak, M. H. (1995). TQM transforms the classroom. *Management Review*, 84, (September), 13-14.

Pike, B., & Mansfield, J. (1996). Adult learning theory increases the success of teaching interns. *Adult Learning*, 7, 5 (May-June), 13-14.

Punnett, B. (1986). Goal setting and performance among elementary school students. *Journal of Educational Research* 80, 40-42.

Tobin, K., and Tippins, D. (1993). Constructivism as a referent for teaching and learning. In *The Practice of Constructivism In Science Education*, edited by K. Tobin. Hillsdale, N.J.: Lawrence Erlbaum, 3-21.

Von Glaserfeld, E. (1995). A constructivist approach to teaching. In *Constructivism in Education*, edited by L. Steffe and J. Gale. Hillsdale, N. J.

Zahorik, J. A. (1997). Encouraging - and challenging - Students' Understandings. *Educational Leadership*, 54, 6 (March), 30-33.

Chapter X

Digital Video in Education

Todd L. Smith and Scot Ransbottom
United States Military Academy, West Point

> "Tis education forms the common mind:
> Just as the twig is bent the tree's inclined."
> -- Alexander Pope

INTRODUCTION

Use of technology to support education is by no means a new concept. Educators have for centuries looked for tools to help stimulate the senses and enhance their students' learning. Though lectures are still the predominant means of delivering material, multimedia is pervasive in educational institutions. For clarity, multimedia is considered the combination of text, graphics, audio, animation and video through electronic means (Vaughan, 1998). This chapter is concerned primarily with video.

The methods for creating videos and the means of delivery continue to change with technological advancements. The earliest educators brought sample objects or hand drawn representations to the classroom in order to provide a visual perspective and enhance understanding. In the mid-1900s, educators began to use analog video signals to show tapes or live shows that were again intended to enhance students' understanding. Today, computing systems are capable of storing and presenting video content on a one-to-one or one-to-many bases.

The key issue is whether the expense and effort associated with multimedia, and specifically, digital video is worthwhile. In this chapter, we discuss the use of digital video in the modern classroom with a focus on learning. Specifically, we base the discussion on Felder's Learning Model, Bloom's Taxonomy , and Kolb's Learning Cycle. First, the Background Section briefly describes these theories and provides some basic information on digital video. Second, we describe a classroom that was constructed to support digital video and detail performance issues. Finally, we discuss the synergy of video in education. The underlying questions that will be explored are (1) How should we use digital video? and (2) What are the technological constraints?

BACKGROUND

Learning Styles

Have you ever had a classroom experience that stimulated your curiosity or perhaps inspired you to explore, to create? Alternately, how often have you daydreamed in a class or been confused by the style of your instructor? How do we best relate to students? What happens in the classroom that causes some students to daydream while others become actively engaged?

Research indicates that students do not all learn or receive information in the same manner. Some respond to aural cues while others

---

The motivation for this work is a research project funded by the Army's Training and Doctrine Command (TRADOC). In 1995, TRADOC initiated a plan to reduce expenses incurred when soldiers travel for training. Through distance learning, TRADOC hopes to leverage technology to provide quality, centralized instruction to soldiers located all over the world. Their plan has two components central to this paper. The first is Classroom XXI, where soldiers at a training post will be able to access digital materials. The second is the Distance Learning Program. Those soldiers not located at training centers will access multimedia-training materials from a digital library through a distributed database. These materials will consist of text, graphics, audio, and video files accessed through either a Hypertext front-end or as a stand-alone application.

TRADOC requested that the Department of Electrical Engineering and Computer Science at the United States Military Academy, West Point, New York, review current technology and assist with the planning and design for Classroom XXI. This initiative will result in the creation and fielding of over 500 classrooms during the next few years.

Figure 1: Felder's Learning Dimensions

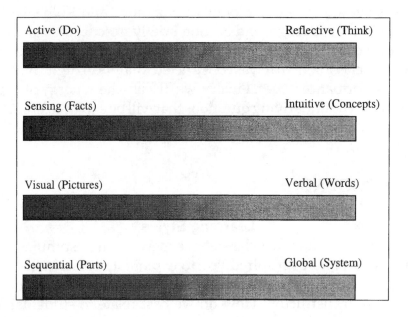

Figure 2: Bloom's Taxonomy of Learning

- Level 1 - Knowledge: Knowing facts with little or no understanding of the meaning.
- Level 2 - Comprehension: Understanding the meaning of the facts.
- Level 3 – Application: Applying the understanding to new problems.
- Level 4 – Analysis: Breaking a complex problem down into smaller parts.
- Level 5 – Synthesis: Building a complex solution from separate areas of knowledge.
- Level 6 – Evaluation: Evaluating the suitability of facts for use in a problem domain.

are visual learners. Some have to see the global perspective before they can digest the parts. Others learn sequentially.

Figure 1 describes Felder's Learning Dimensions concerning these preferences (Felder, 1993).

Bloom's Taxonomy of Learning is a hierarchical representation that characterizes a student's depth of knowledge. Following the 1948 Convention of the American Psychological Association, Bloom took a lead in formulating a classification of "the goals of the educational process (Howard et al., 1996)".

Bloom and his coworkers established a hierarchy of educational objectives, which is generally referred to as Bloom's Taxonomy (Figure 2) and which attempts to divide cognitive objectives into subdivisions ranging from the simplest behavior to the most complex.

It is important to realize that the divisions outlined in the sidebar are not absolutes, and that other systems or hierarchies have been devised. However, Bloom's taxonomy is easily understood and widely applied. The layers vary from a simple knowledge of facts to an ability to evaluate potential solutions.

The Kolb Learning Cycle is another model that describes how students learn (Howard et al., 1996). Figure 3 shows the four quadrants of the cycle. Students progress from asking why are we learning this material to what are the tasks to be learned. They then actively learn the tasks and progress to exploring new ideas related to the topic. The Reflective Quadrants compare to Felder's *Active-Reflective* Dimensions, and the Concrete-Abstract Quadrants compare to Felder's *Sensing-Intuitive* Dimensions.

The United States Army's Training and Doctrine Command (TRADOC) has created a training hierarchy to support its Advanced Technology Classroom design. The hierarchy consists of five levels (Figure 4) that tie the utilization of the classroom to the supported infrastructure. The simplest level consists of a typical lecture style

Figure 3: Kolb Learning Cycle

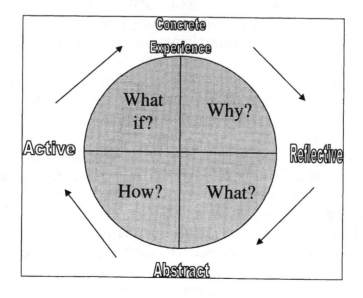

Figure 4: TRADOC Advanced Classroom Levels

Level	Description	
Level 1	Instructor Workstation connected to a LAN or WAN Quality Audio System Video System	**Instructor Directed**
Level 2	Level 1 Capability plus: Networked computer workstations Student Management System for each student	↑
Level 3	Level 2 Capability plus: Multicast Video Digital Video delivery system Distance Learning	↕
Level 4	Level 3 plus: Interactive Simulation	↓
Level 5	Level 4 plus: Virtual Reality Environment	**Student Directed**

classroom with a multimedia capable Instructor Workstation.

At the Second Level, each student has a computer workstation connected by a local network. There is also a student management system that allows the instructor to interact with the student electronically. A Level 3 Classroom supports distance learning and provides Digital Video to each student workstation. A Level 4 Classroom allows students to learn through interactive simulation, and a Level 5 Classroom immerses the student into a Virtual Reality Environment (VRE). TRADOC is currently building Level 3 classrooms and researching the technologies associated with Levels 4 and 5.

Video

Video has many forms. It can be live or recorded, analog or digital, and the recordings can be stored with many copies distributed to user locations or can be centrally stored and served to the user upon request. Recorded video can be watched many times and provides flexibility in scheduling unlike live video transmissions. Live events can be recorded and presented to students at their convenience. However, analog video requires a tape storage and distribution system. Digital video requires substantial storage and/or bandwidth.

The following paragraphs describe some of the advantages and disadvantages of various formats.

Analog Video

Closed-circuit television, video cassette players and reel to reel movie projectors provide analog video in the classroom, but this type of media presentation is a passive activity that limits instructor-student interaction and self-discovery. The use of analog video provides an opportunity to present material that stimulates the visual learner with respect to Felder's Learning dimensions (Figure 1). The media is widely available, and almost every school has televisions and VCR players.

However, the rate of delivery of analog video can not be easily adjusted to individual students in a classroom environment. Recorded analog tapes and movies have other disadvantages such as (Oracle, 1997):

(1) The image quality degrades over time.
(2) It is difficult to search for specific content.
(3) It is expensive if the content requires frequent updates.

Moreover, videotapes use an analog process for storing the video signal. Analog technology is very mature but has reached some physical limits. One of the limits is noise. With an analog signal, it is difficult to distinguish noise from data. The continuous nature of the signal along the tape or other transmission spectrum masks errors in the transmission signal. Another limit is the ability to index and retrieve information. Tapes are sequential and do not allow students to easily scan large quantities of material. As any parent who has made videos of their children can attest, storage and management of tapes is a hard task at even the smallest of levels.

Quality is another issue. The National Television Standards Committee (NTSC) determines the standard for broadcast television in the United States. First, the frame rate is 30 frames per second. This means that there are 30 different frames displayed to the screen each second. Second, the NTSC scans at 525/60, which means that there are 525 horizontal lines that make up each frame. These 525 scan lines are updated 60 times each second. However, the standard specifies a 2:1

interleave, so only every other line is updated during each pass. Third, the aspect ratio for broadcast television is 4:3, so the width of the image is only approximately 390 picture elements.

AVI and ASF Digital Video Formats

The limitations of analog video have resulted in a rapid rise in the popularity of digital formats, though no set standard has emerged. Probably the most popular video standard is AVI, or Audio Video Interleave. This is a defacto standard developed by Microsoft for use on personal computers. AVI is an integral part of the Video for Windows system used by Microsoft's Windows Operating Systems to manage and display video.

The AVI format consists of audio and video "chunks" that are ordered sequentially and interleaved. In theory, you would have a video "chunk" that contained a frame followed by the audio "chunk" consisting of the sound associated with the frame.

An advantage of the AVI format is that the player is included in Microsoft Windows. Likewise, a disadvantage is that there is limited support on other Operating Systems. Also, AVI files are not as compressed as MPEG files and not suitable for Web Based applications. You can edit AVI frames, but this is difficult with the MPEG format (Microsoft, 1998).

Microsoft states that the ASF format will replace AVI's eventually. The ASF file format allows the developer to specify whether the file will be displayed locally or over a network. Skipping most of the details, ASF is composed of objects rather than "chunks." These objects can be synchronized and are more suitable to streaming over a network.

MPEG-1 Digital Video Format

DVD Players and HDTV follow a specification known as MPEG-2 (Motion Picture Experts Group). MPEG-2 is the follow-on to MPEG-1. MPEG-1 is an open standard whose quality is similar to standard VHS tapes. MPEG-1 specifies a frame size of 352 by 240 with 30 frames per second. VGA monitors are 640X480 so this frame size is sometimes called half-size video. The first digital video standards were "quarter screen" video or 176 by 120.

MPEG-1 has proven popular because of its compression and quality. Uncompressed video can be quite large. Sixty seconds of uncompressed video at MPEG-1 quality levels can occupy up to 435 Megabytes of storage. This assumes true color. At this quality, Titanic would occupy 78 Gigabytes. For comparison, a DVD is currently limited to 4.7 Gigabytes. Obviously, for digital video to be practical, we have to use compression. By eliminating unnecessary information and by storing differences between frames rather than entire frames, MPEG-1 can achieve compression rates of over 100:1. Figure 4 shows a typical file size calculation for 1 minute of MPEG-1 quality video.

Actual MPEG-1 files sizes vary depending on the parameters, but the typical file requires from 15-20 MB per minute of video. Gall provides an in depth description of the MPEG-1 standard (Gall, 1991).

MPEG-2 and MPEG-3 Digital Video Formats

MPEG-2, offers resolutions of 720x480 and 1280x720 at 60 fps, with full CD-quality audio. This is sufficient for all the major TV standards, including NTSC and even HDTV. MPEG-2 is used by DVD-ROMs. MPEG-2 can compress a 2 hour video into a few gigabytes. While decompressing an MPEG-2 data stream requires only modest computing power, encoding video in MPEG-2 format requires significantly more processing power. MPEG-3 was originally intended to specify the formats required for future high definition broadcast signals but was determined that MPEG-2 standards already met all of the requirements intended for MPEG-3. The MPEG-3 video format was never completed, but MP3 is a very popular digital audio format. MP3 is an audio coding scheme used with the MPEG-2 video format. It's name is derived from Layer 3, one of the schemes used for compression.

QuickTime

Quicktime is a Video and Animation system developed by Apple Computer that is included with Apple Operating Systems. Quicktime movies are identifiable by the MOV extension. One of the strengths of the Quicktime Media Player is the large number of supported media types and formats. Windows-based personal computers can play Quicktime movies with a freely available player, and the player also supports MPEG, AVI, ASF, music animation, audio and text.

The Quicktime format does not impose any restrictions on the video characteristics. Video can be stored at any frame rate, color depth, resolution, or number of channels. This capability allows

Quicktime to expand to meet future formats while still supporting older formats. In 1998, the International Standards Organization decided to use the Quicktime format as the basis for MPEG-4 (Apple, 1999).

HDTV

In order to overcome some of the limitations of existing analog video systems, the United States is pursuing the transition to the High Definition Television (HDTV) format. HDTV is a digital video standard that specifies up to 1250 scan lines with 60 frames per second compared to 525 and 30 for NTSC and is based on the MPEG-2 standard. The aspect ration of HDTV is 16:9, yielding approximately 700 picture elements in each scan line.

The transition to HDTV is difficult because of the infrastructure that currently exists. Stations broadcast analog signals because consumers have analog televisions. Consumers won't purchase high definition televisions until there is HDTV programming available. Two factors could speed the transition. The first is the introduction of DVD players, which store movies in the same format, specified by HDTV. The second is the growth of satellite as an alternative to cable. Satellite services will be able to adapt to digital transmission easier than the cable companies.

MPEG-4

You might think that MPEG-4 would have a higher quality than MPEG-2. This is not the case. MPEG-4 is designed to "be an extremely powerful standard for video conferencing" providing high quality video while only using from "4.8 to 64 Kbps (Fluckiger, 1995)." One of the tenants of this standard is to scale the video quality to the bandwidth capability of the user. MPEG-4 should provide

- Reusable content
- Intellectual property rights
- A Quality of Service mechanism
- High levels of user interaction (Cox et al., 1998)

Streaming Video

There are basically two methods of viewing video on the computer. The first is to play a movie file that is located on a local drive. The drive may be physically located in the client machine, or it may be on a file server with a logical connection. Software on the client machine decompresses and decodes the video file and displays the temporal information. This is the method most used to view video files, in particular the types mentioned above.

The problem with this method is that video files are quite large. If we assume 20 MB per minute, a five minute video would require 100 MB of storage. Titanic would require over 3 Gigabytes of storage. Equation 1 depicts a sample file size calculation for one minute of uncompressed video. It would be impractical for each user to keep a copy of the video on the hard drive, and downloading videos over a Local Area Network or through a modem can be exasperatingly slow.

Equation 1: Sample File Size Calculation for 1 Minute of Video

$$60 \cdot sec \ * \ 352 \cdot \frac{pixels}{line} \ * \ 240 \cdot \frac{lines}{frame} \ * \ 30 \cdot \frac{frames}{second} \ *$$

$$24 \cdot \frac{bits}{pixel} \ * \ 1 \cdot \frac{Byte}{8 bits} \ * \ 1 \cdot \frac{MB}{1,048,576 \ Bytes} \ = \ 435 MB$$

Streaming is a method of reducing these problems. The file size is still quite large, but there is only one copy of the video. This copy resides on a video server, and users obtain the video from the server similar to the method used to retrieve web pages. The content is stored on the video server in small chunks. These chunks are forwarded to the requesting machine as needed rather than all at once. This allows the user to view the video without downloading the entire file; it prevents the user from storing the file on a hard disk, and it allows the administrator to manage the files. Some video servers can even adjust the quality of the video depending on the user's connection.

NETWORK AND CLASSROOM CONFIGURATION

This case study examines a classroom that was constructed for the purpose of delivering digital video and web content from a video server to a single classroom supporting twenty students. The classroom typically supports the University's Computers Science, Electrical Engineering, and Civil and Mechanical Engineering programs.

Figure 5: Network Configuration Infrastructure

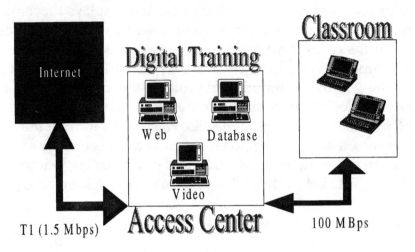

As always, there were several competing requirements that limited the potential designs of the classroom network. The classroom uses portable computers because they are becoming ubiquitous and because the university is considering a requirement that each student own a notebook computer. This restricted the use of Asynchronous Transfer Mode (ATM) to the desktop. A facility at Fort Eustis, Virginia, has implemented ATM (155 Mbps) to the desktop in a similar trial. Adams and Jansen (Adams and Jansen, 1998)give a complete description of TRADOC's Classroom XXI. Funding and personnel were also limiting factors. There exists insufficient funding to hire network administrators for the design and maintenance of the classroom, so instructors installed the network and are responsible for its maintenance. This constraint is not unusual in educational environments.

However, we were able to use a T1 line provided through a grant from MCI for Internet access. This capability freed us of the limitations of the existing campus network. Based on these considerations, we choose a combination of switched 10BaseT and 100BaseT Ethernet using Category-5 twisted pair cabling. The Network Interface Card in the client machines determines the speed of the network connection.

Figure 5 shows the network infrastructure. Each client workstation in the classroom has a switched Ethernet 10/100Base-T connection. All of the machines are connected to a CISCO Catalyst 2924 Ethernet Switch. This switch is then connected to a CISCO Catalyst 2908 Ethernet Switch via Full-Duplex 100BaseT. The Catalyst 2908 is used to support the servers where the web, training database, and video content of the training courses are maintained. The Catalyst 2908 also provides an uplink to the department's T1. The T1 would be used for distance learning via the Internet.

The client machines consisted of Pentium 166 Notebooks with 80 MB of RAM. They have 10/100BaseT 3COM Fast Etherlink PCMCIA Network Interface Cards. The servers included two Dual Pentium 200 MHz machines each with 160 MB of RAM, a Dual Pentium 90 MHz with 48 RAM, and a Pentium 200 MHz with 32 MB of RAM. These servers provide web, database and video content to the students.

In our test, we utilized two types of video, MPEG-1 and RealNetworks RealVideo. Students accessed the MPEG-1 files through a file server located on a switched 100 Mbps segment. We also connected the server to a 10 Mbps segment for performance comparisons. We are currently installing a Video Server capable of MPEG-1 streams for further study. The RealVideo Server was installed on a 100 Mbps segment off of the Cisco 2908.

RealNetworks states that their architecture "is a framework of client and server API's for the development of streaming multimedia applications. It is the third generation client-server system created by RealNetworks, designed to allow independent software companies to build or adapt their software to be streamed from servers and played by clients which support" the architecture. RealNetworks uses their proprietary protocol, The Real Time Streaming Protocol (RTSP). RTSP is a communications protocol for the "control and delivery of real time media" (RealNetworks, 1999). We chose the RealNetworks products because of their dominance in the video server market. We are currently exploring other technologies, as well.

The classroom operating system was Windows NT 4.0. NT provides diagnostics that allow the monitoring of processor and memory utilization. However, we had difficulty installing and maintaining different combinations of PCMCIA cards and installing some software programs. Several MPEG-1 players had difficulty under NT 4.0, but the Microsoft plug-in for Media Player worked on all platforms and on most files. A few files recorded with a digital video camera worked under Windows 95 but not under NT.

Finally, we used the NetXray/Dual Version 3.0.0 sniffer to look at the network utilization, collisions and errors. We first tried to run the sniffer on a Pentium 166 notebook, but it could not handle the network load and locked up. We then switched to a Pentium 200 desktop and were able to measure the impact on the network.

DISCUSSION

As stated, our target client was a notebook with a 166 MHz Pentium processor and 80 MB RAM. We also looked at other clients to determine the impact of the client on system performance. None of the clients had MPEG hardware, but the video cards, video memory, cache, and bus architecture varied greatly in the available machines. Table 1 illustrates the performance of the notebooks compared to other systems. We used Windows NT Performance Monitor to measure the utilization of the processor in the range from 0-100 percent. The P166 was able to play the MPEG-1 file full screen without degradation of quality. The audio was synchronized sufficiently that speech and lip movement seemed natural.

We first streamed/transferred the video file from the Pentium 200 MHz machine with 32 MB of RAM. When using the RealVideo, the server could stream to the maximum number of clients on the network with no performance degradation from either the network or the server. The network utilization varied from 4-7% with no collisions or network errors. At the advertised 45 Kbps, nineteen clients should have registered 855 Kbps or less than 1% of the 100 Mbps segment (8.55% of the 10 Mbps segment). But when we attempted multiple

Table 1 - Client Processor Utilization from NT Performance Monitor

Client Machine	RealVideo	MPEG-1 File
Pentium 100 MHz 80 MB (Desktop)	45%	99%
Pentium 133 MHz 32 MB (Notebook)	70%	100%
Pentium 166 MHz 80 MB (Notebook)	70%	100%
Pentium 233 MHz 128 MB (Desktop)	12%	13%
Pentium 300 MHz 128 MB (Desktop)	2%	11%

Table 2 - Network Utilization, 200 MHz Server, 100 Mbps Segment

	RealVideo	MPEG-1 File
Number of Streams before degradation	19	5
Network Utilization	4%	10%
Collisions	0	0
Errors	0	0

transfers of the MPEG-1 file, the server degraded to the point that we had to disconnect it from the network. We were only able to achieve five simultaneous transfers. The network utilization was 7% at the time of system failure. Assuming a transfer rate of 1.5 Mbps for a MPEG-1 file, five files would require 7.5 Mbps or 7.5% of available bandwidth (75% of the 10 Mbps segment).

Second, we used the Dual Pentium 90 Server located on a 10 Mbps segment. The server showed an average of 5% CPU utilization when streaming 19 RealVideo Streams. The network utilization varied between 7 and 9% with no errors or collisions. This configuration only supported four MPEG-1 files prior to the degradation of video quality. The server was at 32% utilization and the network varied from 65% to 68% utilization on the fifth stream. The audio on all five were unintelligible when the fifth file began.

Finally, we used the Dual Pentium 200 MHz and 160 MB of RAM. As before, there was no degradation in the RealServer streamed video. The significant difference came with the MPEG video file transfer. We were able to achieve nineteen simultaneous MPEG transfers with no degradation of video quality. The maximum network utilization was 32% with no collisions or errors. The server CPU utilization was only 25% on one processor and 4% on the other.

Network utilization was not a factor when the server was connected with a 100Mbps Ethernet segment. The segment never exceeded 35% utilization, and we did not see any collisions on the segment. It was not until we connected the server to a 10 Mbps Ethernet segment that we saw degradation in the video. We were only able to have four simultaneous transfers of the MPEG file without any loss in quality.

USING DIGITAL VIDEO?

Having obtained the necessary hardware and software, the ques-

Table 3 - Network Utilization, Dual 90 MHz Server, 10 Mbps Segment

	RealVideo	MPEG-1 File
Number of Streams before degradation	19 (No degradation)	5
Network Utilization	9%	68%
Collisions	0	30
Errors	0	5

Table 4 - Network Utilization, Dual 200 MHz Server, 100 Mbps Segment

	RealVideo	**MPEG-1 File**
Number of Streams	19 (No degradation)	19 (No degradation)
Network Utilization	7%	32%
Collisions	0	0
Errors	0	0

tion becomes utilization. Video teleconferencing is certainly beneficial in distance education; though there has been limited research that compares the availability of or quality of the video to the educational outcomes. Russell (1997) provides a list of references. Our goal was resident instruction. This reduced the bandwidth constraints and limited the potential platforms and software used by the students.

We have worked with USMA's Behavior and Psychology Department on two projects that studied the utility of digital video. Our goal for the first project was to compare different types of video with a live

Table 5: Project 1 Conditions

Condition	DESCRIPTION	Learning Dimensions
1	An actual class taught by an instructor using a Power Point slide show. Participants were encouraged to ask questions of the instructor. This is currently the mode used in the centralized schools.	Active, Sensing
2	An MPEG video of the instructor teaching the class with Power Point slides. Interaction was not allowed, but students were allowed to collaborate. The video alternated between slides and the instructor.	Active, Sensing
3	Mpeg video showing only the Power Point Slides with the instructor's audio. Neither interaction nor collaboration was allowed.	Reflective, Sensing
4	Power Point slides with student collaboration (Self-paced).	Active, Sensing Visual, Sequential
5	Power Point slides with no student collaboration (Self-paced).	Reflective, Sensing Visual, Sequential
6	An MPEG video of the speaker without slides (Talking Head video). Interaction was not allowed.	Reflective, Sensing Verbal, Sequential

instructor and with text. The content was designed for Levels 1 and 2 of Bloom's Taxonomy.

Seventy-five freshmen students, male and female, ranging in age from 18-21, enrolled in an introductory psychology class and receiving extra credit for volunteering for our research, participated in the experiment. Our goal was to evaluate the student's ability to understand unfamiliar technical concepts through various media. We anticipated that access to an instructor (interaction) would produce a higher degree of understanding given the complexity of the domain and various means of delivery. The delivery means are listed in Table 5.

Following the instruction, proctors gave the participants a sheet with five analytical reasoning questions from a Law School Aptitude Test pretest book to reduce the effects of short-term recall. The proctors then administered an exam of twenty questions based on the material. A committee then graded the exams and compiled the statistics. The results are depicted in Table 6.

Though we predicted that interaction with the instructor and collaboration would produce higher scores, there was no significant difference. This is consistent with other studies (Russell, 1997) that suggest no significant difference in the means of delivery. Two factors that may have affected the outcome of the statistical analysis were the high variance in the results of all conditions and the small sample size of each condition group.

When designing the second project, our goal was to provide an active *student-centered* environment, and allow student's to demon-

Table 6: Project 1 Results

Condition	DESCRIPTION	MEAN	STD DEV	N (Students)
1	Instructor in Classroom. Collaboration.	9.833	2.98	12
2	MPEG Video: Slides, audio, and instructor. Collaboration.	8.0	2.18	14
3	MPEG Video: Slides, audio, no collaboration.	9.0	3.14	15
4	Power Point Presentation: Collaboration.	11.36	3.39	14
5	Power Point Presentation: No collaboration.	7.29	4.66	14
6	MPEG Video: Audio, instructor, and no collaboration.	10.55	3.11	11

Table 7: Project 2 Conditions

Condition	DESCRIPTION	Learning Dimensions
1	A traditional classroom setting with an instructor interactively teaching students.	Active, Sensing, Visual, Sequential
2	A class using a digital radio training manual with a live instructor available.	Active, Sensing, Verbal, Sequential
3	A class using a digital radio training manual with a chat room session.	Active, Sensing Verbal, Sequential
4	A class using only a digital radio training manual.	Active, Sensing Verbal, Sequential
5	A class using digital video with a live instructor available .	Active, Sensing Visual, Sequential
6	A class using digital video with a chat room session.	Active, Sensing Visual, Sequential

strate an *Application Level* of understanding. We wanted students to watch videos in the context of the course of instruction, rather than stop an activity to watch a video. The student should be able to continue the activity with the video as a component. The videos were objects in a lesson, practical exercise or an exam. We wanted the student to be able to increase or decrease the video size in relation to the *learning space* on their desktop. This satisfies both the sequential and global learners from Felder's Model. Table 7 describes the conditions for the second project.

Project 2 required that students be able to employ the digital radio upon completion of the training session. The conduct of the trials was similar to Project 1, and there was a hands on test conducted following the training. There was only one hour allotted to each trial.

Performance scores revealed that the control group performed better than the other condition test groups for the task. The main reason for this was student focus. The instructor had a set agenda to accomplish, and could accomplish it in the allotted time. For the other test groups, many students did not manage their time sufficiently to cover all the material necessary to pass the exam.

FUTURE TRENDS

Undoubtedly, video is a driving force in the current demand for bandwidth. Quicktime, ASF and MPEG are the current formats, but vendors such as RealNetworks, Microsoft, and Vivo Software are fighting to dictate the standard for streamed video. It is certain that quality will improve as compression improves and bandwidth grows. The fusion of television and information technologies is inevitable, and this combination will undoubtedly revolutionize the education process along with the rest of society. It is likely that technology will support a more interactive experience in the future. It is possible that a future student could be immersed in a virtual environment. This environment could provide multiple concurrent video sources to stimulate student reactions which are monitored and provide feedback to the system which interprets this feedback in order to determine the content of the next video segments to be provided to the student. The system of the future will likely allow the student to exercise multiple iterations of a video experience from many perspectives. The student would then be free to experiment in a controlled environment to observe system responses to varied stimuli. This type of a system could cover the spectrum of learning styles (Figure 1) and would allow students to develop through every level of Bloom's Taxonomy of Learning (Figure 2).

CONCLUSION

Automation in general and digital video in particular will have an increasing impact on future learning environments. However, the expense of technology in terms of procurement, training and maintenance mandates a firm theoretical foundation. In this chapter, we have attempted to correlate the use of video with established learning models.

The hardware and software requirements are currently within the reach of many educational institutions. As a minimum, a computer lab consisting of a minimum of PII 233 MHz workstations, a robust file server and a 100 Mbps switched Ethernet network is sufficient to provide digital video to individual students.

The best utilization of video is still an open issue, however. Certainly, multimedia in general and digital video in particular can reach both the *Active* and *Reflective* students. It can compliment text with a stimulating visual display impossible for an instructor to duplicate on a blackboard. It can provide *Facts* and *Concepts* with professional quality. It can satisfy *Sequential* learners, but allow *Global* learners to skip from segment to segment.

It can't provide guidance, however. It can't manage a student's time or provide motivation and inspiration. It can't adjust its teaching style based on the body language or "blank stare" found on the face of the student. It doesn't care what the weather is like outside, or if its homecoming. Instructors will always have a role if only to provide the inspiration to pursue lifelong learning, the motivation to challenge established ideas and forge new ones, and the synergy to collectively challenge creative minds.

REFERENCES

Adams, W. and B. Jansen (1998). *"Distributed Digital Library Architecture: The Key to Success for Distance Learning.,"* presented at International Workshop on Research Issues in Data Engineering.

Cox, R.V., B. G. Haskell, Y. Lecunn, B. Shahraray, and L. Rabiner (1998). "Scanning the Technology, On the Applications of Multimedia Processing to Communications," *Proceedings of the IEEE*, vol. 86, 755-821.

Felder, R.M. (1993). "Reaching the Second Tier — Learning and Teaching Styles in College Science Teaching," *Journal of College Science Teaching*, vol. 23, 286-290.

Fluckiger, F. (1995). *Understanding Networked Multimedia: Applications and Technology*, Hertfordshire, Prentice Hall.

Gall,D.L. (1991). "MPEG: A Video Compression Standard for Multimedia Applications," *Communications of the ACM*, vol. 34, 46-58.

Howard, R.A., C. A. Carver, and W. D. Lane (1996). "Felder's Learning Styles, Bloom's Taxonomy, and the Kolb Learning Cycle: Tying It All Together in the CS2 Course," presented at SIGCSE, Philadelphia.

Microsoft (1998). *How Does ASF Relate to AVI?*, http://www.microsoft.com, Microsoft Corporation.

Oracle (1997). *Streaming Digital Video in Today's Corporation, An Oracle Business White Paper*, http://www.oracle.com.

Quicktime Technology Brief (1999). Quicktime 3.0, http://www.apple.com, Apple Computer, Inc.

RealNetworks (1999). The Home of Streaming Media, http://www.real.com.

Russell,T.L. (1997). *The "No Significance Difference" Phenomenon*, http://www2.ncsu.edu/ncsu/cont_ed/out_ex/oit/nsdsplit.htm.

TRADOC (1998). *The Army Distance Learning Plan*, http://www-dcst.monroe.army.mil/adlp/adlp.htm.

Chapter XI

The Emergence of Distance Learning in Higher Education: A Revised Group Decision Support System Typology with Empirical Results

Caroline Howard
Emory University

Richard Discenza
University of Colorado, Colorado Springs

Although distance learning is not a new phenomenon, recently there has been a huge jump in the number of organizations offering on-line instruction. The National Center for Education Statistics released a two-year survey on distance programs for higher education on behalf of the U.S. Department of Education. The survey reported that one-third of U.S. post secondary schools offered distance education in 1995, and an additional 25% planned to offer courses within the next three years.

Probably the best methodological critique of the emerging literature on the impact of distance learning was contained in the 1996 special issue of *The American Journal of Distance Education*. The issue's intent was to disseminate information and act as a forum for criticism and debate about the practice and research of distance education in the Western world. The lead article entitled, "The Evolution of Distance Education: Emerging Technologies and Distributed Learning," by Chris Dede was followed by well-documented critiques of the distance education literature (Dede, 1996). The issue brought attention to the unique and complicated needs which exist among different kinds of learners. What works for one individual may not work for another. Researchers and practitioners have acknowledged the different needs of students in traditional classrooms for years, and it appears that the needs of distance learners also vary.

A recently released report on distance learning on the material published since 1990 points out that several hundred articles, papers and dissertations have appeared in the form of original research, how-to articles and policy papers. There are at least six journals that stress college-level distance education as their central theme. However, most of what has been written about distance learning consists of opinion pieces, secondhand reports and how-to articles that do not include original research on students and faculty. With few exceptions, the bulk of the writing lacks a theoretical or conceptual framework (Phipps & Merisotis, 1999). Frameworks and typologies provide a basis for researchers to build on the work of others and allow researchers to replicate and strengthen its generality; thus making individual studies more meaningful.

Distance learning programs use a wide variety of types of communication, modes of interaction and electronic media. Given the assortment of distance education programs, it is difficult to research the uses and impacts of the various forms of distance education so that they can be used properly and assessed in terms of the impact of distance education on student learning (Money, 1996). This chapter proposes a typology for categorizing distance learning and reports on the results of a study of 119 MIS programs who responded to an e-mail survey sent to the professors listed in the *Directory of MIS Faculty* (DeGross 1995).

BACKGROUND

Recent distance education programs incorporate similar dimensions to Group Decision Support Systems (GDSS) in terms of the technology used, communication transmission and types of interaction. GDSS is a broad-based term that is used to describe a variety of computer-based tools used to increase the effectiveness of group decision making. Some major categories include electronic meeting systems (EMS) and computer-based systems for cooperative work (CSCW).

Research studies have shown that EMS and CSCW produce significant improvements in factors such as ease of communication, anonymity and public recording or communications (group memory). These tools significantly improve the efficiency and effectiveness of group decision making in business organizations (Jessup & Tansuk, 1991; Nunamaker et al, 1991). Therefore, the literature of GDSS was reviewed as the basis for developing a distance education typology. Also, experimentation in distance education has been ongoing with various techniques incorporating group decision support systems tools, which seek to improve students' knowledge acquisition and classroom experiences. The GDSS employed in these distance education programs supports group work and encompasses systems and software that coordinate various tasks that vary from group writing to voting and group decision support tasks. (Descriptions of these tools may be found in McGrath and Hollingshead (1993) and Bidgoli (1996). Applications for the educational environment can be found in Money (1996)).

The groupware typology developed by DeSanctis and Gallupe (1985) is substantially modified for application to distance education. Their model proposed three levels of GDSS. The first included support to the group processes of generation ideas (brainstorming), evaluating alternatives generated, and finally voting to reach a consensus. The second level GDSS included model support. The third and final level added rules of order that controlled the use of level 1 and level 2 features. This chapter proposes a typology for defining the various forms of distance education through the development of a typology which categorizes distance education along three dimensions: 1) direction of communication flow, 2) predictability of physical location, and 3) communication technology used for communication.

TYPOLOGY FOR DISTANCE EDUCATION

Important aspects of the educational experience are changed in the distance education environment. Traditional face-to-face course delivery is not possible in distance education due to the physical distance between instructor and student. Thus, course delivery methods must be modified for distance courses. Distance education also eliminates other face-to-face interactions between students and instructors. In many cases, interactions among students are also reduced. Finally, when students are independent of the classroom and cannot be seen by faculty members, the traditional assessment vehicles of in-class quizzes and exams are not feasible (Gilson 1994).

The dimensions described in this section appear to have significant impacts on course delivery, student to professor interactions, student to student interactions, and student assessment vehicles. The dimensions are: 1) direction of communication flow, 2) determination of physical location, and 3) medium used for communication. This section defines each dimensions and why it is important, provides examples from the literature and presents the results of the survey of MIS programs.

Face-to-face communication provides instantaneous, bidirectional communications between the instructor and student, but the communication medium used for distance education is not all interactive. Some allow real-time interaction between student and instructor, while others may allow off-line interaction, and still others provide no communication from the student to the instructor. The type of communication flow is critical in determining if and how a course can be suitably delivered, what types of interactions between students and instructors are possible and how students can be assessed. Three types of communication flow are defined in the typology (refer to Figure 1):

1) Simplex communication or one way communication from the instructor to the student

2) Half-Duplex communication is transmission in both directions, from student to instructor and instructor to student, but only in one direction at a time, and

3) Full Duplex communication or simultaneous communication in both directions.

Simplex communication has been used for distance education for many years. Telecourses are a popular form of distance course using Simplex communication (Figure 1: section 2). Hundreds of colleges and universities in thirty-seven states currently use Public Television to broadcast their courses. These are a viable way for nontraditional, remote and handicapped students to easily benefit from college courses which they are unable to physically attend. (Catchploe, 1991). The Western Cooperative of 150 colleges and universities throughout Alaska, Arizona, California, Colorado, Hawaii, Idaho, Montana, Nevada, New Mexico, North Dakota, Oregon, South Dakota, Utah,

Figure 1: Operationalization of the Distance Learning Typology for Predictable Locations

	Simplex	Half-Duplex	Full Duplex
Audio	Intercom transmissions 1	Audio broadcasts to classrooms equipped to listen & provide subsequent response 2	Teleconferencing 3
Video	Televised courses to specially equipped classrooms 4	Televised courses to classrooms equipped with equipment for subsequent video response 5	Interactive television & video conferencing 6
Computer	Computerized materials to libraries & electronic classrooms 7	Course materials distributed on the Internet, World Wide Web or electronic mail 8	Computer conferencing 9
Mixed	Computerized training with audio or video transmission to classroom 10	Televised courses with microphone audio or electronic response 11	Video & computer conferencing combined 12

Communication Technology (vertical axis label)

Simplex
One direction only   **Half-Duplex**
One direction at a time   **Full-Duplex:**
Both directions simultaneously

Direction of Communication Flow

Washington and Wyoming uses telecourses to provide college coursework to rural, handicapped and special needs students.

These courses offer student flexibility in both the time and place in which they attend class. Students can view the programs from any television receiving the broadcast station or can videotape the classes for later viewing. Taping the courses also allows students to review sections of the course with which they are having difficulty or to rapidly advance through sections, which are repetitive or easy. The survey of MIS programs found that 14.71% used television to transmit course programs.

Use of Simplex communication for course transmission has several limitations. Since Simplex communication is one way communication from the instructor to the student, students can not respond to the instructor, answer questions or to provide feedback in a timely

Figure 2: Operationalization of the Distance Learning Typology for Flexible Locations

	Simplex	Half-Duplex	Full Duplex
Audio	Radio transmitted or audio-taped courses 1	Radio or audio-taped course with telephone response 2	Teleconferencing 3
Video	Televised courses on public networks 4	Televised courses with subsequent student video response 5	Video-conferencing & picture phones 6
Computer	Computer assisted learning or tutorials 7	Course materials distributed on the Internet, World Wide Web or electronic mail 8	Courses conducted using groupware or computer discussions 9
Mixed	Televised courses with individual computerized learning component 10	Televised courses with electronic mail or Internet response 11	Television & computer discussions combined 12

Communication Technology (left axis label)

Simplex	**Half-Duplex**	**Full Duplex:**
One direction only	*One direction at a time*	*Both directions simultaneously*

Direction of Communication Flow

manner. Although this method may suffice for traditional lecture courses, class formats requiring student participation are impossible to support using Simplex communication technology. Also, instructors cannot assess students using Simplex communications and need to institute testing vehicles which use other methods to gather information on student performance.

Courses using Half-duplex communication allow communications in both directions. However, since communications can only occur in one direction at a time, interactive communications are not possible. Using Half-duplex communications, instructors can broadcast their courses, and students can later ask questions and provide feedback or comments. The rapid increase in the use of the Internet and e-mail should make these forms of communication increasingly popular for distance education.

These communications are not instantaneous but do allow students to work more closely with their instructors and fellow students. The survey of MIS programs found that 20.59% of their distance education programs used the World Wide Web and 41.18% used electronic mail for instructor and student communication.

More options for class delivery are available through Half-Duplex communication than Simplex communication. Half-Duplex communication can be used in conjunction with telecourses to require students to more actively participate in the learning process. For example, students can use e-mail and the World Wide Web to find information to supplement a lecture presentation. Students can use e-mail to interact and work with other students to complete course activities. Student assessment vehicles can be performed using Half-Duplex communications from student to professor. Tests distributed on the World Wide Web and e-mail submissions of exams are examples.

Full Duplex communication allows simultaneous communication in both directions. Therefore, courses can be truly interactive with both the instructor and students benefiting from real-time interactions, questions and other responses. This type of communication provides a learning environment which is much closer to the traditional classroom. It allows students to actively participate in classes expanding the possible class formats possible from lectures to case studies and discussion classes.

Students can interact in real-time with the instructor. This expands the available assessment vehicles to include grading methods based on student participation. Due to technological advances and reductions in technology costs, we can expect that the future will bring more and more on-line courses using Full Duplex communications. Currently, 41.18% of the programs used technology, which allowed some Full Duplex communications.

Student Location. Students taking a course may be required to be in a predefined setting or predetermined location. Alternatively, some programs allow students to take the course in a setting of their choice. In these cases, student location is flexible. The typology divides student location into predetermined and flexible locations. Usually, the predetermined student locations house expensive equipment such as video conferencing, electronic or library classroom, interactive television or computer conferencing systems in specially equipped classrooms or library locations. The equipment is usually too expensive for individuals to purchase it individually. Usually, students take the course as a group at a scheduled time which allows face to face student interaction. Usually, interaction with the instructor is also possible during the scheduled class. Thus, class delivery options include not only the lecture method but interactive methods such as case study and class discussions. In addition, student assessment vehicles can include group activities and projects.

As the costs of technologies decrease, business and some educational organizations can be expected to increasingly use video and computer conferencing systems to transmit training or course information to distributed groups of employees located in rooms equipped with the appropriate hardware (Figure 1: section 2). For example, SUN and Apple use computers equipped with video cameras for their interactive distance training. The most common location for conducting the distance classes in the MIS programs surveyed was the electronic classroom used by 38.24% of the programs. Other predetermined locations used by the MIS programs are the conference center used by 17.65% of the programs and computer lab used by 8.82%. Flexible, less predictable, locations used by the respondents were anywhere with a television (17.65%), anywhere with a computer (8.82%), and anywhere with a telephone (2.94%).

Technology. Both students and providers of distance education are benefiting from advances and cost reductions in the technologies which expand remote communication options. These include interactive television, video conferencing systems, computer conferencing systems, the Internet and World Wide Web. These technological advancements and related cost reductions allow educational institutions to provide low cost, effective distance education to a diverse group of students in a wide variety of locations.

The choice of technology has an enormous impact on the educational experience provided in the distance education program. First, it is often a determinant of the other two dimensions, communication flow and flexibility of location. Second, the type of technological interaction can have an effect on student learning as experienced by students using virtual reality to teach students about AIDS cells (Winn 1994). Third, the technology also determines student and instructor locations in many cases, especially when expensive technology is being used.

Referring to Figures 1 and 2, courses can be transmitted via audio (audio tape, telephone radio), video (television or video conferencing), computer conferencing (may also use video or audio transmissions) or mixed media (a combination of two or more approaches). At the present time video television transmission is a common form of communication used to transmit video and audio information to individual students and is frequently located in their homes. To transmit courses to groups of students sophisticated computer conferencing systems, incorporating both video and audio conferencing located in business conference settings or sophisticated classrooms, are sometimes used (Dutra 1996). In the survey of MIS programs, 20.59% used audio conferencing, 23.53% used video conferencing, 14.71% used television and 5.88% used computer conferencing.

Often, there is more than one technology used for broadcasting distance education. Television programs broadcast to schools are sometimes accompanied by computer assisted learning materials which allow the student to further pursue the topic at his or her own pace (Figure 2: section 4). Frequently, due to the expense of interactive television, students respond to televised broadcasts using audio or electronic responses (Figure 2: section 11). Business and educational organizations (Kahn et al. 1995) are increasingly using electronic mail, the Internet or the World Wide Web to transmit informational materials to students (Figure 1: section 7). These courses may use electronic mail over the Internet (Figure 1: section 8) or have on-line discussions between groups (Figure 1: section 9) using electronic mail or groupware. Of the MIS programs surveyed, 47.06% of the respondents reported using more than one technology for student-instructor communication.

IMPLICATIONS FOR FURTHER RESEARCH

As can be seen in previous sections, the typology can be used to classify distance education and clarify the dimensions and their impacts. Other dimensions of distance education are important to consider in the research. Is the student taking the course from his/her home or with other students? Does he or she meet face-to-face with other students? For individual students viewing distance courses from their homes, they may not receive the educational benefits which result from interacting with their peers. Also, these students may be lonely. Some programs have made accommodations for students taking classes alone. The United Kingdom encourages computerized student discussions and suggests that students visit the campus for an orientation during the degree program.

Class size is a determinant of the type and quality of interaction. When classes become too big, it is impossible to have students interact with each other. The United Kingdom's Open University uses computer and video conferencing to transmit courses to thousands of students. They call these courses "stadium classes". Obviously, not all the students can interact with each other. To allow students to have quality interactions, they have computerized "breakout rooms" where students can have computerized discussions with a limited number of students. They also have found that the use of a facilitator or multiple facilitators is critical to the success of large classes. In classes too large for the instructor to interact with students individually, facilitators provide

Figure 3: A Distance Learning Typology with Communication Technology, Location and Direction of Communication Flow

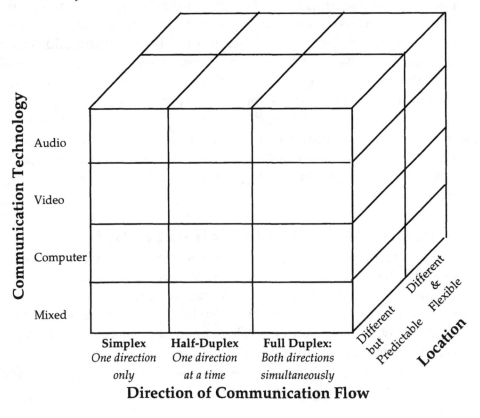

personal interactions with students.

Finally, the maturity of the students may have a greater impact on student learning than in a face-to-face environment. Several faculty in the MIS survey expressed concern that immature students learned less in distance classes than they would in a traditional classroom. They expressed concern that immature students took advantage of being physically removed from the faculty who could not require them to attend and participate in class or oversee their exams. The faculty felt that immature students needed the face-to-face supervision provided in the traditional classroom environment.

CONCLUSION

This chapter proposed a typology for categorizing distance learning which has implications for the use of distance education. Successful distance education requires that classes be developed to encompass appropriate course delivery methods, student/instructor and student/student interactions, and proper student assessment vehicles. The typology proposes the critical dimensions to consider when creating distance education classes, and provides insight into the factors to consider when deciding which courses to deliver via distance education, choosing communication technologies, and defining student locations.

Distance learning has been driven by what many call the "information revolution". Advancements in technology have presented a dizzying array of opportunities and challenges for the general public, universities, students and faculty. This revolution will continue to have a profound impact in the United States and around the world. It is becoming a more visible part of higher education, but research and literature reviewed in this chapter indicate that much has to be learned about how and in what ways technology can enhance the learning process. At times it seems that technology is advancing more rapidly than our understanding of its practical uses. More emphasis is needed on the practical implications to enhance learning and teaching.

The focus on distance learning appears to have several implications for the higher education community. First, is the notion of "access to college." This has reached the point where public policy leaders and politicians are recommending distance education as an alternative to "bricks and mortar" learning. Second, computer-assisted learning requires special skills by students and a more sophisticated technical support system to provide a high quality environment of access. This questions whether the student has the necessary skills to use the technology and whether the student has the financial resources to purchase and maintain a computer with the accompanying software. Third, it is obvious that technology does not replace the human factor in education. Faculty must be more than content experts; they must be motivators, process implementation managers, mentors and interpreters.

Fourth, technology is not as important as some other factors that affect the learning process such as student motivation, learner characteristics, and the professor. In 1987, the American Association for Higher Education published, "Seven Principles for Good Practice in Undergraduate Education," which summarized the research on the undergraduate educational experience (Chickering & Ehrmann, 1996). These principles are:

1. Encourage contacts been students and faculty
2. Develop reciprocity and cooperation among students
3. Use active learning techniques
4. Give prompt feedback
5. Emphasize time-on-task
6. Communicate high expectations
7. Respect diverse talents and ways of learning

While research on distance learning has a long way to go, technology and topologies of this nature can help keep the focus on essential goals of learning and teaching.

REFERENCES

Albrektson, J. R. (1995) Mentored on-line seminar: a model for graduate-level distance learning. *The Journal of Technical Horizons in Education*, 23(3), 102-105.

Andriole, S.J., Lytle, R.H. and Monsanto, C.A. (1995) asynchronous learning networks: Drexel's experience. *The Journal of Technical Horizons in Education*, 23(3), 97-102.

Bidgoli, H. (1996) A New Productivity Tool for the 90s Group Support Systems. *Journal of Systems Management*, 47(4) 56-63.

Applegate, L. (1993) *Leveraging diversity*. A presentation to the International Conference on Information Systems, Orlando, Florida.

Barker, B.O. (1987), Interactive learning by satellite. *The Clearinghouse*, 61(1), 13-16.

Brock, D. (1990) Using technology to deliver education. *Bulletin of the American Society for Information Science*, 16(6), 9-11.

Catchploe, M.J.(1989) Student response to a distance education course incorporating live, interactive television. *The American Journal of Distance Education*, 3(2), 23-41.

Cheng, H.C., Lehman, J. and Armstrong, P. (1991), Comparison of performance and attitude in traditional and computer conferencing classes. *The American Journal of Distance Education*, 5(3), 51-64.

Chickering, A.W. and Ehrmann, S.C. (1996), Implementing the seven principles. *AAHE Bulletin*, 49(2), 2-4.

Dede, C. (1996), The evolution of distance education: Emerging technologies and distributed learning. *The American Journal of Distance Education*, 10(2), 4-36.

DeGross, J. (1995) *Directory of MIS Faculty*, Minneapolis: University of Minnesota and McGraw-Hill.

DeSanctis, G., and B. Gallupe, (1985) Group decision support systems: a new frontier, *DATABASE*, 3-10.

Grudin, J. (1994) Computer supported cooperative work: History and focus. *Computer*, 27(5), 19-26.

Holloway, Robert E. and Ohler, Jason, (1993) Distance education in the next decade in *Instructional Technology* Englewood, CO:Libraries Unlimited, Inc. 250-275.

Hugdahl, E.O. (1982) Once you've got a communications system, how to keep people using it or keeping the show on the road. in *Teleconferencing and Electronic Communications: Applications, Technologies, and Human Factors* comp. L.A. Parker and C.H. Olgren, 253-268, Madison:Center for Interactive Programs, University of Wisconsin-Extension.

Hugdahl, E.O. (1991)Meeting needs of church musicians by audio teleconferencing in Wisconsin. *The American Journal of Distance Education*, 5(4), 63-70.

Jessup, L. and Tansuk, D. (1991) Decision making in an automated environment: The effects on anonymity and proximity with a Group Decision Support System. *Decision Sciences Journal*, (Spring).

Kahn, B.K. (1993) The challenge of IS education in business schools:

Coping with ever-changing demands of students' diversity, business expectations and accreditation. Panel Discussion at the International Conference in Information Systems, Orlando, Florida.

McGrath, J.E., and Hollingshead, A.B. Putting the "group" back in group support systems: some theoretical issues about dynamic processes in groups with technological enhancements. In L.M. Jessups and J.S. Valacich (eds), *Group Support Systems. New York;* Macmillan.

Money, W.H. (1996) Applying group support systems to classroom settings: A social cognitive learning theory explanation. *Journal of Management Information Systems*, 12(1) 65-80.

Nunamaker, J., Dennis, A., Valacich, J., Vogel, D. and George J. F. (1991) Electronic meetings to support group work, *Communications of the ACM*, (July).

Phipps, R. and Merisotis, J. (1999) What's the difference? A review of contemporary research on the effectiveness of distance learning in higher education, The Institute for Higher Education Policy, Washington, D.C., 42.

Pinsonneault, A. and Kraemer, K.L. (1989) The impact of temporal support on groups: An assessment of the empirical research. *Decision Support Systems* 5, 197-216.

Reinhard, R. Schweitzer, J. Volksen, G. and Weber, M. (1994) Computer supported cooperative work tools: Concepts and architecture. *Computer*, 27(5).

Romiszowski, A.J. (1992) *Computer mediated communication: A selected bibliography.* Englewood Cliffs, NJ: Educational Technology Publications.

Shepherd, M. (1995) *An empirical analysis of the factors affecting the diffusion of group support systems in organizations.* Doctoral Dissertation, Graduate School of Management, University of Arizona.

United States Department of Education (1998) *National Center for Educational Statistics Survey of Distance Education Programs* Washington, D.C.: Retrieved October 6, 1998 from the World Wide Web: http://www.nces.ed.gov.html.

Wagner, E.D. and B.L. McCombs, (1995) Learner centered psychological principles in practice: Designs for distance education. *Educational Technology*, 25(2), 32-35.

Wolcott, L. (1995) The distance teacher as reflective practitioner, *Educational Technology*, 25(1), 39-43.

Chapter XII

Commuting the 'Distance' of Distance Learning: The Pepperdine Story

Eric C. Adams
Catholic Diocese of Monterey

Christopher Freeman
University of Tulsa

INTRODUCTION

A primary determinant of the success of an online distance learning program is its ability to develop a sense of community among its online participants. As a participant in the Pepperdine University Educational Technology Doctoral Program, we have firsthand knowledge and experience of the impact deliberate creation of community has on learning outcomes. A vehicle for the cultivation of this community can be found in principles of knowledge management.

PEPPERDINE UNIVERSITY

This is the fourth cadre of students since Pepperdine University began offering a fully accredited doctoral program in educational technology in July 1995 (http://moon.pepperdine.edu/gsep/programs/ET/). The program features 60 percent face-to-face and 40 percent online instruction, although participants are the first to inform you that the 40 percent online in actuality translates to 80 percent when considering the number of hours actually logged on. Online instruction includes the use of Multi User Dimensions, online conferencing, newsgroups, and e-mail. Doctoral students in groups of no more than 25 participate in this lock step program on the Culver City, CA campus. They meet for one week and two weekends each trimester for two years of coursework. This is followed by competency exams, after which the dissertation process is formally begun.

One intention of the Pepperdine Program is to develop a sense of community in our cadre. Joel and Michelle Levey in *From Chaos to Community at Work* describe the development of communities in three stages: De-facto Community, Intentional Community, and Generative Learning Community (1995). The de-facto community was achieved upon our acceptance into the EdTech program; we had not met and did not know each other, yet we still constituted an, albeit unconscious, community. The intentional community began to develop during our first experience with the program, Pepperdine University's "TechCamp." During TechCamp, an intentional effort was made by members of the previous three cadres to make our membership in the community explicit through initiation. Now and ever increasingly, we, as a cadre, are becoming a generative learning community; where we transform the EdTech program as much as it transforms us through the integration of new media and the creation and transfer of artifacts.

COMMUNITY OF PRACTICE

The deliberate attempt to cultivate a community of practice is grounded in the belief that knowledge generation can become self-perpetuating, and that members of the community can have legitimate access to this knowledge. Communities of practice are characterized by people engaged in common activity, dynamic roles of learner and leader, and legitimate peripheral participation; a constant movement from the periphery of the workgroup to active participation and subsequent emergent status as a knowledge member. The use of artifacts, such as knowledge and technology, and an understanding of how they significantly interact as a single learning process facilitate this movement. Our instructors apprentice us into the technological practice. The technological practice functions not as an end, but as a means toward economic, educational, and civic ends. This makes the shared goal of our EdTech community technological use, which is then interpreted and applied individually by students in the broad fields of practice of their current employment.

Knowledge management facilitates the emergence of communities of practice by providing communities of learners and members of these learning communities legitimate access to one another. This access to social interaction is an intrinsic condition for the generation and transfer of knowledge.

KNOWLEDGE MANAGEMENT

One of the difficulties of a distance education program is that of generating, maintaining and transferring knowledge among the members of the community. Because of the absence of physical presence, the challenges of imparting and sharing knowledge among a class of students are greater in the distance education environment. This means that distance education programs will have to begin looking at the principles of knowledge management in order to truly create and maintain successful programs.

Knowledge management, like education, is devoted to information: how to capture it, how to access it, how to transform it into knowledge, how to embed it, and how to transfer it. While business clearly understands the technical end of managing knowledge, education should prove an invaluable resource for understanding the human side of generating the knowledge to manage. Knowledge transfer has always been a goal of education. As corporations redefine themselves as learning organizations, the goal is becoming shared. Yogesh Malhotra (1998), founder of @Brint.com, describes knowledge management as "organizational processes that seek synergy between the data and information processing capabilities of technology, and the creative and innovative ability of human beings" (p. 58). Davenport and Prusak (1998), in their book *Working Knowledge*, categorize the knowledge work comprising the knowledge management process into four sequential activities: accessing, generating, embedding and transferring.

Access: Legitimacy and Transparency

While the Pepperdine EdTech Program is unique in that it provides approximately 60% face-to-face interaction among it's participants, it still encounters the challenge of maintaining and transferring knowledge when the members of the community retreat to their respective home locations. The technological tools act as media of access in this situation. In distance learning environments where participants are sequestered by differences in time and space, these media of interactions have added significance. As in any educational program, the generation of cognitive artifacts is present, but these tools also shape the interactions and learning processes of the participants. More importantly, these technological artifacts help facilitate the cognitive artifact generative process by providing access to other community members.

Tools of practice and access include, but are not limited to:

- E-mail
- Newsgroups
- MOO's and MuD's (TappedIn, VROOM, ICQ) and their logs
- On-line conference: CU-SeeMe, NetMeeting
- Web pages:
  Information pages for cadre members (calendar, annotations, skills bank, etc.)
  Completed projects
  Cadre member's information
- Intraspect (online repository of group memory)

Each of these tools aids in the generation of cognitive artifacts and provides subsequent access to them. They can then be used by the community to grow not only in each individual member's knowledge but also in the continual growth of the whole community's knowledge. Access is the first knowledge activity in the process of transforming information into knowledge. It is what situates the information in the human mind. Where it resides until application transfers it to the realm of knowledge. "If information is to become knowledge, humans must do virtually all the work" (Davenport and Prusak, 1998, p. 6).

Generation: Communities of Interest

The following might be typical uses of the above technology tools following a weekend face-to-face session. An individual class will have several readings, projects and papers to be completed before the next face-to-face monthly meeting. Assigned readings are typically discussed either in newsgroups, affording asynchronous communication or in synchronous environment in groups of 8 to 10 members.

Specific questions are often posted ahead of time in newsgroups for members to discuss over the coming weeks. This allows members to reflect on comments being made and to contribute quality responses that are not rushed by time constraints.

Typically, each class will have at least one synchronous meeting among members to discuss reading selections along with the discussion in newsgroups. This provides a much more personal feel to the communication among community members. While the quality of discourse is often questionable in the fast-paced synchronous meetings, it does create a more personal environment for the discussion. These sessions are typically held in TappedIn (http://www.tappedin.org) or VROOM, which are text-based virtual environments. Some cadre members have been experimenting with audio and video capable collaborative environments such as CU-SeeMe (http://www.wpine.com) and NetMeeting (http://www.microsoft.com/netmeeting/). While there are considerable bandwidth limitations on video transfer over a modem, audio quality is generally high and provides an even more personal touch and clarity to the synchronous sessions. The online sessions are typically logged and either e-mailed to the other cadre members or put into the group memory via Intraspect (http://www.intraspect.com), to peruse at their own leisure. Because each group will generate different content in these sessions, it is often useful to read other members' online sessions to gain insight to their discoveries. This ensures that each community member has access to the knowledge being generated and discussed.

Each member will contribute information and findings via e-mail to the other members of the group. As due dates for projects approach, more synchronous communications begin to occur. These communications typically take place in TappedIn or more recently in CU-SeeMe because it allows for real-time audio transmission over the Web. This usually provides quicker clarification of issues, and when time is really pressed or a very important issue is at stake, members will pick up the phone for immediate feedback. While connectivity is improving, Web-based audio communication will occur more to save on long distance charges among group members.

Many of the completed projects are shared with the professors and other group members via the World Wide Web. This is generally the quickest medium for members to share their results and completed works. Projects are also beginning to be stored in the cadre group memory via Intraspect, which is searchable. This allows for even more thorough knowledge generation as topics are revisited and explored in more depth. In a traditional classroom, other class members typically do not have access to other members' projects for future knowledge sharing and growth.

All of these media of communication and knowledge sharing provide the context for distributed cognition in a distance education environment. In *Things That Make Us Smart*, Norman (1993) discusses the idea of a disembodied intellect, which is a barrier in any distance education program. "People operate as a type of distributed intelligence, where much of our intelligent behavior results from the interaction of mental processes with the objects and constraints of the world and where much behavior takes place through a cooperative process with others" (Norman, 1993, p.146). Students are learning in isolation in most programs and are not afforded the opportunity of learning in context with other participating learners. The above technologies provide the foundation for peer learning and teaching among an online community.

During a recent online session discussing current readings, one member stated, "I have a difficult time reading without you guys". This embodies distributed cognition via the online environment to its fullest. This community member was gaining so much insight and understanding from the newsgroup postings and synchronous discussions of the readings that she expressed the notion that she would be missing out on so much if the texts were being read in isolation, which is an interesting paradox. While each of us is actually reading in physical isolation, we are reading as a collective unconscious because we are so connected technologically. This conceitedness among an online community of learners provides the means for which tacit knowledge can be transferred.

"A key assumption driving the formation of virtual communities is that members will over time derive greater value from member-generated content than from more conventional forms of 'published' content" (Hagel and Armstrong, 1997, p.29).

Embedding: Cognitive Artifacts

Tacit knowledge, that which is experienced and internalized, is the most difficult to codify and pass on to others. While it is relatively simple to codify data and information and disseminate this via the

Web, it is extremely difficult to do the same with tacit knowledge. "Tacit, complex knowledge, developed and internalized by the knower over a long period of time, is almost impossible to reproduce in a document or database" (Davenport and Prusak, 1998, p.70). This is the one of the most difficult aspects of a distance education program in terms of sharing and passing on knowledge to its participants. While it is extremely difficult to codify this tacit knowledge, its added value is worth the effort (Davenport and Prusak, 1998, p.81). The technologies utilized in the Pepperdine program in and of themselves do not provide this tacit knowledge. What they do, however, is to provide a knowledge map that provides pointers to those who hold the tacit knowledge needing to be shared. While these tools do not specifically provide individual's names to search criteria, through their use they inherently provide insight as to whom knows what and provides the means with which to communicate with them.

The data-processing capability of technology provides one means for capturing cognitive artifacts from these situated learning environments. The success of which is dependent on the transparency of the technology, "the way in which using [technological] artifacts and understanding their significance to become one learning process" (Lave and Wenger, 1998, p.103). As they work in these environments, member's work can be captured and maintained as a group memory, making it available for knowledge sharing and reuse.

Artifacts lend a transparency to our community by encouraging engagement and practice. These artifacts influence our sense of community profoundly. Many of the benefits derived from this distance learning program reside not only in the content of the coursework but in the creation of cadre artifacts from the products (logs, hard copies, URLs, etc.) of our technological tools. Knowledge can then be transferred through artifacts. The knowledge encoded in the artifacts is separate from the knowledge creators of it. This provides a stability or permanence to the knowledge, facilitating its renegotiation.

Transfer: Communities of Practice

Another unique aspect of our distance learning is the dynamic relationship created with professors. The static size and population of our lock-step cadre greatly influences the role of our professors in our learning environment. Professors tend to be assimilated into our cadre community and act as temporary brokers of information, providing the common focus around which the community gathers and discriminates from available information the resources most relevant to our focus.

Much of the peripheral learning in our cadre community of practice comes from the modeling of technology driven instructional methodologies by our professors (who are members of a separate, yet overlapping, community of practice), i.e., how they use newsgroup threads for cooperative learning tasks or Web sites for electronic portfolios, etc. As students, we are provided the freedom to participate in these tasks as apprentices (regardless of our previous technological skills), during which we simultaneously evaluate the process. Then we can transform the process for our separate, yet overlapping, communities (corporate, higher education., development, etc.) where we implement the process as a practitioner. We then share our artifacts of application (Competency Exams, Dissertation, class projects, etc.) across our overlapping communities of practice, as a master in each.

Online programs allow for this synergy between academic studies and its immediate application by allowing the doctoral program to run concurrently with practical field experience. This exemplifies the proper use of technology in education. This also models true communities of practice by learning not taking place in a sequestered environment. As we are apprenticed through the program each cadre member is afforded the opportunity and challenged to begin implementation of strategies and concepts immediately in each of their work environments.

CONCLUSION

Each community member brings something different to the community's experience. In many traditional distance education programs, learners are isolated and not afforded the opportunity to learn from their peers. Through the use of technology and knowledge management principles, Pepperdine students are allowed access to each community member's ideas and knowledge. Not just information, but true tacit knowledge by being able to tap into those members' thoughts and experiences and then correspond with them via several modes of technological communication. "The most efficient way to transfer tacit knowledge throughout the organization is through the dialogue that takes place in communities of practice" (Koulopoulos,

1997, p.177). In this way, our face-to-face sessions are actually enhanced by the exchange of knowledge and information online. We come "armed" with questions and information for those we've been communicating with online.

While traditional doctoral programs are isolated experiences for most participants, an online experience can be even more so if not structured properly. These tools and knowledge management principles truly allow members of the Pepperdine EdTech community to learn collectively. As more and more distance education programs develop across the country to meet the growing needs of today's learners, a concerted effort to cultivate a community of practice through good knowledge management principles will be imperative for continued growth and success.

REFERENCES

Davenport & Prusak (1998). *Working Knowledge: How Organizations Manage What They Know.* Boston: Harvard Business School Press.

Hagel & Armstrong (1997). *Net Gain: Expanding Markets through Virtual Communities.* Boston: Harvard Business School Press.

Lave & Wenger (1991). *Situated Learning: Legitimate Peripheral Participation.* New York: Cambridge University Press.

Levey, Joe & Michelle (1995). From Chaos to Community at Work, in K.Gozdz (Ed.), *Community Building: Renewing Spirit and Learning in Business.* San Francisco: New Leaders Press.

Koulopoulos (1997). *Corporate Instinct: Building a Knowing Enterprise for the 21st Century.* New York: Van Nostrand Reinhold.

Malhotra (1998). Knowledge Management for the New World of Business. *Journal for Quality & Participation special issue on Learning and Information Management, v21n4*, pp. 58-60.

Norman (1993). *Things That Make Us Smart: Defending Human Attributes in the Age of the Machine.* Reading, Massachusetts: Perseus Books.

Chapter XIII

The Web as a Learning Environment for Kids: Case Study: "Little Horus"

Sherif Kamel
American Unviersity in Cairo

EXECUTIVE SUMMARY

The Internet and the World Wide Web are demonstrating the growing influence of information and communication technologies in various aspects of the economy. Regardless of the barriers of time and distance, newly introduced information highways are linking the world countries together, their societies and cultures contributing effectively to globalization. One of the growing trends in societal development and growth is investment in people. Therefore, the learning process is a priority issue that information and communication technologies are serving trying to upgrade and leverage human resources to become more competitive as we approach the 21st century with all its challenges and opportunities.

This chapter covers an initiative that was launched in Egypt in 1997 that targets the investment of Egypt's young generation, the kids of the present and the leaders of the future. This initiative is part of a national plan that aims at leveraging the capacities of Egypt's human resources. The focus of the chapter will be the learning process, the Internet and the presence of the first Egyptian Web site for children on the Internet "Little Horus." With the introduction of the Internet since 1993 in Egypt, today there are around 250,000 Internet subscribers, among which are a growing community of schools, teachers and children.

As the Internet grows in magnitude and capacity, perceived to reach over one million subscribers in the coming five years with an estimated 20 percent under the age of 16, the Internet and the World Wide Web could play an active role in the education process in Egypt. The chapter, therefore, will demonstrate the "Little Horus" initiative, the steps that were achieved so far, the plan for the future and the building blocks that represented the critical success factors for the realization of this initiative with relatively modest resources.

INTRODUCTION

The World Wide Web has become the vital means of information and knowledge dissemination in today's global environment. With the variety and diversity of professions from a chief executive officer to a clerk, from a school principal to a first grader, everybody at some point in time is in need of timely, accurate and relevant information. Currently, the World Wide Web is becoming the world's main source of on-line information with implications on many sectors in the economy (Bangemann, 1994). This growing knowledge base available on the Internet represents a building block in the global information highway with implications on the individual, the organization and the society at large.

With the growing role of information and communication technology and its implications on daily life, no one can ignore the vital role played by the Internet (Alvarez, 1996). It is the fastest, easiest and richest means of information and knowledge dissemination not only as information provider, but also as network connector around the world regardless of time and space. This helps to create a global and border-less society of knowledge seekers, providers and coordinators. The Internet as a communication medium has also helped bring the world closer towards the realization of the global village (Naisbitt, 1984).

The Internet is developing a wealth of knowledge through Web sites, Web pages and information sources for adults (Pedroni www.geocities.com). However, if societies are building for their future there is a need to think of the proper formulation of tomorrow's generations. It is important to think of the best way to prepare kids to survive in the cyber environment and the information society. Statistics show that one third of the world's population are kids between the age of 4 and 15 and today over 18 million kids are using the Internet.

These kids need more than games, electronic mail and simple navigation of the World Wide Web. They need to benefit from the body of
knowledge on the Internet in a much more elaborate and constructive
way (Hoffman and Novak, 1994). During the 1990s, the Internet's
popularity grew at a phenomenal rate. The hobby became a necessity
for many people diffusing its use across all sectors. However, in the
coming few years, education will have the priority sector, as the
learning process is becoming a milestone in societal development and
growth.

Today around the globe there are schools and classrooms where
the learning process is being implemented differently. Students and
their teachers are using computing and networking technologies in
exchanging information and knowledge. Both students and teachers
are exploring new frontiers of knowledge and challenging the traditional notions of education which represent the driving force and the
preliminary seeds that will drive the global learning process worldwide in the 21st century (Willis, 1993). Educators feel that the use of
technology in schools will allow teachers to do a better job in today's
challenging environment by motivating students in new ways, allowing for students' different learning styles and by putting special needs
students at a more equal level with their peers. Vice President Al Gore
said "it is a challenge to the United States' communities to use the new
technologies to improve educational opportunities, motivate students and help tap into their natural curiosity" (Educational Technology Report, 1997). This actually applies to the children of the world
pending the availability of the required infrastructure and resources
and where many of the new generation of students have grown up in
a world of computers, information and competition.

The importance of securing an adequate education for children
worldwide has acquired over the past fifteen years a sense of urgency,
with the increase in the diversity of information dissemination channels (Bossert, 1999). Moreover, the expanded global competition and
corporate restructuring have drawn attention to the importance of
preparing the next generation of children to add value within an
increasingly integrated world economy. However, the challenges and
requirements to meet the growing needs with respect to education are
diverse. While a number of different approaches have been suggested
for the improvement of K-12 education in various countries, one
common element has been the more extensive and effective utilization

of information and communication technologies through partnerships involving governments, local communities, schools and the
private sector (Moore et al., 1990).

This chapter explores how the Internet is being used in Egypt, a
developing country, in schooling and kids clubs focusing on K-12, and
how it is affecting their learning processes and the way they get access
to information and knowledge. In recent years, Egypt has been
investing in the buildup of its young generation as "leaders of the
future" to know how to use the Internet in an efficient manner as a
communication, research, and business medium. This chapter covers
a case study, "Little Horus," and its role as a new model for learning
in the 21st century. The case demonstrates the capacities of Web-
enabled technologies in education and how this could imply major
transformation in the curricula and management of the educational
institutions in the coming millennium. Moreover, the chapter highlights the role of Web technologies as a medium for the realization of
globalization while removing barriers and bringing together different
cultures, norms and values.

BACKGROUND

The recent innovation in information technology dramatically
transformed the society in terms of business, economic and social
changes (Naisbitt, 1984). This has led to the emergence of a new
information-based society that is more competitive, more democratic,
less centralized and addresses individual needs. The information
society impacts has changed the way people work, play, learn, enter-
tain, travel and govern (Kamel, 1998) with direct effects on human
knowledge and capacities development, enabling the acquisition and
dissemination of information in different forms, unconstrained by
distance, time or volume. Hence, to survive and compete in the new
information age, education is becoming a priority to have more people
educated to help create more and better employment opportunities
and provide better future prospects (Hoffman and Novak, 1994).
Respectively, within the context of rapid technological changes and
shifting market conditions the educational system worldwide is challenged with providing increased educational opportunities without
increased budgets. Many institutions are facing this challenge by
developing distance learning programs. These programs provide
adults with a second chance education, reach those disadvantaged by

limited time, distance or physical disability and update the knowledge base of workers at their places of employment. However, a key question remains important, which is whether distant students learn as much as students receiving traditional face-to-face instruction. Studies indicate that distance and traditional education could be as effective when the method and technologies used are appropriate, and when there is student-to-student interaction and timely teacher-to-student feedback (Ludlow, 1994).

In a world dominated with fierce competition, the quality of education will determine whether children hold high-skill jobs that add value within the global economy of the 21st century. While a number of different approaches have been suggested for the improvement of K-12 education, the effective utilization of information and communication technologies to support the systemic curricula reform has been the most common (Verduin and Clark, 1991). However, there are a number of factors that need to be put into consideration (Educational Technology Report, 1997). First, the focus should be on learning with technology and not about technology. Although both are worthy of attention, it is important to distinguish between technology as a subject area and the use of technology to facilitate learning about any subject area through the integration of technology in the K-12 curricula. Second, emphasize should be on content and not just hardware. While the widespread of modern computing and networking hardware is necessary if technology is to realize its promise, the development and utilization of useful educational software and information resources, and the adaptation of curricula to make effective use of technology, are likely to represent more formidable challenges. Third, focus should be on professional development. The substantial investment in hardware, infrastructure, software and content will be largely wasted if K-12 teachers are not provided with the preparation and support they need to effectively integrate information technologies into their teaching. Teachers should be provided with ongoing mentoring and consultative support and with the time required to familiarize themselves with available software and content, to incorporate technology into their lesson plans and to discuss technology use with other teachers. Fourth, both government and private sector leadership and funding should be mobilized to help the education sector incorporate technology into the system. Fifth, to ensure accessibility to knowledge building and communication tools based on computing and networking technologies to all students, regardless of socioeconomic status or geographical factors (Educational Technology Report, 1997).

The Role of IT in the Learning Process

The introduction of information technology in the education sector will help improve the quality of education through the use of interactive computer-based systems and enable the possibility of individualizing the educational process to accommodate the needs, interests, knowledge and learning styles of students (Kehoe and Mixon, 1997). It is becoming more and more a reality that the Internet will play an important role in improving and developing a country's educational system (Bernt and Bugbee, 1993). Recently, researchers have begun to focus on the potential of information technology to support certain fundamental changes to the traditional approaches to the educational process. In that respect, greater attention is given to the acquisition of higher-order thinking and problem-solving skills (Ehrmann, 1995). Information technology is also serving as a powerful tool for teachers to monitor and assess the students' progress and maintain portfolios of student work. It can help prepare course work, communicate with students, parents, and administrators, exchange ideas and experiences, access remote databases, acquire educational software and expand their own knowledge and professional capabilities (Williams 1999, Bunderson and Inouye, 1987).

The information technology infrastructure worldwide in K-12 is still lagging behind, although elementary and secondary schools have been for some time acquiring new computing and networking facilities (Kehoe and Mixon, 1994). This raises concern to focus more on K-12 which represents the future generation especially in developing countries such as Egypt. This issue is compounded by a lack of appropriate infrastructure for the operation of innovative computing and networking technology and by a shortage within the schools of trained personnel capable of supporting the use of such equipment. Therefore, the extensive use of computers, particularly where interconnected by a local area network, imposes additional requirements on school buildings that were in many cases not anticipated at the time of their construction; nor were the finances available to do so (Perraton, 1992). Respectively, the access to the Internet and other value-added networks will require that schools be wired.

Information technology plays an important role in the learning process by facilitating student-initiated projects, inquiries, explorations, and problem-solving activities (Educational Technology Report, 1997). For example, computing and networking might be used to implement an environment for the simulation of systems and people, an information retrieval search engine capable of extracting information from the Internet, a vehicle for various forms of interactive exhibits and demonstrations, and an environment for the facilitation of group collaboration.

Significant investments are necessary in computing and internetworking if educational information technology is to be effectively utilized. The ratio of computers to students should be positive and should be more frequently upgraded to be able to execute contemporary applications software. Moreover, computers should be distributed among various classrooms, rather than centralized within a single laboratory to make it easier for teachers to integrate technology within the curriculum because the inadequate physical and telecommunications infrastructure of schools poses a challenge for the effective exploitation of educational technologies (Egan et al 1991).

People-IT Interface in the Learning Environment

Information technology will play a vital role in education in the coming millennium, and both teachers and students will have major inputs in the IT-based educational system (Souder, 1993). This will include operational and managerial implications as well as the methods with which strategies will be developed. Additionally, there will be a significant increase in the degree of interpersonal interaction when information and communication technology will be introduced into the classroom, and where computers will serve as the focal point for extensive collaborative activities (Porter, 1997). In considering the human side of educational technology, it is worth noting that K-12 education takes place within a surrounding environment that includes students, teachers, parents as well as other members of the society, all with significant positive effects on the outcomes (Schlosser and Anderson, 1994).

If computing resources and Internet connectivity are made available within the households for K-12 children, parents will be able to communicate easily and frequently with teachers and the school's administration and involve themselves more actively in the education of their children (Martin and Rainey, 1993). The cultivation of such parental involvement is vital for students whose economic or environmental circumstances would otherwise place them at increased risk of educational failure. Moreover, there is a growing consensus that information and communication technology should foster broader community-wide involvement in the educational process by schools to research centers, universities and libraries making valuable educational resources available to students teachers and the community at large (Porter, 1997).

At school, while the role of the teacher is likely to change within a technology-rich classroom, it is perceived that the potential benefits will decline as class size increases (Porter, 1997). Moreover, teachers will be required to play an important role in helping students to assimilate abstract concepts and develop higher-order thinking skills. Teachers can be expected to spend a great deal of time monitoring, directing, and assisting in the largely self-directed learning process (Chute, 1989 and 1986). However, a major driving force for success will be the training of teachers to lead the students to excel in their comprehension of the cyber environment which has been simplified with the development of user-friendly applications that make it easier for teachers to use. Teachers are known as the "keepers of knowledge" that is transmitted to students. For teachers, the traditional methods of teaching meant tedious preparation of lessons, copying from manuals in grant magnitude, pressures from the administrators to increase the level of students achievement, and the pressures associated with needing to teach a room full of students with varying degrees of knowledge and experience. However, with the introduction of the Internet to schools, teaching methodology has to change because having computers in a corner of the classroom does not guarantee their effective use. There are stories about computers sitting unused in schools because teachers do not know how to integrate this technology into their coursework. Therefore, school administrators need to invest not only in hardware, but also in adequate professional development plans for teachers (Threkeld and Brzoska, 1994).

The acquisition of technology in schools should not depend on a one-time investment rather within a continuous process where technology is upgraded and adapted according to the teaching requirements. Teachers must constantly adapt their curriculum to the changing needs of their students that computing technology can bring about. With the Internet and WWW tools, teachers are no longer the center of instruction, rather students can take control of their own learning at different levels and the role of the teacher will begin to change to that of the person who guides students towards finding and sorting information.

IT AND EDUCATION IN EGYPT

The extent and quality of its work force, human, and intellectual capital will determine Egypt's social and economic future development. Investing in its human resources is a prerequisite for getting ready for the next century. With the emerging global market economy, Egypt, like all other developing countries, is facing great challenges that occurred due to current technological changes. With the emerging global information society, Egypt should get ready to enter the new century or to go back in history, to realize the information society or to dwell with the industrial revolution, to cooperate or to be isolated, to complement and compete or to fragment and stagnate. Egypt, in its strive to realize its socioeconomic developmental objectives, has been recently investing to diffuse information technology in various sectors of the economy with a vision "building an information society that can compete in the global marketplace."

Such a vision can only be realized through the creation of a new profile for its human resources, which is its main asset for development. It would require an educated and information literate labor force with learning facilities and resources that allow them to master the use of information and communication technology. Therefore, students in schools and universities should master the use of information technology while preserving the culture and ethics of their own society. The challenge in the current educational system in Egypt is to prepare the knowledge and information that the students are subject to, in a more effective way through the use of state-of-the-art information and communication technology. The institutionalization of computer-based education and training programs in the learning process throughout its different phases is a must to be able to meet the continuous innovations of the 21st century. Therefore, it has become increasingly important to dramatically transform the way that the learning process is being designed, developed, and delivered. Respectively, Egypt has formulated a massive plan embedding a number of large projects to revolutionize the educational system using information and communication technology. The objectives include improving the learning process through the use of information technology, developing educational software for kids, leveraging computer literacy among students and teachers, empowering students with creativity, structured and competitive thinking skills and teaching them to appreciate the value of information technology.

Examples of these projects include "Educational Software for Children." This project targets realizing computer literacy among children that are more likely to acquire intimacy with computers than adults. The objective is to prepare new generations that can lead in the information age, learn and think using interactive learning media, enhance their skills at young age and evaluate their learning ability using systematic computing methods. The components of the project include learning skill building tools, edutainment packages, the use of experts in children education and psychology, and the collaboration with software houses for children. The project is phased into idea generation and formulation, development of educational material, and finally implementation in kindergartens and preschool educational institutions. The feedback from children will be important in evaluating the project. The duration of the project is four years to be implemented in 200 schools with an estimated cost based on 15 packages per year of US$ 1.8 million.

Another example is the "Educational Software for Students" project. The project includes the development of courseware in a series of formats covering topics such as science and technology, languages, history, and geography. This project targets the Egyptian student populations of approximately 13 million currently enrolled in schools. The objectives include enhancing the effectiveness of students' basic skills, encouraging them to learn about different subjects by introducing computer-based competitions, motivating students to search and acquire information, and encouraging students to communicate through the electronic media. The components of the project include authored content of educational curriculum support packages in various fields, languages teaching packages, and edutainment packages. The project is based on the collaboration of various educational institutions at different levels, setting standards for each level, authoring the educational material, and subcontracting the private sector software firms to develop the educational packages. The phases of the project include software applications testing, training of instructors, software installations in schools' labs and libraries, and feedback from students. The duration of the project is 10 years, where the production volume is expected to be 30 packages per year with an estimated cost of US$4.5 million.

CASE STUDY: "INVESTING IN EGYPT'S FUTURE"

Computing and internetworking are going to change the way kids think and learn, just like how tractors changed farming. In the last few years, the information and communication revolution has been influential, such as the industrial revolution has done in the past. Today, computing is not only important in the business environment, however, it is the means by which students orchestrate the use of information technology to share information dissemination and knowledge acquisition. The role of information technology is growing in the organization of knowledge and becoming a vital aspect in today's formulation plans for future leaders to compete in the next millennium.

The Internet has a wealth of knowledge and information sources for both kids and adults. Therefore, its major investment area is the child of the present soon to be the leader of the future. One third of the world's population are children under the age of 15 and one half under the age of 20, while only 18 million of them are Internet users. These children need more than games and electronic mail. They need to benefit from the Internet in a much more elaborate, informative and educational way. In that respect, the world should be mobilized towards preparing the kids for the 21st century by putting this issue on top of the countries' agendas. Otherwise, there will be a two-tiered global society. The information *haves* and *have-nots* and the gap between those who can communicate and those who can't be linked to the external world will widen with direct implications on societal development and growth.

In Egypt, an initiative was put together "Investing in Egypt's Future" to prepare the kids of the nation for the next millennium. The initiative was developed primarily to help kids talk about tomorrow's language, communicate with their peer group in different parts of the world and allow them to compete and work in a global environment regardless of time and distance barriers. This initiative is mainly targeting the *have-nots*. It includes a number of activities among which are the establishment of the 21st century kids clubs, the development of a Web site in the cyber space and supporting the development of a software industry for kids in Arabic. The objectives are creating a better learning environment for kids with state-of-the-art practices, exposing kids to new ways of thinking to be able to compete globally, promoting collaboration among kids worldwide and improving the quality and methodology used in the learning process. The generation of the future needs to be exposed to new ways of thinking and learning about new tools and apply new methodologies using state-of-the-art information and communication technologies. Kids have to learn how to share things and learn how to work and cooperate with their peer groups regardless of the difference or similarity in time, distance, culture and values. Kids have to believe in the motto "make one friend a day." This has been the driving force behind establishing "Little Horus."

21ˢᵗ Century Kids Clubs

During the preparatory phases for Egypt's kids of the 21ˢᵗ century, the concept of introducing new technologies was highly needed, especially with the growing influence of information and communication technologies and their implications on various socioeconomic aspects of life (VITA, 1995). Therefore, the idea of providing the latest relevant information technology applications to the new generation was formed and presented in the establishment of the 21ˢᵗ century kids clubs. These are information technology empowered clubs where kids enjoy their time and learn about the computing environment. They contain journals, books and multimedia software in the field of edutainment. The success of the clubs, since their inception, encouraged its initiators to share with kids around the world this experience through creating virtual clubs in cyber space. This has been formulated to virtually share with kids of the world the ideas and experiences that were witnessed through the traditional kids clubs.

The 21ˢᵗ Century Kids Clubs project was launched with the establishment of the first club in Cairo in June, 1997 with 26 personal computers, 300 software packages and full Internet connectivity. The clubs are available to kids to learn about computers, importance of information technology, the Internet, as well as to use the facility for both training and enjoyment. The kids at the club have the facilities to use the Internet extensively, get exposed to new technologies, talk tomorrow's language and work in a global environment. The success of the pilot of the Cairo Kids Club encouraged the project team to establish 12 additional clubs throughout Egypt in the remote areas prior to July 1998. These areas are considered to be the least privileged and the technology investment was an attempt to minimize the gap between the *haves* and the *have-nots*. By December 1998, there was at least one club in each of Egypt's 26 provinces. This represents a two-phased project that should be completed with the establishment of a club in each of Egypt's districts by the year 2000.

The growth rate in the establishment of the clubs was mainly due to a great collaborative effort by the private sector, the government, and non-governmental organizations. There are more than 4,500 students who have attended the 1998 summer training program. Capitalizing on the success implementation of the 21st Century Clubs in 1998, a plan is being set to establish 150 more clubs in Egypt. The idea of these clubs has proven to be appealing not only at the kid's level which represents one third of the population but also at the youth and the family level.

LITTLE HORUS (http://www.little-horus.com)

"Little Horus," the first Egyptian Web site for kids in cyberspace was written both in Arabic and English. Launched in June 1997, it contains more than 400 pages of information and illustrations covering Egypt's 7000 years of civilization, telling the kids about the land of civilization with its Ancient, Greco-Roman, Coptic, Islamic, as well as modern civilization. It gives snapshots of Egypt today, including its economic, culture and social life. Kids can have fun while visiting selected favorite places in the tour section and also playing games in the entertainment section. Under the motto of "make one friend a day," kids can make friends, exchange ideas and enjoy being a member of "Little Horus" club. Kids get to learn how to deal with each other, regardless of time or distance barriers and form a network of friends at a global scale.

The objective was to create an environment for Egyptian kids in cyberspace, giving them the opportunity to communicate with kids from all over the world and exchange friendship and knowledge. The impact of "Little Horus" was not only felt in Egypt. However, its role and impact in building Egypt's young information society has been disseminated across Egypt's borders. Little Horus was mentioned in the white paper that was forward by Bill Gates, chief executive officer of Microsoft corporation titled: "Empowerment 2001, Government Technology for the 21st Century" that was published in January 1998. Such initiative was also acknowledged by the global Bangemann challenge, which is one the leading awards in the world in the field of information technology that addresses information technology projects that have positive impacts on people, communities and the environment (Bangemann, 1994).

The objectives of "Little Horus" as an interactive Web site for learning were set to include learning through edutainment, cross-culture dissemination, building a global interactive kids network, providing a avenue to market innovative kids' idea and establishing a presence for the kids of the world in the cyber environment. The Little Horus Web site is developed for kids, teachers, educators and young Internet users worldwide who want to invest their time to learn more about the history of their cultures and the current issues worldwide in an attempt to shape them as the future leaders of the world. The site was developed for kids to train, and learn while having fun. They have the chance to learn about Egyptian culture.

In February 1999, the number of hits has reached 5.5 million. It was recognized by a number of international organizations for its content. In addition, it is being used by fifth and sixth grade students in the United States in 22 different states as a reference for their studies. Because of its educational value, it was published on a CD-ROM and distributed among 10,400 schools in Australia. The site is being updated weekly which attracts kids to check its information content frequently. "Little Horus" has recently won first prize in the 1999 Cable & Wireless Child-Net International Awards in Sydney.

Periodically, there is a review on how the site is being perceived by kids, parents, educators, Internet users, and other interested parties all over the world and its impact. From that perspective, statistics show that the number of visitors per week is more than 2,500 on average coming from 32 countries and 77% are from 26 different states in the United States. This number is justified where there are about 15 million kids using the Internet in the United States. The average number of messages on a daily basis is 30. These messages contain different subjects, among which include making friends from Egypt, wanting to know more about particular issues related to Ancient Egypt and kids games.

The Internet can be used as the main link for kids all over the world and can become an educational and entertainment tool to expose them to a pool of learning resources. Little Horus represents a virtual knowledge valley in the cyber environment. It demonstrates a new venue to accelerate the learning process and to have a fair distribution of knowledge among young Internet users worldwide. This will have greater implications in developing countries, where most of the infrastructure is centralized in the large cities, and other remote areas lag behind in many aspects including education. The ultimate mission of such virtual knowledge valley is preparing kids of the world for the 21st Century.

Through "Little Horus," Egyptian kids were put on the cyber map and were able to play an active role in this virtual world. The realization of the global village among kids from different parts of the globe can be achieved where channels of communication and circles of knowledge are created. This will help reach more than 75 percent of the population, paving the way towards creating a true information society and reducing the gap between the different clusters of the society.

Arabized Software for Kids

One of the most important activities of "Investing in Egypt's Future" initiative is to build the software industry for kids in Arabic. A number of activities have taken place to create the awareness of the need to establish an Arabized software industry for kids in the region. Therefore, a national contest for both professionals and beginners was announced in 1998. The impact of the contest has created the interest among the software industry leaders to start investing in this area and place it on top of the agenda of the software industry in Egypt.

Within the framework of allowing the students to participate in international projects, the ThinkQuest program was introduced in Egypt in 1998. It is an international program that allows Egyptian students to work and compete with their peer groups from different countries. Students design and develop their projects on the Internet and that helps influence the knowledge level of the whole society even though it is mainly targeting kids.

FUTURE RESEARCH

As we approach the 21st century, future research aimed at K-12 schools should focus on a number of elements, such as developing new forms of educational software and studying the most effective approaches to using information and communication technology in the learning process. In that respect, future research should be targeting:

- Studying learning-related disciplines, such as cognitive and developmental psychology, artificial intelligence, and the interdisciplinary field of cognitive science and fundamental work on various educationally relevant technologies.
- Developing innovative approaches to information technology application in education that aim at new forms of educational software, not only in science and mathematics, but also in languages, social studies and creative arts.
- Determining not only whether computers can be effectively used within the school, but also which approaches to the use of technology are in fact most effective and cost-effective in practice.

However, funding for research and development remains a global problem. In that respect, it is recommended that a government-private sector partnership be formulated to promote collaboration for the development of a new generation that is accustomed to the information and communication technology of the 21st century.

RECOMMENDATIONS

This chapter highlights a number of recommendations related to the use of information and communication technology in the learning environment of the next millennium (Educational Technology Report, 1997). This includes:

- Focusing on learning rather than technology. It is important to note that computing skills are vital, however, they should be integrated throughout the K-12 curriculum, and not simply used to impart technology-related knowledge and skills.
- Emphasizing content. The diffusion of cutting-edge computing and networking facilities is important but not sufficient. This should be complemented with the development and utilization of useful educational software and information resources, and

the adaptation of curricula to make effective use of information technology.

- Giving special attention to professional development. The substantial investment in hardware, infrastructure, software, and content will be largely wasted if K-12 teachers are not provided with the support needed to effectively integrate information technologies into their teaching.
- Ensuring accessibility. Access to knowledge building and communication tools based on computing and networking technologies should be made available to all students, regardless of socioeconomic status or geographical locations.

CONCLUSION

The Internet can play a major role in educational reform with students taking more responsibility for their own learning. However, teachers need to adapt themselves to a changing technological society to prepare productive citizens who are adjusted to the information and communication technology. During the next millennium, traditional methods of teaching will no longer be valid. There will be a major transformation in the role of teachers, becoming more like facilitators and co-learners providing richer learning environments, experiences and activities, and creating opportunities for students to collaborate to solve problems and share knowledge and responsibility.

Students will switch from passive to active learning, becoming more of explorers of the universe of learning. Such exploration will provide students with opportunities to make decisions, while figuring out the attributes of events, objects, people and concepts. Both teachers and students will excel in their learning of using the Internet in a variety of ways to enhance their teaching and learning experiences. This chapter examined the potential use of modern information and communication technology in the learning process with a focus on kids. In the case of Egypt, such experience over the last three years has created an environment for the acquisition and transfer of information and knowledge by kids all over the country. For, example, "Little Horus," served as a vehicle to access knowledge using a simple and user friendly interface helping students to realize higher levels of achievement because they are more engaged in their learning activities.

The importance of such an environment is the motivation generated by the use of the Internet resources that appeals to students of all ages and abilities therefore, motivating them to get involved and increasing the time and quality they need to study. Respectively, the Internet has the potential to drastically change the way students learn by controlling their learning process. As the global society embarks into the 21st century, innovative information and communication technology will create many great challenges and opportunities for growth and development in the next millennium. Moreover, with the growing knowledge management needs of the society at unprecedented rates, integrated information and communication technology solutions will enable individuals and organizations to address learning issues facing them in the 21st century and help people build a smarter community, a smarter society, and a smarter world.

REFERENCES

Alvarez, L.R et al. (1996, May/June). *"Why technology?"* Educom Review, 31(2).

Bangemann, M., et al. (1994, May). *"Europe and the global information society."* Unpublished Recommendations to the European Council.

Bernt, F.L. & Bugbee, A.C. (1993). *"Study practices and attitudes related to academic success in a distance learning program."* Distance Education. 4(1), 97-112.

Bossert. P. (1999, March). *"Educating children in the next decades: problems and possibilities with a strategic vision."* Proceedings of the Cairo Internet Conference and Exhibition Cainet. [Web Site] http://www.ise.org.eg

Bunderson, V.C., and Inouye, D.K. (1987). *"The evolution of computer-aided education delivery systems."* In R.M. Gagné (eds.), Instructional technology foundations. Hillsdale, NJ: Erlbaum, USA.

Chute, A.G., and B.W. Hancock. (1986). *"Instructional communications model."* AT&T International Training Conference, Chicago, IL, USA.

Chute, A.G., and L.S. Shatzer. (1989). *"Designing for international tele-training."* International Teleconferencing Association Yearbook.

Egan, M.W., J. Sebastian, and M. Welch. (1991, March).*"Effective television teaching: perceptions of those who count most distance learners."* Proceedings of the Rural Education Symposium, Nashville, Tennessee, USA.

Ehrmann, S.C., (1995, September/October). *"The bad option and the good option."* Educom Review,30(5).

Groth, J. *"Physical or virtual networks?" Connecting Swedish schools to the Internet.* [Web Site] http://www.pi.se

Hoffman, D., and T. Novak. (1994). *"How big is the Internet?"* Internet Society News, 3(2).

Johnston, W.B., and A.H. Packer. (1987). *"Workforce 2000."* Indianapolis Hudson Institute, Indianapolis, USA.

Kamel, S. (1998). *"IT & Trends in Global Education in the 21ˢᵗ Century."* Information Management Journal. 11(3-4), 9-12.

Kehoe, B.P and Mixon, V. (1997). *"Children and the Internet: A Zen guide for Parents and Educators."* Prentice Hall, New Jersey, USA.

Ludlow, B.L. (1994) *"A comparison of traditional and distance education models."* Proceedings of the Annual National Conference of the American Council on Rural Special Education, Austin, TX, USA.

Martin, E.E and L. Rainey (1993) *"Student achievement and attitude in a satellite-delivered high school science course."* The American Journal of Distance Education, 7(1).

Moore, M.G, et al. (1990) *"The effects of distance learning: a summary of the literature."* Research Monograph No#2. University Park, Pennsylvania: The Pennsylvania State University, American Center for The Study of Distance Education, USA.

Naisbitt, J. (1984). *"Megatrends."* Warner Books, New York, USA.

Pedroni, G.E. *"The Importance of the World Wide Web in Education K-12."* [Web Site] http://www.geocities.com

Perraton, P. (1992). *"A review of distance education."* In Paud Murphy and Abdelwahed Zhiri, (eds.). "Distance education in anglophone Africa: experience with secondary education and teacher training." EDI Development Policy Case Series, Analytical Case Studies, No#9, World Bank, Washington DC, USA.

Porter, L.R. (1997). *"Virtual Classroom, Distance Learning with the Internet."* New Work: Wiley, USA.

President's committee of advisors on science and technology. (1997, March). Panel on Educational Technology Report to the President on the Use of Technology to Strengthen K-12 Education in the United States.

Schlosser, C.A and M.L. Anderson. (1994). *"Distance education: A review of the literature."* Iowa Distance Education Alliance, Iowa State University, Ames, Iowa, USA.

Souder, W.E. (1993). "The effectiveness of traditional vs. satellite delivery in three management of technology master's degree programs." *The American Journal of Distance Education*, 7(1), 37-53.

Threlkeld, R., and K. Brzoska. (1994) *"Research in distance education."* In B. Willis (ed.), Distance Education: Strategies and Tools. Englewood Cliffs, Educational Technology Publications, Inc, New Jersey, USA.

Verduin, J.R and T.A. Clark. (1991) *"Distance education: the foundations of effective practice."* Jossey-Bass Publishers, San Francisco, California, USA.

Volunteers in Technical Assistance (VITA). (1995, January). *"Community Information Centers."* Unpublished topic paper prepared for this project. Arlington Virginia, USA.

Williams, N. (1999, March). *"The child and the Internet: Opportunities and challenges in children's use of new communications technology."* Proceedings of the Cairo Internet Conference and Exhibition Cainet. [Web Site] http://www.ise.org.eg.

Willis, B. (1993). *"Distance education: a practical guide."* Educational Technology Publications, Englewood Cliffs, New Jersey, USA.

Chapter XIV

Web-Based
Instruction Systems

Jens O. Liegle
Georgia State University

Peter N. Meso
Kent State University

INTRODUCTION

Education is expensive and takes time. Instructors from both industry and educational institutions have employed one of two methods, besides traditional classroom instruction, to deliver knowledge to learners more cost effectively. One approach has revolved around automating the education process through the use of Computers. The other has focused on using the existing instructors more efficiently by employing video conferencing technology to disseminate lectures to many more geographically dispersed learners concurrently. The advent of the Internet and the World Wide Web (WWW) provides for the merging of both approaches into what can be termed a Web-Based Instruction System (WBIS).

A WBIS allows for the delivery of knowledge to a well-defined set of learners via the WWW by enabling both instructors and learners to fulfill all the roles that they would otherwise fulfill in a conventional learning environment. With the WBIS, it is not mandatory that the instructor and the learners be in the same physical location at the same time. Neither is it necessary to use physical means of correspondence, such as postal mail, to facilitate the learning process. Further, the facilitation of the learning process need not be synchronous. Their geographic and temporal distribution not withstanding, a WBIS allows the participants in the learning process to interact with each other and with the knowledge being delivered in such richness, it enables them to receive an equitable quality of learning to that obtainable in a conventional learning environment (Liegle and Madey 1997; McCormak and Jones, 1998).

This chapter examines the WBIS from the system's perspective. Critical issues and problems relating to WBIS are presented. The chapter proceeds to present a taxonomy for classifying the various types and technologies of WBIS currently in existence and to show how the taxonomy can guide the evaluation and selection of WBIS technologies during the development of a WBIS. It ends by assessing current technological and socioeconomic trends on the future of WBIS.

BACKGROUND OF WEB-BASED INSTRUCTION SYSTEMS

The origin of WBIS can be traced back to the early computer-based training (CBT) systems (Figure 1) that ran on mainframes and were entirely text based (Alexander, 1998).

With the advent of the personal computer and graphical user interfaces, CBT systems that supported multimedia emerged. As local area networks and later the Internet matured, systems that supported multiple users were developed. These computer-mediated instruction (CMI) systems supported multimedia and eventually hypermedia, and since multiple users were connected at the same time, collaboration among them became possible. It is at this point that the use of information technology to provide education became feasible. The emergence of the WWW made possible the provision of computer-based instruction to an even larger population of users, via more types of media. These early Web-based training (WBT) systems were then institutionalized by academic institutions to provide credential based education, hence the emergence of Web-based instruction systems (WBIS) (Szabo and Montgomery, 1992; Laffey, Tupper, Musser and Wedman, 1998; Alavi, Yoo and Vogel, 1997).

Figure 1: Chronology of Web-based Instruction

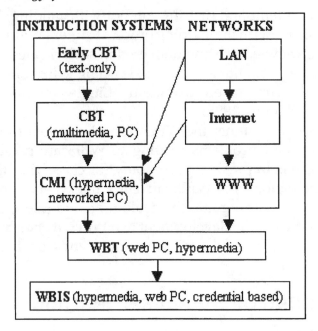

SYSTEMS VIEW OF WEB-BASED INSTRUCTION SYSTEMS

The six core components of a Web-based instruction system are the Learner, the Peers, the Instructor, the Author, the Systems Administrator and the Content. The *learner* is that individual who receives an education from the WBIS. The collection of individuals who receive the same education from the WBIS within the same time frame and from the same instructor are referred to as *peers*. The *instructor* is the subsystem of a WBIS that facilitates the delivery of pedagogical resources by performing a number of administrative tasks including: course moderation, course-content sequencing, learning-progress assessment, learner guidance and authorization of the learners' advancement to higher modules. The instructor may be an individual or a computer program such as an intelligent tutoring system (ITS).

Systems Administrators are the group of individuals responsible for placing the course content on the Web and maintaining the WBIS. The knowledge resources that are shared by the participants in the WBIS enabled learning process collectively constitute the content on the WBIS. Content found on the WBIS could be administrative or pedagogical in nature. Administrative content constitutes all the knowledge resources associated with the management of the course including enrollment and registration instructions, participant directory, syllabus and schedule, announcements and bulletin board, learner assessment feedback, course assessment feedback, and WBIS assessment and end user support. *Pedagogical content* refers to all the knowledge designed to enhance the learner's competence or level of understanding. This content comprises of: a) hypermedia lecture documents, b) assignments, projects or experiments, c) exercises (individual/collaborative), and d) tests and quizzes. A *course* is a subset of the content, possibly supported by external knowledge resources (e.g. textbook, Web sites), facilitated by one instructor and delivered to a well-defined set of learners. Some experts suggest that the concept of a course is outdated and will be replaced by a system of micro-subject units that will be organized on the basis of a set of prerequisites, with learners taking only those units required to achieve a certain level of proficiency (Schank, 1998).

The group of individuals who create the course content fulfills the role of *author* and consists of graphic designers, content authors, programmers and Web experts. Authoring software attempts to support all the roles of an author. However, by restricting authors to the use of a template approach, it limits their creativity and the variability in content that they produce.

The effective interaction and inter-linking of the six components of a WBIS is made possible by interfacing software. This software includes Browsers, Group-ware, Authoring Software, Course Management Software, and Communications Software. *Browsers* enable learners to access and interact with Web content. Software that facilitates collaboration between temporary and geographically dispersed peers is termed *Group-ware*. *Authoring Software* is the set of programs that facilitates the creation of pedagogical resources (see Table 1 for examples). The key limitation in present-day authoring software is their incompatibility, which prevents the sharing and reuse of content. Further, they demand the use of templates or require knowledge of HTML and scripting languages.

Communication software enables peer-to-peer and instructor-learner communication. Of these, synchronous communication software enables real-time communication and includes chat-rooms, voice/video conferencing, among others. Asynchronous communication software,

Table 1: Course Authoring Systems

System, Company	Description
KoTrain, Kobixx Systems (www.kobixx.com)	Web-based, HTML editor w/ templates, Chat and email, Search engine, Quizzes, Reports
Allen Communication (www.allencomm.com)	*Designer's Edge*® (pre-authoring, design) *Quest*® (multimedia authoring) *Manager's Edge*™ (training delivery, mgt.)
ToolBook II, Asymetrix Learning Systems, Inc. (www.aimtech.com)	Authoring and support products Learning Management products
CBT Systems (www.cbtsys.com)	Offer various online courses. Can be integrated into instructor led course.
Director&Authorware, Macromedia (www.macromedia.com)	Various industry strength tools for online course development
Mentorware Enterprise Education Server (www.mentorware.com)	Web-based courses and authoring tools, tests, reports, email
TopClass, WBT systems (www.west.ie)	Web based and offline authoring; targets corporate training
IBT Author, Docent Software Inc. (www.docent.com)	Web based training and assessment; Authoring system; targets corporate training
OnTrack, DK Systems (www.dksystems.com)	Targets corporate training; works with Oracle, SQL Server, etc.
Registrar, Silton-Bookman Systems (www.triadinc.com)	Training Administration Software
Phoenix Net Works, Pathlore (www.pathlore.com)	Web-based; Targets corporate training; Online authoring
VCampus™, UOL Publishing, Inc (www.uol.com)	Supports educational institutions/ professors to put course material online
WebCT Educational Technologies (homebrew1.cs.ubc.ca/webct/)	Web-based authoring; Targets universities Chat, group projects, etc.; Free trial version
CyberClass, SAM, Course Technology (www.course.com)	Offers multiple courses only, tools can be used to create/support own courses.

which includes e-mail, listservs, and forums, supports non real-time communication (Williams, Sawyer, & Hutchinson, 1999; Dede, 1996). *Course Management Software* supports the administrative aspects of Eeb-based instruction such as enrollment and registration of learners, learner assessment and instructor-to-peer message broadcasting.

An ideal WBIS integrates all the components discussed using the technologies outlined in the previous section. Both the components and the integrating technologies are important to the system. Each integrating technology facilitates the effective linkage of a set of components, ensuring that the functions and transactions exchanged between those components can be completely and correctly completed.

To the developer, the systems perspective provides a structured foundation on which to design a WBIS. It assists in the identification of software needs, system architecture, hardware requirements and how these fit together to make a WBIS. Thus it ensures that the system developed is able to address all the functions and satisfy all the roles evident in WBIS.

The systems perspective provides the *instructor* with a clear understanding of how pedagogy, technology and the learners relate to each other and to the instructor in a Web-based instruction environment. With this understanding, the instructors are better able to tailor the course content to fit the medium of instruction. Instructors are also able to assess whether the various learning activities they desire to implement are in fact suited for WBIS. In so doing the instructors are able to prepare the content in ways that will maximize learning via the WBIS.

By understanding the nature of relationships among the key components of the WBIS and the types of interfacing technologies required to facilitate interaction among these components, systems *administrators* can manage the technology on which the entire WBIS is founded more effectively. The systems view helps them to analyze issues relating to bandwidth, traffic control, storage capacity, security features, and usage trends of the WBIS, hence providing better systems management solutions.

The content *authors* need to understand the systems perspective, too. The authors need to tailor the material they place on the Web and the scripting methods to 1) the infrastructure in place, 2) the course delivery style: whether the system tutors individuals or lectures to classes, 3) the orientation of the WBIS: whether the system supports a traditional classroom setting or is completely Web-based, 4) the kind of authoring system is used by the organization, and 5) the other interfacing technologies that are part of the WBIS. In case of adaptive systems, multiple versions of the content need to be written to support visual vs. textual oriented people, field-dependent vs. field-independent people, explorers vs. observers, and abstract vs. concrete oriented people. In reality, fully integrated WBIS are rare, and the few that exist are fairly rigid (example Course Technology and Prentice Hall's online courses.

Common practice has been to purchase individual technologies and try to incorporate them into a working system. Owing to differences in standards and protocols, the resulting systems are usually cumbersome. They exhibit limited functionality and are prone to a myriad of management and maintenance problems. Therefore, there is a real need for better WBIS. However, several issues, as discussed in the following section, prevent the emergence of such improved WBIS.

CRITICAL FACTORS FOR WBIS

Most existing WBIS use the Web to support the information distribution from the instructor to the student. The most common technique is to give each course its own Web site on which the syllabus and homework assignments are posted. Some instructors go further and include a glossary of terms, a list of frequently asked questions (FAQ), notes and slides, and links to outside readings. The above features can be incorporated with a simple HTML editor or by converting existing documents into HTML, which demands knowledge of HTML, FTP, and how to access a Web Server. Further, space on a Web Server is needed to host the material. In the development of more comprehensive WBIS, a number of critical issues, important to the successful deployment of the system, become apparent: build or buy, security, infrastructure, content vs. layout, standards, dynamic features, management issues and pedagogical issues.

Build or Buy: Currently, very few commercially available systems support all the components of a WBIS. Hence, the predominant approach used by most institutions to build their own systems: they rely on different components from various sources and then try to incorporate them under one umbrella as links from the course homepage. A good example for this approach is one from the IS Department at the University of Missouri, St. Louis. For the syllabus and assignments, a course homepage is used with material authored by the instructor. A set of books is used for the course material, an online testing tool from Course Technology for the quizzes, and eRoom (a shared Web-based workspace software) to enable interaction between peers.

Other institutions decided to develop their own systems. A great example is the ORION system by G. Steinberg at Kent State University. This system supports instructors with all of the following without requiring them to know HTML: syllabus creation, course material authoring, and online testing with an authoring component, grade book, and assignment grading. The assignment grading feature is unique among all the systems that we reviewed, and demonstrates the potential power of such systems: students submit online their Excel, Word, Power Point, etc. assignments, and a computer program grades them, updates the grade book, and provides feedback within seconds.

Most institutions rely on existing components and integrate them according to their needs. Hardly any system development methodologies for such undertakings exist. The closest that we are aware of are hypermedia development methodologies such as Relational Management Method (RMM) and the Object Oriented Hypermedia Design Model (OOHDM) (Balasubramaniam et al, 1995).

Access authorization and content security remain key issues for all Web-authors, since unauthorized agents can easily replicate the posted material. Therefore special measures such as password protection and encoding of material need to be considered. Such features require sophisticated programming knowledge, which the authors may lack. Another emerging strategy is the use of intranets to limit content-access to authorized personnel (Alavi, Yoo and Vogel, 1997; Benyon, Stone and Woodroff, 1997).

Infrastructure: A computer running a Web Server program, termed a host, is required to store the content and the supporting applications. Commonly used Web Server programs are Microsoft Internet Information Server (IIS) and WebSite from O'Reilly on a Windows NT computer or Apache on a Linux or NT server. Most instructors rely on department or school Web Servers, which takes away a lot of the maintenance and backup work, but could prevent the regular instructor from running or developing applications. Further, a Web Server needs to be connected to the Internet, and for that it requires an Internet Protocol (IP) address, better a registered name.

From the learner's perspective, access to the WBIS requires a computer with Internet access. Such access could be initiated at home using a modem to dial into an Internet Service Provider, or from a computer lab within the institution. For the developer this means that the users will have different connection speeds with various degrees of bandwidth, different types of graphic cards, monitors, browsers and browser versions, even different computers and operating systems, each of them displaying the material in a slightly different way. This requires tradeoffs in developing a WBIS and authoring content for it: the more advanced the features incorporated into the system, the less the number of people able to access it with their local computer system (Burkowski, Henry, Larsen and Mateik, 1997; Dennis, Poother and Natarajan, 1998).

Content vs. Layout: Most Web-authoring basically entails the encoding of documents in the Hypertext Markup Language (HTML). However, the same HTML document looks different on different computers, operating systems, browsers, monitors, and graphic cards. For standard documents this is not a problem. However, using standard HTML code to develop sophisticated graphical user interfaces (GUI) such as those currently used by Macintosh and Windows applications, and to make them look good on all user machines, is a very difficult, if not impossible task. For real layout control and interaction, Cascading Style Sheets (CSS), Dynamic HTML (DHTML), and scripting is needed (Liegle and Madey, 1997; Alloway et al., 1997).

Standards (Or lack thereof): The browser wars of the late 1990s have caused differences in the capabilities of the browsers. While there is a commonly agreed upon HTML standard, this standard is still evolving, with browser developers inventing new features daily. This compels authors either to use programming tricks to overcome the existing incompatibilities or to create multiple versions of the same document (Alloway et al., 1997; Dennis et al., 1998).

Dynamic Features: Three competing techniques exist that allow the incorporation of dynamic features in a Web page. These are 1) scripting languages (Java Script and Visual Basic Script) in conjunction with DHTML, 2) the use of 3rd party software such as the Shockwave plug-in, and 3) Java Applets. The author has to select between these technologies with the understanding that all Browsers do not equally support these technologies.

Pedagogical issues: Web-based education is a new field and few systems exist that utilize Web technology beyond plain hypertext (Benyon, Stone and Woodroff, 1997). Little is known about the effectiveness, appropriateness, and the implementation of pedagogy on the Web (Alavi, Yoo and Vogel, 1997). What we do know is mainly deducted from our knowledge of hypermedia and related navigation problems, e.g. the infamous "lost in hyperspace" syndrome. By using the Web for instructional purposes, we add additional layers between the learner and the training material: the computer and the operating system, the browser, and the interface that is used by the WBIS. Designers only have control over the last item whose display depends on the computer used by the learner. This makes it difficult to guarantee a certain "look and feel" for all users. In addition, the issue of academic dishonesty becomes increasingly important. The nature of WBIS makes it difficult to prevent cheating. Therefore, some institutions choose not to enforce any supervisory mechanisms, others rely on academic honesty, while the rest use controlled test environments. As an example, Kent State University controls the testing environment by using proctors in the computer lab (Janicki and Liegle, 1999).

Attendance and participation, or their verification, is another major pedagogical problem. While on the one hand electronic systems tend to encourage participation by otherwise shy students, typing skills, difficulties with grammar, and the elimination of face and body language impede the quality of participation. Discussion groups face the additional issues of lurking, moderation, and logging.

Management issues: There are different dimensions to management of WBIS: 1) Web-site administration to ensure that all course related information is stored in subdirectories, 2) content administration to ensure that content is current, correct, and that there are no lost links, 3) measurement of the system's effectiveness, and finally 4) cost effectiveness and cost estimation standards, principles and best practices regarding the management of WBIS are just beginning to emerge (Burkowski, Henry, Larsen and Mateik, 1997; Dennis et al., 1998).

TAXONOMY OF WEB-BASED INSTRUCTION SYSTEMS

There are three basic *types* of Web-based instruction systems (Janicki & Liegle, 1999): an *instructor-based system* utilizes the web primarily as a means of communication. Examples are software that allows an instructor to remotely-control students' Web browsers, pointing them to various sites in the course of the lecture. Real-time Web-based communication systems such as Palace, Pow-Wow, and IRC can also be used to teach over the Web. They employ a combination of video, voice, and text-only communication.

Computer-based systems lack an instructor. They present material, monitor progress of the learner, grade exams, give homework, etc. (all automatically. These are commonly called Intelligent Tutoring Systems (ITS) if they track individual progress and adapt to it, or Computer Based Training (CBT) systems if they do not personalize the material.

Semi-automated systems utilize computers for what they do best, e.g. grading multiple choice exams, while letting the instructor do what instructors do best (lecturing and answering questions).

WBIS have two main *cardinalities*: a *tutoring style* uses a one-to-one mode of communication between the system and the learner, while the lecturing style uses a one-to-many mode of communication between the system and many learners. A tutor does not necessarily have only one learner. Rather, the system personalizes the content delivered to each learner by customizing the instruction to suit the learning pace, the learning style, and the background knowledge exhibited by the learner. A *lecturing style*, on the other hand, does not personalize the course content. Each learner receives the same content in the same way and is expected to complete the same learning activities completed by all the other learners. However, each learner can access the content at different times and proceed through the learning process at a different pace in comparison to other learners.

There are two main *strategies* of WBIS utilization: in the *Web-mediated strategy*, the web is the predominant medium through which learners interact with the other components of the WBIS. The *Web-supported strategy* uses the WBIS to support a traditional instructional learning environment. Therefore, for this strategy the Web is not the predominant mode of interaction; rather, the traditional lecture remains the key means through which instruction is provided.

Table 2 gives an idea of what different types and combinations of WBIS are possible and could be used.

In an education setting or degree-granting program, it is very rare to find a computer-based system that does not require an instructor. The reason is that employers or other institutions do not yet accept computer granted degrees or grades. Thus, such WBT systems are used in settings where it is important for the individual to learn a particular knowledge or skill without the need to receive a certificate for it, and WBIS with an instructor are used when degrees or certificates matter. An examination of existing systems with respect to the pedagogical functions they perform ensues. These functions include lecture, testing, teamwork, course material and authoring.

Lecture: The mode of lecture differentiates between a Web-mediated and a Web-supported system. Online lectures were found in the education department of Kent State University and at the University of Missouri - St. Louis. Here, classes meet only very few times, especially in the beginning of the semester, to get to know each other

Table 2: Online Courses/Degrees

Course, Institution	System	Description
Hypermedia Structures and Systems, Eindhoven U. of Technology	Flexible Hypertext Courseware Calvi, L. and De Bra, P. (1998)	165 pages, 23 images. Enables links only if student is able to understand the knowledge it is pointing to.
MIS, U. of Missouri - St. Louis,	eRoom (Instinctive Technology) Course Technology	Uses web and textbook; eRoom for discussion, assignments. Uses course technology for tests/quizzes
Multiple Courses in IS Department, Kent State University	ORION developed by G. Steinberg (orion.kent.edu)	Web-based syllabus, lecture material in addition to book, extensive web-based testing and assignment grading.
Electronic Commerce University of Illinois at Springfield	COURSEWARE proprietary system developed by R. Hadidi	Web-based class was offered next to traditional class in Fall 99. http://mis.uis.edu/ecomm2/
Western Governors University	No specific system	Entire degrees are offered online using distance learning technology. http://www.wgu.edu/wgu/
University of Phoenix Online Campus	Apollo Learning Exchange (Alex®)	Offers online degree programs http://www.uophx.edu/online/
MBA, MS IS Drexel University	TopClass http://www.west.ie	Offers online degree programs http://www.drexel.edu/irt/distance/
Multiple Courses, New York University	Lotus Notes, Web	http://www.scps.nyu.edu/on-line/ http://www.scps.nyu.edu/virtual/
MBA U. of Akron, OH	Web, developed by B. Vijayaraman et al.	Offers online and traditional MBA. http://www.uakron.edu/cba/
LISP, Dep. of Psychology, U. of Trier, Germany	ELM-PE, G. Weber, M. Specht, P. Brusilovsky, F.Steinle	ITS teaching LISP. http://www.psychologie.uni-trier.de:8000/projects/ELM/elm.html

face to face. The rest of the lectures are then conducted online, either synchronously, using chat software, or asynchronously, using message boards, listservs and e-mail.

For nontraditional students, a large degree of asynchronous instruction eases the scheduling of their time. Current bandwidth limitations prevent meaningful real-time online discussions with more than 7-9 people; thus, lecturing in such a setting is either done in the traditional manner with one instructor "talking" (or typing in chat rooms) and the learners only asking questions. The alternative is to lecture in the conventional way in the classroom requiring physical presence of students in the class. For smaller groups in electronic classrooms, this type of lecture can be supported by WBIS.

Testing: For testing purposes, WBIS can only be used if the problem of authentication and identification is solved. This means that the system must be able to ensure that the person taking a test is in fact the person who he or she claims to be. In our opinion, all forms of Web-based testing should either be conducted in an open testing environment (where no restrictions are placed on the student) or in a strictly controlled testing environment such as a proctored testing center.

Testing is the one component of a WBIS that is very easy to implement and that also increases efficiency of the instructor. Computer programs are very good at distributing and grading standard types of tests, e.g. T/F, multiple choice, short answer and matching. They can even grade standard office-application homework assignments such as spreadsheets and power point presentations. Because of these reasons, most WBIS will include a module for automated testing (Janicki and Liegle, 1999).

The dimensions of electronic testing are: a) the tests/assignments are submitted electronically via e-mail, ftp or uploaded through special scripts, b) the grading is done by a computer program or by an instructor, and c) the test is done under supervision to prevent cheating, or it is a taken as an open book take-home exam. Table 3 gives examples for the different possible combinations.

Teamwork: Working with peers is a widely encouraged pedagogical practice. Potential advantages are 1) preparation for the real world, 2) fostering of learning from others and 3) learning by observing. Teamwork can easily be implemented in a WBIS using software like workflow, chat, and groupware (Chaffey, 1998; Alavi et al., 1997,

Table 3 Combinations of Testing

Submit	Electronic		Hand in	
Grading	**Computer**	**Manual**	**Computer**	**Manual**
Test Unsupervised	I Orion System: Students upload assignments, web-based programs grade, store scores in grade book.	II U. of Missouri, St - Louis: Electronic take-home, responses are emailed to instructor.	V Take home assignments. Instructor inserts student's disks and runs grading programs.	VI regular way of giving assignments or take-home exams by just posting them on the web
Test Supervised	III Orion System: Students show ID to take online-test in lab.	IV Traditional lab tests. Students take exam in lab, email or send results to write-only FTP sites.	VI Interim-state to III where the system is automated to accept assignments electronically.	VIII Traditional lab tests where students take part of exam in lab

McCormak et al, 1998).

Many commercial software packages exist and are used by instructors, e.g., Palace at KSU and eRoom at UMSL. This type of software eliminates one of the biggest problems faced by students that have to work in teams: scheduling meeting times and places. This technology can be successfully used even with the current bandwidth limitations, but from the work that has been done in examining the success of virtual teams we know that such teams can only be productive when the participants have met in person before (Liegle and Bodnovich, 1997).

Course Material and Authoring: The traditional course material consists of text book(s) and handouts. This type of material can be placed on the Web, too. We find a wide variety of combinations that are used in practice at this point in time. One issue is the problem of copyright protection on the WWW (Stallings, 1998). Since digital signatures are still not standardized and material placed on the Web can be easily replicated by downloading, many instructors and publishers remain hesitant to place their lesson plans and course notes on the WWW. Computer labs frequently complain about the skyrocketing number of students printing out the material instead of copying it. This has led many institutions to implement printout-charging mechanisms.

There is another pitfall that authors have to watch for. Early enthusiasts of hypertext systems rewrote their entire course material as a sequence of individual pages referencing to each other. Such a hypertext can be extremely useful as a reference tool when linked to a powerful search engine. However, students are disadvantaged when they cannot perceive structure in the course content and are unable to determine examinable material from the rest of the content. As long as exams and lectures follow a structured approach, the training material must also be organized in a standard way, requiring that Web pages are accessible via a sequentially organized table of contents.

Many instructors who are willing to place their material online find themselves in an awkward position: 1) the administration does not give them any additional support to do so, 2) it takes a tremendous amount of time, and 3) their limited HTML, scripting, programming, and graphic design skills inhibit the development of quality Web sites. Yet despite all their effort, students still prefer paper copies to electronic notes. This can be attributed to the discomfort of reading material on a screen and an inability of most systems to allow for annotations to the displayed material; however, a number of systems that support this feature are emerging (TopClass and WebCT), but for "homegrown" systems, this still requires programming knowledge (Janicki & Liegle, 1999).

For those instructors without HTML knowledge, a number of options exist: 1) some departments and schools provide Web-authoring services and convert existing material, 2) many of the existing word processors, spread sheets, and presentation software come with an save-as-HTML option, 3) a number of WBIS come with sets of templates that do not require the content author to know HTML (Tool Book II, Orion), or 4) learn HTML.

IMPACT OF TECHNOLOGICAL TRENDS ON WEB-BASED INSTRUCTION

Information technologies evolve rather rapidly. Because Web-based instruction systems heavily depend on information technologies, any advances in these technologies are expected to radically impact their quality, functionality and efficacy. Technological impacts on WBI can be analyzed from three perspectives: software, hardware, and networks. Of these, advances in software and network technologies are expected to impact WBI the greatest. Not only are the developments in each individual area meteoric, the integration of these areas promise unending possibilities in the enhancement of WBIS (Figure 2).

Figure 2: Next Generation WBIS

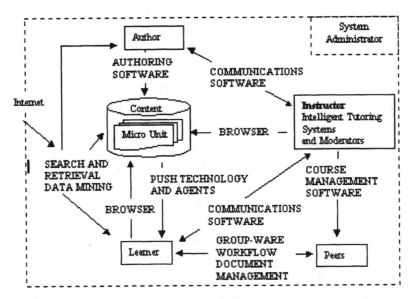

Core developments in *software* are progressing in nine key areas: groupware, messaging, Web browsers, document management, search and retrieval, data mining, visualization, push technologies, and intelligent agents (Hibbard, 1997; Meso and Madey, 1998). Recent years have seen the emergence of Web-accessible *group-ware* packages providing powerful collaboration tools for use in WBIS (Chaffey, 1999). Emerging *messaging tools* allow for application and hardware platform independent sharing of messages. The adaptation of universal mail and messaging standards and the domain name system has provided a structured means by which content can be easily accessed on the Web leading to an influx in the population of Web users. Increasing usage of XML (extended markup language) is expected to simplify the classification of documents through the use of tags that define both the display and the content properties, making *search and retrieval* and overall document management much easier (Chaffey, 1999; McGormak et al, 1998).

Emergent Web-based *document management* technologies are expected to enhance the collaborative authoring, distribution, and the electronic sharing of documents throughout the community of users (Chaffey, 1999; Laudon and Laudon, 1998).

Electronic document management systems are increasingly being linked to workflow systems. *Workflow systems* define, create, and manage the execution of workflow through the use of software. They facilitate the completion of a job by providing a checklist of tasks conducted, the sequence in which these tasks are to be conducted, and the status of a job (Chaffey, 1999).

Push technologies and *intelligent agent technologies* are aimed at identifying content of interest to a user and making it accessible for the user. This means that students do not have to search for information, but it is delivered to them. For example, when the author updates the course content, or when a peer posts new information to the Web site, the student is immediately informed (Hibbard, 1997; Williams et al., 1999).

Intelligent agents go further to provide filtering services, automatic reply services, organization of content and provision of advice to the user with respect to the content. Advances in these technologies promise to increase the interactivity of WBIS. Combined with *data mining* and *search* and *retrieval* technologies, they allow the learner to source for high quality content from a wide cross section of sites external to the course and incorporate this content into the learning activities currently being undertaking on the WBIS (Hibbard, 1997; Laudon and Laudon, 1998).

The overall cost of computer *hardware* is dropping rapidly. While writing this chapter, the first "free" computers were made available to people willing to endure commercials while using the computer. This trend will continue making it possible for anybody to afford the basic technology needed to access WBIS. It is expected that processing power, storage capacity, screen size and resolution will continue to improve, and thus overcome the capacity and feature limitations inherent in current WBIS (Williams et al., 1999; Laudon and Laudon, 1998).

More and more people will be able to access, and thus, use the Internet, representing a growing potential market for WBIS. Additionally, the standards regulating the storage and transmission of multimedia on the Internet are beginning to mature. WBIS can now be developed for these standards and thereby reach any potential learner regardless of location, time of day, infrastructure and software.

The drastic rise in the population of people using the Internet and the volumes of data being exchanged is placing tremendous pressure on the Internet's channel capacity. Sufficient bandwidth remains a major obstacle to the potential growth of WWW. This in turn limits the growth of WBIS. However, the bandwidth limitation will become a thing of the past once current high-speed networks such as Internet2 and Internet Next Generation are commissioned by the end of this millennium (Stallings, 1998).

IMPACT OF ECONOMIC AND SOCIAL TRENDS ON WEB-BASED INSTRUCTION

Traditionally, education occurred in a linear format by starting at school, going to college, and obtaining the necessary skills for a lifelong career. As the employees in their career realize the need for further training, they would return to school for graduate studies. As competition increased, corporations became less willing to release their employees for long periods of time to receive training. This lead to an influx in evening programs which allowed employees to work and go to school concurrently. However, they confined the employees to a particular location.

The transition from the industrial to the knowledge economy has revolutionized organizational structures and the work paradigm (Alavi et al, 1997; Guglielmino et al, 1997; Bernstein, 1998). The employee of today is expected to be more flexible, more mobile, and multi-cultural. This demands that the employee engages in continuous learning or frequent retraining in an environment that allows access to the pedagogy regardless of location and time of day. This new model of learning cannot be satisfied via traditional methods like evening programs, hence the growing demand for Web-based training.

This development of skill specific learning can lead to a new training paradigm: like many existing courses that teach a particular skill, employees want to learn only those skills necessary to be able to do their job. We will therefore have a large number of micro courses, each of them relying on a clearly defined set of prerequisite skills, and each of them teaching only one particular element (Schank, 1998). This means that we will no longer have an "Introduction to MIS," but a micro unit on word processors, one on spreadsheets, one on databases, etc. An employee who wants to learn an advanced level micro course only has to learn that subset of micro courses that teach the knowledge required to learn the higher level course. And here is the difference between a simple CBT/WBT system and a WBIS. The training systems teach the skills but do not provide the learner with an accredited certificate for successfully completing the course.

Employers will want to see from new hirers some documentation of proof that they can do the job. Therefore, WBIS are needed that not only teach the material like CBT/WBT systems do, but also perform some form of quality control in the form of practice and testing, ending with a quality seal in form of a certificate or grade. At the same time, a standard is needed that defines the content of these micro-courses and how a level of proficiency is to be demonstrated in them. This could be done by some controlling governmental organization, but most likely such a standard will be defined by the company that develops the first successful and widely used WBIS (Alavi et al, 1997; Guglielmino et al, 1997; Bernstein, 1998).

CONCLUSIONS

This chapter began by presenting the systems perspective of WBIS and by explaining its relevance to the development, implementation, and management of Web-based instruction. The components, the integrating technologies, and the critical issues related to a WBIS were discussed and a WBIS taxonomy presented. The WBIS taxonomy and the systems perspective were used to classify and analyze existing implementations of Web-based instruction with a view to identifying their completeness and functionality. The impacts of the social, economic and technological changes that are expected to influence WBIS were then presented.

Current WBIS implementations are designed to support traditional methods of instruction. They automate testing, make lecture notes available to students and provide messaging services to support team work. None of the systems reviewed met all of the requirements of a WBIS. Most implemented only a fraction of the functions in a WBIS and were severely constraint by technological limitations, incompatible standards and lack of pedagogy-oriented design.

Advances in information and communication technology are contributing to the emergence of improved WBIS through the incorporation of new technologies such as push technology, intelligent agents, workflow and document management systems, search and retrieval and data mining. The maturing Internet standards will make it easier to incorporate interfacing technologies into a WBIS. Further, advances in networking technology eliminate access and data transfer limitations that impede present WBIS.

The socioeconomic changes currently taking place are changing the learning behaviors and expectations of learners. Globalization, a highly mobile society, the need for continuous learning and access to learning on demand require an entirely different educational paradigm. This has led to a growing demand of a flexible, adaptive, time and geographic independent learning environment.

This chapter illustrated that WBIS meet the functionality and flexibility requirements needed to support this new instructional paradigm. At the same time, this emerging instructional paradigm is made possible by WBIS.

REFERENCES

Alavi, M., Yoo, Y. & Vogel, D. (1997). Using Information Technology to Add Value to Management Education, *Academy of Management Journal*, 40 (6), 1310-1333.

Alexander, S. (1998). Teaching and Learning on the World Wide Web. Debreceny, R. & Ellis, A. (Eds.), Innovation and Diversity - The World Wide Web in Australia. AusWeb95 - *Proceedings of the First Australian World Wide Web Conference*. Lismore, NSW, Norsearch Publishing.

Alloway, G., Bos, N., Hamel, K., Hammerman, T., Klann, E., Kradjcik, J., Lyons, D., Madden, T. Magerum-Leys, J., Reed, J., Scala, N., Soloway, E., Vekiri, I., Wallace, R. (1997). Creating an Inquiry-Learning-Environment using the World Wide Web. *Journal of Network and Computer Applications*, 20, 75-85.

Balasubramaniam, V., Ma B. M., Yoo, J. (1995). A Systematic Approach to Designing a WWW Application. *Communicatinos of the ACM*, 38(8), 47-48.

Benyon, D., Stone, D., Woodroff, M. (1997). Experience with Developing Multimedia Courseware for the World Wide Web: The Need for Better Tools and Clear Pedagogy. *International Journal of Human Computer Studies*, 47, 197-218.

Bernstein, D. (1998). WBT: Are We Really Teaching? *Inside Technology Training*, 2(2), 14-17.

Burkowski, E., Henry, D., Larsen, L., Mateik, D. (1997). Supporting Teaching and Learning via the Web Transforming Hard-copy Linear Mindsets into Web-flexible Creative Thinking. *Journal of Network and Computer Applications*, 20, 253-265.

Chaffeey, D. (1998). *Groupware, Workflow and Intranets: Reengineering the Enterprise with Collaborative Software*. Boston: Digital Press.

Dede, C. (1996). Emerging Technologies in Distance Education for Business. *Journal of Education for Business*, 71(4), 197-204.

Dennis, A., Pootheri, S., Natarajan, V. (1998). Lessons from Early Adopters of Webgroupware. *Journal of Management Information Systems*, 14(4), 65-86.

Guglielmino, P., Murick, R. (1997). Self-directed Learning: The quiet Revolution in Corporate Training and Development, *SAM Advanced Management Journal*, 62(3), 10-16.

Hibbard, J. (1997). Knowing What We Know. *Information Week*, October 20, 46-64.

Janicki, T., Liegle, J. (1999). *Are Web-Based courses built on a foundation of accepted learning pedagogy?* Manuscript submitted for Publication.

McCormak, C., Jones, D. (1998). *Web-Based Education System*. New York: Wiley Computer Publishing.

Meso, P., Madey, G. (1998). Developing Web-Based Agents for Knowledge Management. In Hoadley, E., Benbasat, I (Eds), *Proceedings of the Association for Information Systems Americas Conference*, Baltimore, MY, 183-185.

Laudon K., Laudon, J. (1998). *Management Information Systems: New Approaches to Organizations and Technology* (5th Edition). Upper Saddle River, NJ: Prentice Hall.

Laffey, J., Tupper, T., Musser, D., Wedman, J. (1998). A Computer-Mediated Support System for Project-Based Learning. *Educational Technology Research & Development*, 46(1), 73-86.

Liegle, J., Bodnovich, T. (1997). Information Technology in Virtual Organizations: A needs Assessment from the Perspective of Human Resource Management. In Gupta, J. (Ed), *Proceedings of the Association for Information Systems Americas Conference*, Indianapolis, IN, 536-538.

Liegle, J., Madey, G. (1997). Web-Based Training: A Case Study on the Development of an Intranet Based Training Course. In Gupta, J. (Ed), *Proceedings of the Association for Information Systems Americas Conference*, Indianapolis, IN, 521-523.

Stallings, W. (1998). *Data and Computer Communications* (5th Edition). Upper Saddle River, NJ: Prentice Hall.

Szabo, M., Montgomery, T. (1992). Two Decades of Research on Computer-Managed Instruction. *Journal of Research on Computing in*

Education, 25(1), 113-133.

Schank, R. (1998). Horses for Courses. *Communications of the ACM*, 14(7), 23-25.

Williams, B., Sawyer, S., Hutchinson, S. (1999). *Using Information Technology: A Practical Introduction to Computers & Communications* (3rd Edition). Boston: McGraw-Hill.

Chapter XV

A Case for Case Studies via Video-Conferencing

Ira Yermish
St. Joseph's University

INTRODUCTION

Demands are being placed on educational institutions to provide course content in new and complex forms to address the needs of an ever more mobile student body. This chapter explores the issues of delivering a normally highly interactive graduate level course using these new technologies within the demands of organizational missions and constraints. We will argue that a course covering topics of organizational technology assimilation is the ideal place to begin this process. It will describe the problems and issues that were faced in one typical course. We will also suggest that this is an ideal area to focus future research in organizational adoption of new technologies that address missions and strategies.

The "passing of remoteness" is how one commentator described the phenomenon of the rise of the Internet and other distance-shrinking technologies. Ever since the advent of television, educators have wrestled with the viability of using this technology to reach wider audiences. Educational television facilitated the distribution of high-quality program content in a one-directional fashion. Yet for many educators, this approach lacked the interactive give-and-take so important to the educational process. Video-conferencing has been used heavily in industry to reduce the costs of travel within far-flung organizations. This technology made it possible to meet "face-to-face," even if the faces were a little blurry and movements were jumpy at best. The visual cues so often considered important in determining if messages were being properly communicated were now available. Immediate visual feedback leads to more productive dialog.

Educational institutions have always lagged behind industry in adopting these technologies for two critical reasons. First, there is the psychological barrier that faculty must cross adapting new technologies. One could argue that despite the popular view of "radical academia", the reality is much more conservative. Changes in curriculum or program delivery can be glacial. Second, and perhaps more critically, the investment in the infrastructure to support these technologies was beyond the means of the organization. Yet these same constraints are tipping the balance toward the requirements to adopt these technologies. Resource constraints, particularly in the area of a scarce, high-quality faculty, competition among educational institutions for market share, and the declining technology costs and improvements in transmission quality are combining to drive experiments in this area.

In graduate business education, there has always been an emphasis on the interactive approach to education. Universities pride themselves on, and like to print, glossy brochures about the interactive classrooms where the faculty and students conduct highly charged dialogues on topics of immediacy. One popular form of this dialogue is the case study approach. Similar to the kinds of activities one might find in a law school moot-court experience, potential managers must, with often limited and yet at the same time overwhelming data, process situations, explore options and develop recommendations. The instructor may provide a gentle push based upon the direction the class takes but shouldn't, assuming good case study pedagogy, be dominating a one-sided presentation. Unlike a lecture in nuclear physics, there is no way to predict the exact direction of the class interests - a very dynamic approach is required. How can the video-conferencing technologies address the needs of this very complex form of the educational experience? This chapter will review our experiences and organizational issues surrounding this issue and raise some future research questions that should be addressed to improve the quality and efficiency of this specific form of education.

INSTITUTIONAL BACKGROUND

St. Joseph's University is a medium-sized Pennsylvania institution serving primarily the Delaware Valley markets. With 2,800 full-time undergraduates and nearly 5,000 part-time undergraduate and graduate students it has, especially since the 1960s, served the "non-traditional" student market. Part-time MBA, Executive MBA, and industry specific masters' programs (e.g., Food Marketing, Pharmaceutical Marketing and Public Safety) were developed to reach specific educational market niches important within the general geographic area. As one narrows the focus of particular programs the need to serve larger geographic areas is inevitable. From the point of view of the program directors, any means of expanding this reach and, hence filling up classrooms (read: generating more income) is desirable. Competition among the many institutions in this region continually places a premium on innovative delivery mechanisms. This region has a large concentration of pharmaceutical companies, and this market has been an especially valuable one for St. Joseph's. But, given the vagaries of highway arteries, students can be excused for their reluctance to brave rush-hour traffic to attend courses at our main campus. The approach frequently taken at institutions like St. Joseph's is the creation of "satellite campuses" in corporate training centers or in the facilities of other educational institutions closer to the students but without similar programs. Though only thirty miles from the main St. Joseph's campus, the campus of Ursinus College in Collegeville, Pennsylvania, has provided an excellent alternative for students to attend the evening MBA program. This campus is located near a concentration of pharmaceutical companies from which we draw a significant student population.

The approach to these "distance-education" sites has been simple: have the faculty face the expressway rush-hour traffic or fly to the remote city, instead of the students. A "customer-first" business strategy if ever there was one. From the administrator's point of view this worked beautifully and would continue to work well if it weren't for a countervailing pressure. In the effort to add more sections at the remote sites for student flexibility, the academic department chairs found it necessary to hire adjunct faculty to cover the increased number of sections. This actually exacerbated the problem, making these distance education sections even more profitable. Unfortunately, the pressures of perceived quality, largely brought on by the requirements of accreditation (AACSB, in this case) made the situation untenable. Full-time regular faculty coverage demands made scheduling problems a nightmare.

The president of St. Joseph's University, Nicholas S. Rashford, S.J., has always been interested in the use of technology in delivering education. He and his academic cabinet have been strong supporters of technology. To this end, they created an *ad hoc* committee, the Distance Education Task Force, to explore how technology could be used to address these frequently conflicting organizational goals:

- Expanding Programmatic Content
- Expanding Geographical Reach
- Improving Educational Quality
- Reducing Educational Costs

One of the outcomes of this Task Force was a joint program with Ursinus College to establish a direct link between two technology-equipped classrooms. These facilities would be used to provide simultaneous classes on the two campuses, particularly to serve a number of graduate education programs (e.g., MBA and Health Administration). The two institutions agreed to invest in the technology to implement these classrooms to address these needs. Each site included a PictureTel facility for two-way video and audio including their LiveShare computer projection facility. This facility makes it possible to share computer applications running on PCs at either end of the T-1 dedicated line connection (with ISDN backup). On a large projector students could see PowerPoint presentations, videotapes, slides, or share comments on a whiteboard while the instructor or other students were being shown on one of the two monitors at the front of the class. The most important aspect of this design was the equivalence of the two sites. The faculty member could conduct classes from either site easily. This goal was nearly met with minor differences.

From a programmatic point of view, the most significant issue was the scarcity of faculty resources. For many narrowly focused courses, it was impossible to adequately cover the needs of the two campuses. This seemed like an ideal opportunity. As a member of the task force, I volunteered to offer my upper division, MBA course "Case Studies in Information Resource Management" as one of the first courses using the new facility.

COURSE DESCRIPTION

This course has been an integral part of our management information systems specialization in the traditional MBA (evening) program at St. Joseph's for many years. Using traditional textbooks (e.g., Applegate, et al 1996), updated Harvard case studies as well as some additional sources of special cases (e.g., Liebowitz and Khosrowpour, 1997 or Wysocki and Young, 1990), students explore through written and oral presentation, the current issues in strategic information technology management. During the fifteen-week semester students prepare individual case analyses and make formal group case presentations. Table 1 shows an outline of the assignments and course flow. A major goal of the course is to improve analytical and critical thinking skills. Creativity and cross-functional thinking is stressed throughout. There is very little lecture, just enough to emphasize critical conceptual issues. Our goal is to get students to apply the theoretical concepts learned in foundation courses and to think in cross-functional and interdisciplinary ways.

The course is divided into three major phases:
- Individual Case Analysis
- Group Informal Presentation
- Group Formal Presentation

During the first phase, all students prepare the same set of cases for general class discussion. Short two or three page analyses are submitted at the time of the class to guarantee student preparation. The major goal of this phase is to address the conceptual issues and to give students feedback on the quality of their analytical processes. It is here that we can correct many of the defects in logical analysis. For example, students will frequently make one-sided recommendations without adequately exploring the possible negative arguments.

In the second phase, the class is arranged in teams of three to four students. Each team is responsible for the presentation and discussion of a case. All students are required to read all cases. To foster creativity and to give students an opportunity to get more comfortable with the process of presentation, this phase is ungraded. This does not mean, however, that there is no feedback. On the contrary, there is much greater feedback from both the instructor and the students. Students in the class evaluate each presentation on the basis of content and presentation quality. There are often lively debates in this phase concerning the styles used. The only grading that is done during this phase addresses student participation.

In the final phase, each team makes a formal presentation of one of the cases (or case series). The instructor formally grades each

Table 1 - Course Outline

Date	Site	Assignment
Sep 1	SJU	Introduction, Minicases
Sep 8	URS	Text Chapters 1-5 (read text material only) Case 5-1 Mrs. Fields Cookies
Sep 15	URS	Text Chapters 6-9 Case 2-1 KPMG Peat Marwick: The Shadow Partner HBR 9-397-108 KPMG **Written case assignment number 1 on KPMG series**
Sep 22	SJU	Text Chapters 10-13 Distance Education Workshop, Chat Rooms, Minicase
Sep 29		**Yom Kippur - No Class**
Oct 6	URS	Case 9-1 Toyworld Discussion, Developing Presentation Strategies that use the technology to its fullest
Oct 13	SJU	Electronic Commerce and the Virtual Organization Case 1-1 Veriphone, HBR 9-398-030 Veriphone Case 4-4 Open Market, HBR 9-198-006 Ford Motor Company **Written case assignment number 2**
Oct 20		**Spring Break - No Class** Paper evaluations will be e-mailed
Oct 27	SJU	**Informal presentations (with immediate evaluations)** **Written case assignment number 3 due with presentation** Group 1 Presentation: HBR 9-396-283 China's Golden Projects Group 2 Presentation: Case 4-5 Proctor and Gamble
Nov 3	SJU	Group 3 Presentation: Case 10-1 Xerox: Outsourcing ... Group 4 Presentation: Case 11-3 Chemical Bank: Tech Support
Nov 10	URS	Group 5 Presentation: HBR 9-198-007 Network Computing at Sun Microsystems
Nov 17	SJU	Review Evaluations - Group Meetings for Formal Presentations
Nov 24	SJU	**Formal presentations (e-mailed evaluations)** **Written case assignment number 4 due with presentation** Group 3 Presentation: National Mutual Series Group 4 Presentation: Air Products Series
Dec 1	SJU	Group 5 Presentation: Singapore Series Group 1 Presentation: Frito-Lay Series
Dec 8	URS	Group 2 Presentation: Burlington-Northern Series
Dec 15		Chat Room with Final Comments, Etc.

presentation for content, flow, graphic presentation and ability to reply intelligently to questions.

I'm not sure I knew what I was getting myself into when I volunteered for this course. Despite participating in a short seminar for faculty describing the techniques of video-conferencing courses, I was not prepared for the new environment. As a freewheeling instructor, rarely locked into one place in a classroom, the demands of the technology often were frustrating and negatively affected the quality of the instruction. Add to this a problem of over-subscription (thirty-five students at the two sites instead of the normal twenty-five student limit) and we have the ingredients for disaster. Fortunately, we were able to get by some of the technical problems almost guaranteed for such a new facility. There were times when I would lose the train of thought while trying to make sure that each student was being shown properly on the screen for the remote site. Within about six weeks, we could handle to controls and still maintain control of the class content. But the lessons were learned. More about the administrative issues later.

From the students' standpoint there were a number of interesting opportunities in this first attempt in the fall of 1997. For most of the students, despite working for large companies with corporate communications operations including video-conferencing, this was their first opportunity to engage in discussions that crossed the electronic video frontier. It didn't take long to get both sides of the connection to participate in normal class discussions. The interesting events began during the informal presentation phase. Working with document cameras, presentation programs, automatic following video cameras and the like was a good experience for the students in learning one of the key concepts of the course: technology assimilation. They quickly learned that it was not easy to walk up to the podium, press the buttons and make a quality presentation. The interaction of technology and content became obvious to them.

A number of technical issues that are not present in local presentations surfaced. For example, the high quality graphics with complex color schemes that could be incorporated into a local presentation often took noticeable and annoying minutes to be transmitted between the stations. "Cute" presentation tricks like dissolves and fades didn't work smoothly. For this ungraded opportunity to gain facility, they were very grateful. During the second, a graded phase, they demonstrated significant improvements, demonstrating that most had learned the lessons of the first phase. These were translated into quality distance presentations that used the media to convey the message without being an intrusion.

In short, the students were able to learn how one information technology could be best incorporated within an organizational context. They learned how to modify their approaches to deliver messages and to engage in creative dialog across distances. Ideas easily flowed across the electronic barrier.

ADMINISTRATIVE ISSUES

This facility addressed one critical issue quite easily: faculty coverage. Given the number of students in this upper division course across the two campuses it resolved a need for adjunct faculty. This has been an important issue as St. Joseph's as it strives for AACSB accreditation. The requirement for greater coverage by regular full-time faculty has also been marketed by the University as providing a higher quality educational opportunity. Increasing opportunities and flexibility for students has always been a desire of the program directors while at the same time creating scheduling nightmares for the academic department chairpersons.

Another important institutional benefit from both the St. Joseph's and Ursinus perspectives has been the publicity associated with the electronically based alliance. As institutions compete more intensely for shrinking populations, this advantage could be significant.

From the academic standpoint, the faculty is gaining experience in using new technologies to deliver course content in new ways. In addition to the video-conferencing mode, we are beginning to use web-based technologies to share comments and conduct discussions. In this second semester of this course (fall 1998) I have added a small component of this to the course structure. MBA students, often working full time and traveling in their work, appreciate the ability to write cases, transmit messages and get feedback from any location in the nation. Where some institutions are going toward completely remote distance education, St. Joseph's maintains the critical importance of a "home base" around direct student/teacher interaction within the structure. The terms of the alliance required that the instructor be at both locations during the term (see Table 1). From a business standpoint, students are addressing case issues in remote modes so similar to the kinds of problems described in some of their cases (e.g., Veriphone in Applegate, et al 1996).

Not all, however, is "sweetness and light" with this concept. From a student standpoint, there must be some diminution of perceived quality when the instructor is a small figure on a TV screen instead of a live being in a face-to-face environment. Several sets of course evaluations have echoed this issue. For some students, normally attending the main site, their perception was that their course "value" was being diminished by the part-time lack of an on-site lecturer. Some students balanced this by the increased flexibility in their educational opportunities afforded by this structure. From the faculty point of view there is a course organization that is much more complex. There are issues of materials distribution (via FedEx, fax, e-mail, courier) and personal travel. There is the difficulty in getting to know students at remote locations. When dealing with a course like "Case Studies" these issues can be quite complex.

One of the most important technologies that proved invaluable in this environment has been the use of web-based course support software (e.g. CourseInfo or WebCT). These tools have made the immediate distribution of materials and the submission of papers and reports much simpler. Faculty, however, have a greater job coordinating these activities. One cannot just take a stack of papers home, mark them, and then hand them out at the next class.

From the organizational perspective, these advances do not come cheap. In addition to the technology infrastructure required for the operation of these courses, there is additional overhead (e.g., technicians, hardware and software maintenance and equipment upgrades). The bar has been raised in education and institutions must invest to maintain growth and reputation. During the first year the faculty member was responsible for running the technology at the site he/she was working from. A technician would be available on the remote site only. It was clear that this was not an adequate mode of operation. In the case mode of teaching, there must be so much interaction between the teacher and the student that asking the faculty member to also attempt to control the technology is untenable. During the second year, technicians were provided at both sites for controlling the operations.

Finally, there is the faculty compensation issue, an issue that St. Joseph's is struggling with at this time. Given the increased workload associated with distance learning course structures, how should faculty be compensated? A highly interactive course like "Case Studies" brings these issues to light rather clearly.

SUMMARY AND FUTURE TRENDS

"Case Studies in Information Resource Management" provides

an excellent laboratory for studying how new technologies can be implemented in education. At a "meta" level, we can examine how the institution explores and adopts this technology for its educational "value-chain." How do we integrate video-conferencing, web-technologies and traditional printed materials in a seamless, effective way? When is it appropriate and how do the organizational missions and strategies affect the technology implementation strategies? This author sees this as an important new line of research in technology management within a critical industry.

The future for these technologies will be web-based. It is already clear from the economics examined in this experiment that dedicated communications facilities (e.g. T1 lines) do not come cheap, especially when used only for a small fraction of the time. Constantly examining the balance between video transmission rates and costs of delivery will be the responsibility of university technology managers. Furthermore, the technologies (both hardware and software) must become more seamless to eliminate the requirements for technological support. When these hurdles are crossed, there is no doubt that this mode will become the norm and not just an experiment.

REFERENCES

Applegate, Lynda M., F. Warren McFarlan, James L. McKenney, *Corporate Information Systems Management: Text and Cases*, Fourth Edition, Irwin, Chicago, IL, 1996,

Liebowitz, Jay and Mehdi Khosrowpour (editors), *Cases on Information Technology Management in Modern Organizations*, Idea Group Publishing, Hershey, PA, 1997.

Wysocki, Robert and James Young, *Information Systems: Management Practices in Action*, John Wiley & Sons, New York, 1990.

Chapter XVI

Web-Based Training for the Network Marketing Industry

Janet M. Hugli
University of Ottawa, Canada

David Wright
University of Ottawa, Canada

The Internet is radically changing the way we do business and in the ways we deliver information and training. Companies must use effective methods for distributing information and training materials in a timely manner to ensure their competitive edge.

With globalization, dispersed workforces, remote management and an ever increasing information glut, ensuring that employees are properly trained to represent the company and the industry to which they belong becomes on ongoing challenge, if not a nightmare. One industry that is particularly vulnerable to the challenge of providing consistent, high-quality training, is the Network Marketing Industry.

This chapter will look at the Network Marketing Industry training requirements in light of the industry needs and available training sources. An assessment of the fit for the inclusion of Web-Based Training (WBT) as a support tool will be made. A global overview of the potential market sizing will be reviewed with a look at future trends and opportunities.

The objective of this chapter is to determine the potential fit of WBT for the Network Marketing Industry. More specifically, this chapter will:

- Define the training requirements at each stage in the network marketing discovery process.
- Compare the current methods being used to offer training.
- Highlight deficiencies/opportunities with the current training systems.
- Suggest a role for WBT in the Network Marketing Industry.
- Calculate the potential market size within the industry.
- Highlight the challenges for using WBT in the Network Marketing Industry.
- Identify the benefits of WBT for the Network Marketing industry.

BACKGROUND

Network Marketing

Network marketing is simply a form of distribution for products and services. It is the movement of products or services from the manufacturer or producer to the end user via word of mouth marketing which is one of the most effective and cost-efficient methods of distribution. According to Rod Nichols (1995), Network Marketing is "conversational marketing" — people talking to people.

J. P. Getty further explains the concept of network marketing when he says that he would rather have 1% of the efforts of 100 people than 100% of the effort of one person. Network Marketing is all about having many people work together, either part-time or full-time, and distribute a small amount of consistent volume of products or services.

Network marketing works on the concept of geometrical growth. As each new distributor (company representative) introduces their company's products or services to their own circle of influence, word of mouth advertising expands to new circles and continues exponentially to expose increasing numbers of people to the products and the individual companies. Products are normally ordered through the use of 800 numbers with delivery being direct from the home company to the end user. The distributors are rewarded for their "word of mouth" advertising through a company specific compensation plan.

Products which have been proven to be successfully distributed via network marketing include health care products, consumables, and telecommunications.

Web-Based Training (WBT)

WBT is currently in its infancy. It links into the power of the WWW which is a wide area hypermedia information service. The end user requires a computer and a modem to allow access to the Web. The Web allows computer users to access large information databases and interact with a wide range of information sources. It can include everything from simple information gathering, to a much more integrated training approach which could include audio, video, graphics, animation, and/or live interaction with a facilitator and/or other students.

WBT extends the capability of classroom training and/or of conference calls. From the end user point of view it is interactive, ubiquitous, easily accessible, inexpensive, allows learning at one's own pace and offers total flexibility in terms of time availability and scheduling. From a course delivery point of view, WBT allows a broad geographical reach, multi-platform capabilities, flexibility to use concurrently with other training systems and great ease for the updating of the training materials. It can also offer the option of integrating the WBT with live support via audio or video-conferencing.

For individual Network Marketing companies who offer WBT to their employees additional benefits can be derived in terms of JIT (Just in Time Training), training of the masses concurrently, tracking and billing options, impact analysis.

Although WBT is very early in its life cycle process, with the evolution of technology, the increased penetration of computers, increased access to the Internet, faster speeds on modems, the introduction, adoption and use of the Internet as a training tool will undoubtedly increase rapidly.

ISSUES AND OPPORTUNITIES

Overview

Critical training challenges exist in the network marketing industry as the responsibility for the training of each new distributor lies with their "sponsor" (the person who introduced them to the business). Varying levels of expertise and time availability of the sponsor are major determinants of a new distributors success in the business.

Although there are many current forms of training being used within the network marketing industry such as audioconferences, one-on-one coaching, traditional classroom training, printed reference, and many others, each with their own set of strengths and weaknesses, there are several key overall industry challenges which the existing forms of training are not currently addressing well. Some of the most critical challenges for training (and trainers) in the network marketing industry, include:

- credibility of the actual training, both from a content and from a delivery perspective.
- consistency in the delivery of the training materials.
- timeliness in the training and development of new distributors, and availability of ongoing training for more experienced distributors.
- accuracy regarding the content of the training (specifically regarding product training and the explanations of compensations plans).
- dilution of the training programs (short circuiting the full delivery, or inaccurate presentations).
- inexperience or inability of the trainers.
- overall quality of the training .

Each distributor operates as an independent business entrepreneur, therefore added costs for training development and time commitments required to attend training events often limit the participation levels.

Traditional one-on-one training with sponsors continues to be very effective; however, it is very time consuming for those with large organizations (large sales forces), and its success is largely dependent on the sponsor commitment, experience, credibility, and availability. In many cases, the sponsor may have been someone who has only recently joined the company and may in fact not have even received their own training.

Three way calls (which include on-line training), teleconferences, and printed materials all play an important role in the development of new distributors; however, with globalization, and efforts to build businesses outside one's local territory consistency, timeliness and quality of training run the risk of becoming diluted. Access to WBT could undoubtedly minimize the inconsistencies, increase the quality, and extend the ability for JIT (Just in Time) delivery of training components fitting the new distributor's time schedule. More importantly, enthusiastic distributors can immediately gain access to proper training without waiting for their own sponsor to go through the learning curve.

Network Marketing Conceptual Model

The Network Marketing Conceptual Model (exhibit 1), outlines the thinking process potential network marketers experience. For each of the stages, it identifies:

- WHO the key learners would be (audience).
- WHAT kind of training requirements would be necessary (needs).
- WHERE the network marketers are currently obtaining the required training.
- WHY alternative training sources are required.
- WHAT types of results could be generated from the integration of WBT with current training methodologies (WBT Benefits).

It is recognized that potential network marketers may not consciously go through the full thought process outlined, as many are introduced to the industry and the specific company directly by their potential sponsor without any reference points for comparison. However, the decision process will include all of the aspects identified at some point in their network marketing experience. Putting discipline into the decision-making process will help enhance the overall credibility of the Network Marketing industry.

The potential for WBT to support the network marketing industry varies at each stage in the conceptual model and in its potential application and delivery of training. WBT is viewed as a powerful "future" delivery mechanism for effective training as the life cycle of development and sophistication for WBT is in its infancy, and the network marketing industry is still striving to gain mainstream acceptance as a viable alternative distribution method. WBT can provide the capability for full interactive training with appropriate measurements and feedback mechanisms. In addition, WBT can be an excellent integrating tool for existing training processes.

With the network marketing population being widely disbursed, WBT makes good sense. Travel times to training locations can be eliminated and consistency and quality of the message can be maintained. The end result is that participation levels in industry training programs can be increased by making the training ubiquitous, and retention rates of distributors within the companies can be increased.

TRAINING IMPACT

Measuring the impact of training initiatives is always challenging as the results may be influenced by other factors working in tandem with the training programs. However, clear targets and objectives need to be established at the onset to validate the extent to which training has had an impact.

Specific measures need to be evaluated at each of the stages of training to ensure that the training is not simply a "warm bath". The following list identifies a sample measurement criteria for the key stage of learning cycle - IMPACT. Tracking of these elements would confirm the extent to which WBT was effective for the Network Marketing Industry, once again recognizing that there are likely many other support mechanisms that would be operating simultaneously with the training initiatives.

Reaction level (enjoyment levels of the training experience), *learning level* (the degree to which the learner is successful during the training session in meeting the training standards), and *transfer level* measurements (the trainee ability to transfer the new knowledge/ skills to the workplace) should also be developed for cognitive, psychomotor and affective learning.) For the purpose of this chapter, the focus will be on impact level measurements.

IMPACT LEVEL - TRAINING MEASUREMENT CRITERIA
a) **Independent Distributors**
- increased pay checks, increased organizational size, higher volumes of product being moved
- reduction in the training time, and duplication of effort by distributors (personal and training time extended to new distributors)

- faster speed in building the sales organization
- faster attainment of management levels

b) **Network Marketing Companies**
- longer retention levels of the distributors, decreased drop out rate
- increased sales volumes, increased profitability
- decreased distribution support costs
- increased market penetration
- enhanced corporate image

c) **Network Marketing Industry**
- heightened credibility, respect, leveraging power
- increased distributor retention rates
- increased lobbying power
- increased speed, and consistency in the delivery of key industry information

d) **Educational Institutions**
- increased enrollments, increased revenues
- increased profile for the institution - recognition for innovation and forward thinking

MARKET POTENTIAL

To determine the market potential for WBT in the Network Marketing Industry, statistics were reviewed for the:
- Overall Population of North America
- Network Marketing Industry
- Computer Use / Internet Access
- Overall Demographics

Although statistics for a direct correlation of network marketers, with Internet access were not available, projections were made using population statistics and demographics. As the Network Marketing population is viewed as paralleling the overall population statistics (Wood, 1999), these projections are viewed as an accurate estimate for base line analysis.

Exhibit 2 summarizes the overall market size and indicates an initial target potential of 3.39M within North America. The market size was estimated several ways to confirm the final numbers. Age, gender and general population numbers were consistent in estimating the market size at approximately 3.4 million. This number represents people who are currently active in their Network Marketing businesses and have access to the Internet.

The overall population of North America is 300.965M. There are currently 85 million people who have access to the Internet, representing 28.24% of the total population. As the network marketing industry parallels the general population, 28.24% of the active network marketers (12 M), results in a forecast of 3.39M in the target market.

Overall Population of North America (Canada & U.S.)

The overall population of North America (Canada and the U.S.) as shown in Table 1 is used as the base line for determining the potential market size for WBT for the Network Marketing industry.

Several factors reinforce the utility of using North America as the forecasting base:

- The penetration of computers is currently the highest in North America positioning the continent for faster acceptance of alternate training methodologies.
- English is generally the common language, which will minimize translation/adaptation challenges with learning materials.
- The use of Network Marketing as an alternate distribution method in North America represents the highest initial numbers globally.

It is recognized that Network Marketing is a global industry, and thus the potential numbers for WBT could be significantly increased. However, limited information is currently available on global statistics, and the North American numbers provide useful statistics for a baseline.

As the Network Marketing industry is viewed as a parallel for the overall population statistics, Figure 1, can be used as an indication of the age distribution of the industry. Figure 1 shows only those individuals between the ages of 18-79, as there is a legal requirement in the Network Marketing industry for individuals to be a minimum of 18 years of age to conduct business. Retirement ages are not imposed and distributors can be actively involved in their businesses to their age of choice.

The population base of Network Marketers between the ages of

Table 1: Overall North American (NA) Population

Total North American Population	U.S. (000's)	Canada (000's)	Total (000's)
Total	270,290	30,675	300,965
Male	132,489	15,184	147,673
Female	137,801	15,492	153,293

Source: U.S. Bureau of the Census, International Data Base

NOTES:
- Canada represents 10.19% of the total North American (U.S. & Canada) population
- Gender split for both Canada and the U.S. is 49% male, 51% female

Figure 1: North American Age Distribution

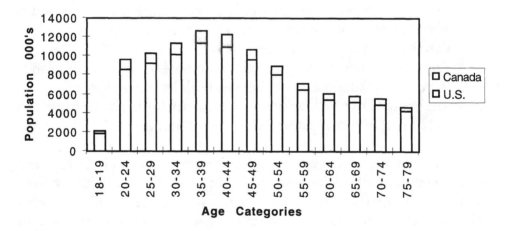

Source: U.S. Bureau of the Census, International Data Base

NOTES:
- 30% of the target population is in the age categories between 25-49 (baby boomers)
- both Canada and the U.S. show a significant distortion in the overall age distribution due the impact of the baby boomers
- 28.8% (86,716.8K) of the total population is not involved/eligible for Network Marketing (<18, >79)
- 32.4% (97,355.2K) of the total population is between the ages of 18-40
- 38.8% (116,894K) of the total population is between the ages of 40 - 79

18-79 (those eligible to conduct business) is 214,245K as shown in Table 2.

Target Market for WBT in the Network Marketing Industry Ages 18 - 79 (North America)

Having determined the total existing population of North America as over 300 million, and reviewed the overall age distribution, the forecast for WBT for the Network Marketing industry is further refined by age in Table 2. The forecast model includes ages 18 -79.

Of the target market of Network Marketers (214,249.2K), the age distribution is:

- 45.4% are between the ages of 18 and 40
- 54.6% are between the ages of 41-79

Table 3 uses 214,246K as the baseline for estimating the growth in the overall potential market target of network marketers. Using growth rates forecasted by the U.S. Bureau of Census, the overall population growth indicates a potential for network marketing from the population base of 221,272K by the year 2002.

Network Marketing Statistics

According to Doris Wood (1999), president emeritus for the

Table 2: Target Market for WBT in the Network Marketing Industry

North American Population (Ages 18 - 79)	U.S. Totals (000's)	Canadian Totals (000's)	North American Totals (000's)
Total	191,772	22,474	214,246
Male	93,785	11,140	104,925
Female	97987	11,334	109,321

Source: U.S. Bureau of the Census, International Data Base

NOTES:
- 49% of the target population is male, 51% of the target population is female, for both Canada and the U.S. (the gender statistics are consistent with the overall population)

Table 3: Growth Projection of Overall Target Market (NA)

Gender/Year	1998 (000's)	1999 (000's)	2000 (000's)	2001 (000's)	2002 (000's)
Male	104925	105774	106631	107495	108366
Female	109321	110206	111099	111999	112906
TOTAL	214246	215980	217730	219494	221272

Source: U.S. Bureau of the Census, International Data Base

NOTES:
- growth rate for the U.S. population is .8%
- growth rate for the Canadian population is .9%
- weighted average growth rate for the North American population is .81

Multi-Level Marketing Industry Association (MLMIA), there are now more than twelve million distributorships in North America. These distributorships include:

- one person distributorships
- couples, and
- business entities.

As a result, the total number of people involved in the Network Marketing Industry is understated, however statistics are currently not available on the percentage distribution among the three categories. The potential for double counting of individuals who are involved in more than one Network Marketing company is also not reflected, however, the multiple participation levels will help adjust the overall numbers in the situations where more than one person is involved in one distributorship).

Using the 12 million statistic, the representation of network marketers in North America represents 5.6% of the target population. Industry trends suggest that Network Marketing participation levels will continue to grow. Some of the key trends stimulating the growth of Network Marketing include:

- corporate downsizing, fear of restructuring, search by many business professionals to look for a "Plan B".
- increased awareness of the power of the industry. Doris Wood states that there are over 1200 network marketing companies in

North America, representing over $22 billion in sales annually, with an expectation that the growth level will climb to over $88 billion and a network of over 20 million distributorships within the next decade.

- increased credibility of the industry as high profile companies implement network marketing distribution methods to complement existing distribution.
- individuals' desire to pursue alternate/additional business opportunities while maintaining existing work commitments.

The Direct Selling Association (1997) reported the total Network Marketing participation levels for the years 1993-1997. Using these numbers, the MLMIA statistics, and a projected growth rate of 13 percent, Figure 2 displays the ten year forecast to the year 2009.

Growth factors ranged between 10% and 18% during the years 1993-1997. A 13 percent growth factor has been used to forecast future growth to the year 2009.

The gender comparison is quite different from the overall population statistics, with females representing 64.9 percent of the network marketing population base, males representing 35.1 percent (1997). This compares to the overall population statistics where females represent 51% of the population, males 49%.

COMPUTERS / INTERNET

Statistics on computer penetration and Internet access are challenging to validate. They fluctuate regarding the individual population, as well as regarding the overall household numbers. For reference, a number of household statistics, and computer/Internet sources are compared in Table 4 and Table 5.

To begin, household statistics are presented in Table 4. These numbers are important in calculating the overall Internet access, recognizing that in many cases the network marketing distributorship is a partnership or couple.

The aspect of forecasting that is not difficult to validate is the overall rapid growth. However, few experts appear to agree on just what the growth level will be. For WBT to be a viable delivery mechanism for training for the Network Marketing industry, users must have a computer, and also have access to the Web. The growth

Figure 2

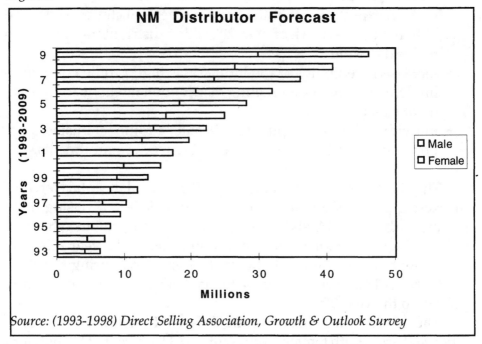

NM Distributor Forecast

□ Male
□ Female

Source: (1993-1998) Direct Selling Association, Growth & Outlook Survey

rates for each of these elements vary considerably.

Table 5 provides a variety of sources quoting computer and Internet statistics. These numbers are combined with the statistics in Table 4 to compute the forecast of overall Internet access in North America.

Based on the widely varying statistics, the 1998 total base line for *individuals* with access to the Internet used in this report for forecasting is eighty-five (85) million.

This baseline number of 85M individuals indicates that the overall

Table 4: Household/Family Statistics

Statistics	Sources
Average size of a household in the U.S. = 3.02	15
Total Households in the U.S. = 102,528	16
Mean size of Family = 3.18	10
Average Size of Household = 2.64	10

Table 5: Computer/Internet Statistics

Statistics	Sources
People on line in the U.S. = 101 million	22
Households on line in U.S. = 35M	17
Less than half of the U.S. households (43%) own computers (March 1998), a number expected to jump to 50% by the end of this year.	1
Only 2/3 of the U.S. households with modems subscribe to an on-line service or Internet provider, however it is expected that virtually every household with connection capability will have Internet access by the end of the decade.	23
Domestic On-line Internet households are rapidly expanding (U.S.) = 29.1 million	24
American computer users are wired to the Internet = 60% (3Q 1998) American adults with Internet access (3rd Q, 1998) = 72.6 million	22
Computer penetration in Canadian households = 60%	6

NOTES:
- individual population access to the internet ranges from 79 million to 111 million (adding to the quoted numbers a 10% increase for Canada)
- using an average household size of 2.64, multiplying the reported household access numbers, and adding a 10% factor for Canada, the individual population access for North America ranges from 83 million to 112 million

North American Internet access is currently just over twenty-eight percent of the total population.

Figure 3 indicates the overall forecast for Internet growth by gender the next five years.

The Network Marketing population is consistent with the overall population statistics (Wood, 1999). Demographic information is important at the design stage of WBT to ensure that the training addresses the specific needs of the users groups. Additional primary research will be required to further support the training initiatives as there is limited (if any) available at this time.

WBT Potential for the ACTIVE Network Marketing Population

Using the previous numbers forecasted for the overall network marketing industry and Internet access, the estimated number of ACTIVE network marketers having access to the Internet, and thus become potential users of WBT is shown in Table 6.

Figure 3: Internet Access Forecast

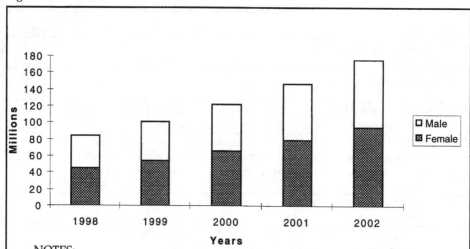

NOTES:
- the growth rate used for forecasting the growth of Internet access for the next four (4) years is twenty (20) percent, from the 1998 baseline of 85 million
- the four (4) year forecast shows internet access levels at 176 million in 2002, representing fifty-nine (59) percent of the overall population
- the Internet gender representation, while closer in its match to the overall population, also shows a variance with females at 54%, and males at 46%

The total *number* **of internet users by gender would be as follows:**
- Female 54% of total internet access of 85 million = 45.9 million
- Male 46% of total internet access of 85 million = 39.1 million
  Using population statistics to bring these numbers to *overall percentages*:
- the number of females who have access to the Internet as a percentage of the total population = 45.9 million / (300 million * 51%) = 30%
- **the number of males who have access to the Internet as a percentage of the total population = 39.1 million / (300 million * 49%) = 26.6 %**

Table 6: WBT Potential for the ACTIVE NM Population

Active Network Marketers	12 M
% of population with access to the internet	28%
Estimated Target Market for WBT for the Network Marketing Industry (1998)	3.39 Million

NOTES:
- 28% represents 85M individuals with internet access based on the total population of 300.9M

To further confirm the forecast, the numbers have been reworked based on age, and based on gender.

1. Age

Of the target market of Network Marketers (214,249.2K), the age distribution based on overall population numbers is:
- 45.4% are between the ages of 18 and 40
- 54.6% are between the ages of 41-79

The Internet access numbers are slightly different. From Figures 4 to 5:
- 55% of the Internet access population is between the ages of 18 and 40
- 40% of the Internet access population is between the ages of 41-79

Using the Internet access and age distribution numbers, the percentage of Internet assessors is:
- 18- 40 (85 million total accesses * 55% = 46.75 million. 46.75 million / (.45 * 300) = 34.6% of the total population in the age group 18-40
- 41-79 (85 million total accesses * 45% = 38.25 million. 38.25 million / (.55 * 300) = 23.18% of the total population in the age group 41-79

Taking the Network Marketing numbers, and the previous sets of data into account, the number of active Network Marketers with Internet Access is:

12 million (97,355.2/214,249.2) * 34.6% + 12 million (116,894/214,249.2) * 23.18% = 3.404 million

Figure 4: Active NM with Internet Access

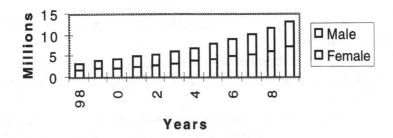

Figure 5: Computer Users — Ages

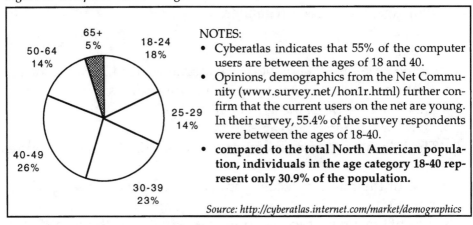

NOTES:
- Cyberatlas indicates that 55% of the computer users are between the ages of 18 and 40.
- Opinions, demographics from the Net Community (www.survey.net/hon1r.html) further confirm that the current users on the net are young. In their survey, 55.4% of the survey respondents were between the ages of 18-40.
- **compared to the total North American population, individuals in the age category 18-40 represent only 30.9% of the population.**

Source: http://cyberatlas.internet.com/market/demographics

2. Gender

Further validating by gender, the Network Marketing industry gender distribution is as follows:
- Female representation is 64.9%
- Male representation is 35.1%

The Internet gender representation while closer in its match to the overall population, also shows a variance, although much smaller.
- Female at 54%
- Male at 46%

The total numbers of Internet users by gender would be as follows:
- Female 54% of total Internet access of 85 million = 45.9 million
- Male 46% of total Internet access of 85 million = 39.1 million

Using overall population statistics to bring these numbers to overall percentages:
- the number of females who have access to the Internet as a percentage of the total population = 45.9 million / (300 million * 51%) = 30%
- the number of males who have access to the Internet as a percentage of the total population = 39.1 million / (300 million * 49%) = 26.6 %

Taking all three (3) sets of information into account, the number of Network Marketers with Internet access is estimated as follows:

- 12 million * 64.9% * 30% = 2.336 million
- 12 million * 35.1% * 26.6% = 1.12 million
- TOTAL   3.456 million

Working the numbers by age, gender, and general population, the results consistently show that the current potential target market for WBT in the Network Marketing industry is over 3.4 million. These people are currently active in their Network Marketing businesses and have access to the Internet.

Looking to the future, and using the Network Marketing average growth rate during the past four years of 13 percent, the following chart indicates the ten-year forecasted growth for WBT for the Network Marketing Industry in North America.

The current gender profiles are continued at 64.9% female, 35.1% male. The forecast indicates a market potential for WBT of 13.134 million within North America by the year 2009.

WBT Opportunities for the Network Marketing Industry

With 1998 target market size now determined as 3.39 million active network marketers who access to the Internet, the specifics of training content need to be reviewed.

Table 7 highlights some of the potential applications where WBT can help support the Network Marketing industry and specifies some key potential content areas for course offerings. Courses could be delivered as individual modules or packaged within general subject areas.

FUTURE TRENDS

Network Marketing Trends

The Network Marketing industry is forecasted to continue to grow. Technology will help support the growth of this industry, which is conducted by a widely dispersed population that puts a premium on time and flexibility. Effective training, delivered just in time with ease of access will be required to support the industry and

Table 7: Applications and Course Contents

Potential Audience	Need/Application	Course Contents / Key Subject Areas
Corporate Business Managers a) small b) medium c) large	• enhance understanding of the network marketing industry • evaluate the potential of network marketing as a distribution method for existing or planned products • obtain a credible, unbiased overview of the industry, existing companies and compensation structures • determine the fit of network marketing for the distribution of company products/services • establish a selection criteria and guidelines • anonymity for research & evaluation	• industry overview • compensation structures • industry success factors • company reference lists
Network Marketing Companies	• enhance overall professionalism of distributor teams • ensure consistent, quality training and communications • reduce development and training time and costs • offer distributors quality education • offer a tool for ongoing support • increase retention levels	• industry overview • industry success factors • general management training • leadership development • accounting • legal guidelines • recruiting support
Existing Network Marketing Distributors	• obtain quality, consistent, timely training • reduce reliance on upline support team • enhance personal confidence, and personal credibility • JIT @ the distributor's convenience	• general management training • leadership development • accounting • legal guidelines • tools to manage the business • recruiting support • advertising methods and ideas
Potential Network Marketing Distributors	• obtain a credible, unbiased overview of the industry, existing companies and compensation structures • avoid high pressure solicitation from specific company distributors • anonymity	• industry overview • compensation structures • industry success factors • company reference lists • distributor success factors
Universities / Colleges / Business Students a) accreditation b) continuing education	• certification, program accreditation • demonstrate leading edge technology and product distribution methods • include new option(s)/course offerings to support education curriculum • offer special interest development • expand new student markets	• industry overview • compensation structures • industry success factors • company reference lists • distributor success factors • advertising methods and ideas • demographic analyses

help build the overall industry credibility.

Demographers like Faith Popcorn in her book "Clicking", and David Foote in his book *Boom, Bust and Echo*, highlight trends which make Network Marketing the ideal opportunity for a growth business in the near future, and introduce new challenges in delivering proper training to the network marketing distributors. One of the key trends which will challenge the delivery of effective training to the masses includes the concept of "cocooning" whereby a large shift to work at home is occurring. Extended travel times, suburban living, high charges for metro parking, reallocation of office space are all phenomena encouraging traditional employees to work from home.

"Cashing out" is becoming a common preoccupation with middle management, many of whom are making "mid-life" reevaluations of priorities and shifting their focus towards enhanced family lives. There is a strong desire among most for less work related stress, and more time with families. Network marketing allows the pursuit of all of these objectives. For those "traditional" employees, who exercise the option of "buy outs", the termination packages provide sufficient funds to allow themselves time to initiate their new businesses. This "safety net" is particularly well suited for those reviewing the network marketing option. Delayed gratification and delayed financial rewards are experienced by most in this business, and "buy out" packages can help cushion the void while the new distributors work to build their organizations to a sufficient size and product volume to sustain their business efforts.

For those not choosing to elect the option of a "buy out", many employees are actively looking for a "Plan B" opportunity that will allow them to continue in their current positions, however offer a safety net to support the existing uncertainty. Use of the Internet for research, learning and personal training is increasing, and for the network marketing industry offers tremendous opportunities for support in terms of providing wide sources of references, and flexible access.

Burke Hedges, the author of "Who Stole the American Dream" believes that the network marketing industry is where franchising was 30 years ago and has only recently begun to receive the respect it deserves. He believes that network marketing will experience the same growth patterns of franchising, which contributes to over one-third of the U.S. Gross National Product.

Paul Pilzer, the author of "Unlimited Wealth" believes that "network marketing sales will double every 3 to 5 years". This industry is definitely in growth mode. Increasing numbers of professionals are joining the business both on a part-time as well as a full-time basis. The potential of the network marketing industry is unquestionable. By supporting its development and the training of the independent distributors with technology tools such as WBT, network marketing will skyrocket through its momentum stage.

Computer/Internet/WBT Trends

Within the past 30 years (since the introduction of the Internet), the way that people do business has dramatically changed. The explosion of Internet hosts from barely 1000 during the first 15 years of Internet life, has exploded to over 30 million hosts by 1998, representing over 100,000 interconnected networks and well over 70M users in 240 countries (Zimmerman and Mathiesen, 1998). The annual growth rate of hosts has been 40 to 50 percent during the past few years demonstrating unbelievable commitment and potential for the new technology.

Modem speeds are increasing with more than two-thirds of the users with speeds above 28.8. The increased speeds allow for not only faster surfing, but also the use of more complex graphics and video. The key reasons for people accessing the Internet are research and e-mail. Although the percent of people purchasing on the net is still less than 1%, significant time is spent obtaining product information. Products that sell particularly well on the Internet include: hardware, software, books, travel and electronics.

IMPLEMENTATION CHALLENGES

Although the use of WBT shows great potential for the Network Marketing industry, its introduction and adoption will not be without challenges. Some of the anticipated challenges which may delay the adoption of the technology as a key training tool, or limit the full integration, include the following:

- *User readiness.* WBT is a new (and in many cases untested) way of delivering training. The end user will need to be willing to change the way they are accustomed to learning, moving out of their comfort zones.

- *Learning styles.* Course designs will need to take into consideration different learning styles to ensure the greatest impact. WBT may prove most successful with experiential learners. Others may experience challenges, and participate with limited commitment.

- *Access to a computer.* Growth in penetration of computers is positive, however, for those without access, WBT is not an option. Initial set up costs may be a prohibiting factor for some potential users. Although computer costs have declined significantly, and access fees to the Internet are nominal, there is still hesitance on the part of many network marketers to invest money in their personal development until their businesses are profitable. It is a bit of the case of "which comes first, the cart or the horse".

- *Access to the Internet.* Use of the Internet is also growing rapidly, however, without access, WBT is not an option. Incremental costs may be a factor for the end user.

- *Speed of modem.* End users modem speed will impact the training experience. Slow modems will undoubtedly cause frustration, and negatively impact the learning experience. Cost will be a factor for the end user.

- *Industry sponsor.* Content credibility, non-bias presentation of the learning materials will be important for generic course offerings. Alternative sponsor could be educational institution.

- *Executive support and demonstrated commitment.* Support will be required in the form of initial investment, as well as in ongoing maintenance support. Company leaders will need to ensure a long-term view to WBT support to ensure it does not become "another flavor of the month," and diminish the quality, accuracy, and timeliness of the training provided.

- *Basic literacy.* Literacy levels vary greatly in North America, and even more around the world. The utility of WBT will be largely dependent on the user's ability to read, and to comprehend the information being delivered.

- *Language.* In a global environment translation capabilities will be required. Although some Internet providers currently provide translation, quality is still a challenge.

- *Basic computer literacy.* Computer literacy levels vary greatly.

Comfort with a computer and knowledge to use the computer and access the Internet will be foregone required necessities.

- *Suite of programs.* Enticing end users to participate in WBT will require a product portfolio that is perceived as useful interesting and constantly updated and enhanced. A one course offering will do little to encourage repeat visitors to the site.
- *Web performance.* The Web is slow for highly interactive applications which may limit the use and flexibility of different training options. Delays may be experienced, frustrate the user, and limit future participation.
- *Technology.* Bandwidth and browser limitations may restrict the instructional methodologies used. Limited bandwidth will result in slower performance for sound, video and graphics. Plug-ins can be downloaded; however, online support will likely be required in the initial stages.
- *User support.* Introduction of a new way of learning will undoubtedly require on-line user support. The question arises over who will provide, and who will fund. Mediated WBT will be useful to support WBT during the transition phases, to build user confidence, and minimize initial frustrations with new methodologies.
- *Security.* Information integrity will be important. Effective security measures will need to be used to authenticate the user of the training course. Although information integrity is already provided by TCP on all Web accesses, end users will require assurances that they exist.
- *Ownership rights.* In a highly competitive industry, ownership of the generic materials will be contested.

Despite the many current challenges anticipated with the introduction of WBT to the Network Marketing industry, the Web is changing the way we do business around the world. Planning for its integration within the existing training initiatives now, will be critical for the future success of the industry. Once the end users, industry associations and individual network marketing companies embrace the concept, WBT will takeoff with the potential to revolutionize the industry.

CONCLUSION

This chapter has reviewed the Network Marketing industry and its potential fit for WBT. It has uncovered many training areas which although in some cases are being addressed, are experiencing challenges regarding quality, consistency and JIT delivery. Current training methodologies were reviewed in light of the Network Marketing conceptual model to identify possible opportunities for WBT. Many WBT opportunities were identified at each stage in the conceptual model.

The market potential was analyzed for North America. The numbers indicate that almost six percent of the overall population is currently involved in Network Marketing, and over 28 percent of the population has access to the Internet. This results in a market potential greater than an estimated 3.4M for WBT. The Network Marketing industry is growing at an average of 13 percent, and access to the Web is growing well over 20 percent per annum. These numbers suggest a very healthy opportunity for WBT within the industry.

Despite the rosy picture, there are many challenges to be addressed to ensure the successful implementation of WBT. End user readiness, and psychological acceptance of an alternative learning methodology will likely be the greatest hurdle. However, the industry needs to position itself for the future success and demonstrate leadership in the adoption of technologies that will help support the industry as a whole.

Introducing WBT will excite primarily the early adopters who are already comfortable with a computer and with using the Web. However, with the rapid increase in computer penetration and Web access, with an intensively competitive industry, and an industry who is striving for mainstream acceptance in the marketing world, leveraging tools that will help position the industry as leading edge will entice the early majority to follow quickly. Careful attention must be placed on technology limitations of the end users when designing the training programs. Inadequate equipment by the users to view and/or participate in the training will cause high levels of frustration and diminished participation levels.

WBT is not intended to replace existing forms of Network Marketing training, rather to enhance them and extend their capabilities. JIT training , improved quality and consistency and more flexible access to the end users are just some of the key benefits discussed that will make WBT a perfect fit for the industry. WBT shows great promise for the Network Marketing industry. The potential size of the market is huge, the potential users are widely disbursed, and access to inexpensive high quality training on a regular basis are all important elements to the end-user industry distributor. WBT appears to be an excellent fit for the Network Marketing industry.

Partnerships among business, industry, government and educational institutions will be important for full adoption and continuity of WBT programs. They will help serve to augment the potential of WBT within the Network Marketing industry.

REFERENCES

BOOKS / ARTICLES

Angus Reed Polsters. (1999). CTV Television Interview. *Computer Penetration Levels in Canada.*

Broersma, M. (1998). ZDNN, *Survey: 20% of the U.S. households don't want PCs.*

Candon, Don (1999). President, Candon & Associates, Strategic Planning and Training.

Direct Selling Association (1997). Industry Facts. *Growth & Outlook Survey*, Washington.

Marks,W. (1996). *Multi-Level Marketing - The Definitive Guide to America's Top MLM Companies,* Second Edition, (Arlington, TX: The Summit Publishing Group.

Nichols,R. (1995). *Successful Network Marketing for the 21st Century,* Grants Pass, OR: The Oasis Press/PSI Research.

Poe, R. (1997). *The Wave 3 Way to Building your Downline*, Prima Publishing.

Statistics Canada, *Market Research Handbook* - Catalogue 63-224 Annual.

Wood, Doris (1999). President Emeritus, MLMIA (Multi-Level Marketing Industry Association).

Zimmerman, J. & Mathiesen,M. (1998). *Marketing on the Internet ,* Third Edition. Gulf Breeze, FL: Maximum Press.

INTERNET SOURCES

Industry Canada - Strategis- Information and Communications Technologies, Paul T. Dickinson (in co-operation with Statistics Canada)

"Access to the Information Highway: Canadian Households"
http://ferret.bls.census.gov/marco/031998/quint/15_000.htm. U.S. Bureau of the Census, International Data Base. *Annual Demographic Survey - March Supplement - 1998.*

WWW.filename.com/wbt/pages/advdis.htm. *Web Based Training Information Centre*: WBT Online Learning, Distance Education.

http://ccwf.cc.utexas.edu/~mcmanus/wbihtm#Why. *Delivering Instruction on the World Wide Web.*

FreeEdgar - Forester Research - *Newbridge Profile Corporate.*

http://www.mds.org. Quarterman's Estimates. *Network Marketing Trends/Growth.*

www.focusoc.com/cities/coto/house.html. *U.S. Household Statistics.*

http://ferret.bls.census.gov/macro/031998/quint/3_000.htm. *U.S. Household Statistics.*

www.communitysystems.com/households_online.htm. *U.S. Household Statistics.*

Computer/Internet Demographics

http://cyberatlas.Internet.com/market/demographics/ages.html

http://cyberatlas.Internet.com/market/demographics/education_levels html

http://cyberatlas.Internet.com/market/demographics/income_levels.html

http://cyberatlas.Internet.com/market/demographics

http://www.cyberatlas.com/big_picture/demographics/mainstream.html

www.adsl.com/pressroom/adsl_pc_growth.html. Kim Maxwell. *Growth of PC Households*

www.cityweb.com/cmp/presentation/internethouseholds/html. Jupiter Communications. *Domestic On-Line Internet Households*

http://tenb.mta.ca/phenom. Dr. Thomas L. Russell, *"The No Significant Difference Phenonema"*

www.survey.net/hon1r.html. Opinions, Demographics from the Net Community

Network Marketing Conceptual Model

- interested prospects
- committed entrepreneurs
- new network marketers
- network marketers

CURIOSITY SEEKING STAGE

Audience
- speculative entrepreneurs

Needs
- general industry knowledge
- company overviews & compensation plans
- general product overviews

Current Sources
- word of mouth from existing distributors

Current Challenges
- info. biases
- info. accuracy
- distributor pressure

WBT Benefits
- ubiquitous access
- anonymity
- accuracy of info.
- flexible timing

Audience

INTERESTED PROSPECT STAGE

Needs
- detailed industry knowledge
- industry success criteria

Current Sources
- company sponsored info. sessions
- sponsor literature

Current Challenges
- info. biases
- info. accuracy
- info. quality

WBT Benefits
- accurate, consistent info.
- credibility of info.
- customization for industry, company or product grouping

Audience

EVALUATION STAGE

Needs
- detailed, unbiased, credible training on overall industry
- evaluation criteria and methods

Current Sources
- minimal
- sponsors looking for new prospects

Current Challenges
- strong biases from recruiting sponsor
- minimal overall knowledge among industry network marketers

WBT Benefits
- heightened awareness of industry potential as well as challenges
- increased confidence of new business partners

Audience

SELECTION & DECISION STAGE

Needs
- company specific information on products, compensation plan & company

Current Sources
- audio, video tapes
- company meetings
- sponsor
- conference calls
- literature

Current Challenges
- participation levels
- measurements
- credibility of sponsor and / or upline

WBT Benefits
- eliminate sponsor learning curve (time lag)
- integrate with existing tools
- minimize obsolescence of print materials

Audience
- active business building

EXPERIENCE STAGE

- passive wholesale customers

Needs
- general management
- leadership
- business / accounting
- budgeting
- marketing
- team building
- presentation

Current Sources
- ad hoc company functions
- own initiative

Current Problems
- travel times
- investment
- timing of events

WBT Benefits
- easy access
- minimal investment
- quality / consistency
- time flexibility
- expanded reach
- JIT

EXHIBIT 1 Candon & Associates ©

Exhibit 2: Market Sizing - Distance Learning Potential
Network Marketing

NORTH AMERICAN POPULATION
N = 300.9M

INTERNET USERS
N = 85M

Active Network Marketing
Distributors
N = 12M

Network Marketers
with Internet Access
N = 3.39M

About the Authors

Linda K. Lau, Ph.D. (Rensselaer Polytechnic Institute) is a financial consultant associate with Salomon Smith Barney, Inc. in Richmond VA. For the past five years, she was Assistant Professor and Discipline Coordinator for MIS in the School of Business and Economics at Longwood College, Farmville VA. She was the author and coauthor of numerous articles and an ad-hoc reviewer of the *Information Resources Management Journal* and *SAM Advanced Management Journal*. Her name was also published in the Who's Who Among America's Teachers, 5th edition (1998) and International Who's Who of Professionals for the Year 1997. Her past research interests include using Behavioral Anchored Rating Scales (BARS) for employee performance evaluations, developing Web pages, writing applets using Java programming language, and distance learning.

* * *

Eric C. Adams is a Technology Coordinator for the Catholic Diocese of Monterey. Eric's primary duties include providing technical support and professional development to school staff personnel on the integration of technology with classroom curriculum and the use of technology to support instructional methodologies. He also manages the acquisition, installation and troubleshooting of technological hardware, software and infrastructure on the school site. He has previous experience training teachers and developing curriculum for schools in Shanghai, P.R.C. and Hiroshima, Japan. Adams received a BBA in Entrepreneurship from Pace University in 1992, and a MST in Elementary Education from his alma mater in 1995. Eric is presently a Doctoral student in Pepperdine University's Educational Technology program.

Mitchell Adrian is an Assistant Professor of Management at Longwood College. He earned his D.B.A. in Management from Mississippi State University and has published in a number of academic journals and proceedings including the *SAM Advanced Management Journal, Journal of the Academy of Business Administra-*

tion, Southern Business Review, and the *Journal of Education for Business.* His research interests include human resource aspects of quality management and the continuing developments of electronic communication tools and their effects on human interactions.

Zane Berge is currently Director of Training Systems, Instructional Systems Development Graduate Program at the University of Maryland UMBC Campus. Of his work in computer-mediated communication in education, most notable are his series with Mauri Collins. In 1995, a three volume set, *Computer-Mediated Communication and the Online Classroom,* was published that encompasses higher and distance education, and then in late 1997 a four-volume set of books, *Wired Together: Computer-Mediated Communication in the K-12 Classroom* was published. In 1998 he co-edited the book, *Distance Training: How Innovative Organizations are Using Technology to Maximize Learning and Meet Business Objectives,* (Jossey-Bass). berge@umbc.edu.

Richard Discenza is Dean of the College of Business of the University of Colorado, Colorado Springs. His primary research areas are Production and Operations Management, Information Systems; and Productivity and Quality Management. He has authored over 100 publications in the area of business. He is married to Suzanne, a speech pathologist who is currently pursuing a Ph.D. in Public Administration with a Health Policy Emphasis. They have four grown children.

Christopher Freeman is currently a Master Teacher at the University of Tulsa working on a NSF funded grant to improve Math and Science education in Oklahoma. One of Chris' main duties at TU is revising math and science courses that are taken by pre-service teachers. Chris is also working on an internally funded mini-grant to develop web based instructional material and the development of a faculty technology-training center at TU. Chris also helped revamp the masters in Mathematics and Science Education program at TU, which has a large emphasis on technology. He has previous experience teaching math and science in grades 7 through 12. He has his B.S. in Physics & Mathematics from Auburn University and his M.S. in Mathematics and Science Education from the University of Tulsa. Chris is presently a Doctoral student in Pepperdine University's Educational Technology program.

Caroline Howard is on the faculty of the Goizueta School of Business of Emory University where she teaches Information Systems and Statistics. Her primary areas of research are information systems with an emphasis on distance education, using telecommunications to substitute for transportation and systems development. She is married to Peter Dolid, a manager for Hewlett Packard. They have two children, Anne age 12 and Tommy age 9.

Janet Hugli is a recent graduate of the Master of Business of Administration program at the University of Ottawa. She also holds an honors undergradu-

degree in Business Administration from Brock University and a Diploma in Adult Education from St. Francis Xavier University. Janet has over 20 years experience in corporate management in the telecommunications industry, which has included roles in strategic planning, business development, marketing, sales and training. She has been involved with the network marketing industry for the past five years, and has developed leader-led training materials to support the development of the associates.

Sherif Kamel is an Assistant Professor of Management Support Systems at the American University in Cairo. He is also the director of the Regional Information Technology Institute in Cairo, Egypt. His research interests include management support systems and information technology transfer to developing countries and its implications on socioeconomic development. He is a graduate of London School of Economics and Political Science and the American University in Cairo. He designed and delivered professional development programs in information systems applications for public and private sector organizations in Africa, Asia, the Far East and Eastern Europe. He is one of the founding members of the Internet Society of Egypt. He serves on the editorial and review boards of a number of information systems and management journals and has published several articles and chapters on the application of information and communication technology in developing countries.

Dennis S. Kira is an Associate Professor of MIS in the Department of Decision Sciences and MIS at Concordia University, Montreal. He received his BSc in Mathematics from Simon Fraser University, and Ph.D. from University of British Columbia. He has published in *Management Science, IEEE Transactions, Journal of the Operational Research Society*, and *Omega* as well as many other scientific journals. His research interests include e-commerce, web design, distance learning, decision making under uncertainty, neural networks, Artificial Intelligence, financial modeling, and knowledge management.

Jens O. Liegle has recently joined the CIS faculty of Georgia State University. He received his Ph.D. in Management Information Systems at Kent State University. His areas of specialization are web-based intelligent tutoring systems and Web-based system development. He has participated in the development of the Web-based training system PageMaster for Goodyear Tire and Rubber, developed the Web-based surveying tool IntQuest, and is currently developing an adaptive Web-based intelligent tutoring system for computer programming languages.

Peter N. Meso is a doctoral student at Kent State University majoring in Management Information Systems. His areas of specialization are Knowledge Management and Information Infrastructure. He developed an intelligent web-based knowledge acquisition system, designed course supplemental web sites for the MIS department, and has experience in computer-mediated communication technologies and educational administration.

Lorraine Meyer-Peyton was a foreign language teacher and a career counselor before her life changed with the advent of personal computers. Thoroughly hooked on technology, she started teaching computer science. She eventually joined the Department of Defense Education Activity's distance learning program in its infancy, at first teaching Pascal programming and AP Computer Science. When tasked with exploring the educational possibilities offered by Lotus Notes, Lore and a colleague were soon piloting projects in several countries. Today Lore provides technical support for DoDEA schools in Europe and the United States as well as database development support for the DoDEA Electronic Schools' instructors. Lore can be reached at lore_peyton@hotmail.com.

Valerie N. Morphew, Assistant Professor of Education at West Virginia Wesleyan College in Buckhannon, West Virginia, received her doctorate in Curriculum and Instruction from West Virginia University in 1994. She taught education and science at Longwood College in Farmville, Virginia, before joining the faculty at West Virginia Wesleyan College in Fall 1999. Dr. Morphew's areas of expertise include science education, curriculum and instruction, and obsessive compulsive disorder education. Dr. Morphew is the author of two books and numerous articles. She enjoys writing nonfiction and fiction.

Dat-Dao Nguyen is an Assistant Professor of MIS in the Department of Accounting and MIS at California State University, Northridge. He holds a BA in Economics, a BCom in Quantitative Methods, and an MSc in Decision Sciences. He is finishing his Ph.D. in MIS at Concordia University, Montreal. His current research interests include Artificial Intelligence methodology and applications, behavioral decision theory, knowledge management, distance learning, and e-commerce. His works have been presented and published in Proceedings of AIS, ASAC, DSI, APDSI, NEDSI, WDSI, SCI, and other conferences.

Daniel F. Purcell Sr has been working in the Information Technology industry for over 20 years. He is currently employed by Logicon Incorporated on a contract to a government agency providing information technology and project management support. Mr. Purcell is also a member of the on-line faculty for the University of Phoenix On-line where he teaches primarily project management within a text-based asynchronous environment. His e-mail address is dfpurcel@email.uophx.edu.

Rita Purcell-Robertson is a consultant with the Arcadia Group Worldwide, Inc., in support of the International Medical Program of the Partnership for Peace Information Management System. She has developed, facilitated, and taught graduate and undergraduate level courses using distance media including the World Wide Web, the internet, two-way audio/one-way video, and two-way audio-video. Her current position involves telehealth instructional media for central and eastern European countries.

Arkalgud Ramaprasad is a Professor in the Department of Management and Director of the Pontikes Center for Management of Information. He teaches and conducts research in Strategic Management and Management of Information, and promotes industry-university cooperation in education and research related to management of information. He obtained his Ph.D. from the University of Pittsburgh in 1980. Prior to that he obtained his MBA from Indian Institute of Management, Ahmedabad, India, and B.E. (Electrical) from the University of Mysore. He has published in *Behavioral Science, Management Science, Academy of Management Review, Omega, Decision Sciences,* and other journals. He has received research grants from major corporations such as Comdisco, Chrysler, IBM, and Bozell Worldwide.

William E. Rayburn teaches Management Information Systems classes at Austin Peay State University. His research interests include the strategic management of technology and the role of technology as an agent of change. His recent research has focused on the organizational aspects of distance learning technology. He obtained his DBA degree from Southern Illinois University in Carbondale in 1997. Prior to that he obtained his MBA degree and BE degree from Vanderbilt University.

Lynne Schrum is an Associate Professor in the Department of Instructional Technology at the University of Georgia. She received a Ph.D. in Curriculum and Instruction with an emphasis on Distance Learning and Educational Telecommunications from the University of Oregon. Prior to her university work, she taught in an elementary school for several years. She is currently President of the International Society for Technology in Education (ISTE), a 47,000 member organization focused on implementing technology in schools. Dr. Schrum's current research and teaching focus on distance learning, online course development and delivery, ethical electronic communications, telecommunications, and technological innovations in education. She has written two books and numerous articles on these topics.

Major Todd Smith and Major **Scot Ransbottom** are United States Army Officers who have served in a variety of Command and Staff positions both overseas and in America. They have been responsible for training combat soldiers and educating future leaders. They are currently Assistant Professors at the United States Military Academy at West Point.

Ira Yermish is an Assistant Professor of Management and Information Systems at St. Joseph's University in Philadelphia, Pennsylvania. His education includes degrees from Case-Western Reserve University, Stanford University and the University of Pennsylvania in operations research and computer science. His areas of expertise include strategic applications of information technology, database systems and systems analysis and design. With over thirty-five years of experience in the computer industry as a software developer and consultant he provides a balanced approach for his undergraduate and graduate students.

Index